Management consulting

A guide to the profession

Edited by M. Kubr

International Labour Office   Geneva

ISBN 92-2-101165-8

First published 1976
Fifth impression (with modifications) 1980

ILO publications can be obtained through major booksellers or ILO local offices in many countries, or direct from ILO Publications, International Labour Office, CH-1211 Geneva 22, Switzerland. A catalogue or list of new publications will be sent free of charge from the above address.

Printed by " La Tribune de Genève ", Geneva, Switzerland

CONTENTS

FOREWORD

Management consulting is a professional service that helps managers to analyse and solve practical problems and transfer successful management practices from one enterprise to another. Since its inception in the early 1950s the Management Development Programme of the International Labour Office has, therefore, paid great attention to the development of management consultants and the promotion of effective consulting practices. The ILO has assisted many of its member States in establishing consulting services (in a number of cases attached to national management and productivity institutes) to serve the various sectors of the economy.

The demand for a comprehensive book on management consulting has been expressed by many individuals and institutions; this has been known to us for some considerable time. Drawing on the experience accumulated over the years, we have, therefore, attempted to fill this need.

Purpose of the book

In this book consulting is viewed primarily as a *method* for improving management practices. It is one which can be provided by independent private firms, internal consulting and advisory services in large public or private organisations, management development and productivity institutes, small business advisory centres, and other institutions interested in and capable of making a specific contribution in this field. The book is, therefore, based on experiences from a number of industrialised and developing countries, with private, mixed or public enterprise economic systems.

The main purpose of the book is to contribute to the upgrading of professional standards and practices in consulting and to provide information and guidance to individuals and organisations wishing to commence or improve consulting activities. The book is an introduction to the consulting profession, its nature, methods, organisational principles, behavioural rules

1

and training practices. It also suggests guidelines to consultants for operating in various areas of management. It is not, however, intended to replace handbooks and manuals which deal in depth and detail with various management functions and techniques: for this the reader is referred to special sources, some of which are suggested in this guide.

The book is intended for:

— new entrants to the consulting profession;

— independent management consultants and consulting firms, bureaux and services;

— consulting departments of national and sectoral productivity and management development institutions;

— departments and divisions performing management consulting and advisory functions in large private and public organisations, including the organisation and methods and similar services in governments;

— management teachers, trainers and research workers, who may be part-time consultants, and whose work is closely related to that of consultants;

— managers wishing to use consultants more effectively.

Terminology

The most common terms used in management consulting in various countries are explained in the text of the book. But the meaning and use of two basic terms warrants a definition at this early point:

— the term *management consultant* is used in the book as a generic term and applies to those persons who perform all or some of the typical consulting functions in the field of management;

— the term *client* is also used as a generic term and applies to any manager, administrator or organisation using the services of management consultants in private businesses, public undertakings, government or elsewhere.

Plan of the book

The guide is divided into 28 chapters grouped in 6 parts. These are followed by 8 appendices.

Part I (Chapters 1-5) presents and over-all view of the management consulting profession. Emphasis is placed on the consultant-client relationship and on the role of management consultants in the processes of change.

Part II (Chapters 6-10) deals with the preparation, planning and control of individual consulting assignments. It focuses on the management survey of organisations, and provides a detailed description and explanation of a financial appraisal of business organisations.

Part III (Chapters 11-15) is a guide to the general methodology of the four major steps in typical management consulting assignments: fact finding, fact analysis, developing and presenting proposals, and implementation.

Part IV (Chapters 16-22) provides an introduction to consulting in specific areas of management. The areas covered are general management, finance, marketing, production, management information systems and data processing, personnel and small enterprise management.

Part V (Chapters 23-25) is devoted to the organisation of management consulting. The main aspects covered are the specialisation and organisation of consulting units, headquarters' support and client services, and the internal management and administration of a consulting unit.

Part VI (Chapters 26-28) focuses on careers in consulting, the initial training of new consultants, and the further training and development of experienced consultants.

The appendices provide some useful information supplementing the main text of the book (Appendices 1, 2, 3 and 8) and materials for a deeper study of consulting methods and communication techniques dealt with in various parts of the book (Appendices 4-7).

Authors and acknowledgements

This book is the result of a collective effort.

The main authors are James Dey, George Kanawaty and Milan Kubr of the ILO Management Development Branch, Frederic Latham, formerly of Urwick Orr and Partners and ILO expert in Jamaica, Philip Neck of the ILO Management Development Branch, and J. Geoffrey Rawlinson of PA International Management Consultants.

Other authors and contributors include Derek Bowland of the ILO Management Development Branch, Gerry Y. Elliot and W. J. C. McEwan of PA International Management Consultants, Alan Gladstone of the International Institute for Labour Studies attached to the ILO, Colin Guthrie of the ILO Management Development Branch, Alan C. Popham and W. Trevor Utting of PA International Management Consultants. Edgar H. Schein of the Massachusetts Institute of Technology and P. W. Shay of the Association of Consulting Management Engineers gave us their kind permission to use their contributions on consulting originally published in other works. Business Books in London authorised us to reproduce several tables and paragraphs from E. G. Wood's publication *Bigger profits for the smaller firm*.

There are, furthermore, many specialists in ILO field projects whose experiences, ideas and suggestions made possible the publication of this book.

Many secretaries of the ILO Management Development Branch assisted the authors in the preparation of the book at various stages of the project. Nivie van Ginneken was particularly helpful in finalising the manuscript.

Milan Kubr edited the book technically and prepared it for publication.

●

The authors recognise that their attempt to define a broad conceptual framework for management consulting and prepare an international guide for consultants cannot be more than a first step in this field. The ILO Management Development Branch would be grateful to the reader for any comments and suggestions on how this book could be further improved and its usefulness to management consulting practice enhanced.

PART I

MANAGEMENT CONSULTING IN PERSPECTIVE

NATURE AND PURPOSE OF MANAGEMENT CONSULTING

1

1.1 Definition

In its guide to membership, the Institute of Management Consultants in the United Kingdom defines management consulting as:

> "The service provided by an independent and qualified person or persons in identifying and investigating problems concerned with policy, organisation, procedures and methods; recommending appropriate action and helping to implement these recommendations." [1]

Definitions used by other professional associations of management consultants, such as the Association of Consulting Management Engineers in the USA, are very similar. This shows management consulting to be a special service, to which managers can address themselves if they feel a need for help in problem solving. The consultant's work begins with some condition judged to be unsatisfactory and capable of amelioration; it ideally ends with a condition in which a change has taken place, a change that must be seen as an improvement.

Some particular features of management consulting need to be emphasised at the outset.

First, consulting is an *independent service*. This is characterised by the detachment of the consultant, which is a major feature of his role. But this independence means at the same time that consultants enter into a very complex relationship with their client organisations and the people working within them. The consultant has no direct authority to decide on changes and implement them—but this must not be viewed as a weakness. He has to master the art of being a deeply concerned change agent without giving up his

---

[1] *Guide to membership* (London, Institute of Management Consultants, 1974).

7

independence. He must, therefore, ensure the utmost involvement of the client in everything he does, so that ultimate success becomes a joint accomplishment.

Secondly, consulting is essentially an *advisory service*. This means that consultants are not recruited to run organisations or take delicate decisions on behalf of desperate managers. They are advisers and their responsibility is for the quality and integrity of their advice; the clients carry all the responsibilities that accrue from taking it. Of course, in the practice of consulting there are many variations and degrees of " advice ". Not only to give the right advice, but to give it in the right way and at the right time—this is a basic skill of a consultant. The client in his turn needs to become skilful in taking and utilising the consultant's advice. These points are so important that we shall be returning to them many times in the text that follows.

Thirdly, consulting is a *service providing professional knowledge and skills relevant to practical management problems*. An individual becomes a management consultant in the full sense of the term by accumulating considerable knowledge of varying management situations and problems and acquiring skills needed for problem solving—for identifying problems, finding relevant information, analysing and synthesising, choosing between alternative solutions, communicating with people and so on. But managers, too, need to possess these particular types of skill. What is unique to consultants is that over the years they pass through many organisations and learn how to use experience from previous assignments to handle new assignments skilfully. In addition to this, professional consultants keep continuously abreast of developments in management methods and techniques, including those that take place in universities and research institutions; make clients aware of them; and help in applications. They function thus as a link between the theory and practice of management.

Fourthly, consulting is *not* a service providing miracle solutions to difficult managerial problems. It would be an error to assume that once a consultant is brought in, life becomes easy for management. Consulting is difficult, systematic and disciplined work based on the analysis of hard facts and the search for imaginative but feasible solutions. Strong management commitment to solving the problems of the organisation and client-consultant co-operation are at least as important to the end result as the quality of the consultant's advice.

1.2 Why are consultants used

Managers would see no reason for using consultants if the latter could not provide something that is missing in a particular organisation. As a rule, consultants are used for one or more of the following reasons:

Providing special knowledge and skill

Consultants are called in when an organisation is short of people able to tackle a given problem with the same chance of success. It may often involve new techniques and methods in which a consultant has acquired special expertise. In other cases, the problem submitted may be of a general nature, if the organisation is failing to achieve its principal purpose and the gaps in knowledge concern general management policy, planning, co-ordination or leadership.

Supplying intensive professional help on a temporary basis

A deep examination of major problems, such as the company organisation or marketing policy, would require the full attention of senior management for long periods of time. But the day-to-day running of business leaves little time, and, what is worse, it is difficult to concentrate on operational and conceptual problems simultaneously. Consultants not only provide the time but will leave the organisation once the job is completed.

Giving an impartial outside viewpoint

Even the best people within an organisation may be too influenced by their personal involvement and existing traditions and habits to see a problem in its true light and propose feasible solutions. Because he is independent of the client organisation, a management consultant can be impartial in situations where no one from within the organisation would be.

Providing management with arguments which justify pre-determined measures

From time to time consultants are approached with a request to undertake assignments, and submit reports, so that a manager can justify his decision by referring to the consultant's recommendation. In other words a manager may know exactly what he wants and what his decision will be, but prefers to order a consultant's report to obtain support for his views. This is a not unreasonable course but, as a matter of principle and in their own interest, professional consultants should be careful not to accept assignments in which their services might be misused for in-company politics.

The above-mentioned reasons may be present in such varying degrees and may be so inter-related that the consultant is confronted with quite a complex situation. He should nevertheless endeavour to maintain a clear view of the reasons for which his services are being used, even if in the course of an assignment the initial reasons change or entirely new ones are discovered.

1.3 Who uses consultants

Management consulting as a professional service and method for implementing change is not confined to a particular type of organisation or economy. In the course of its development consulting has been spreading to new areas of human activity and this has led to varying patterns of specialisation.[1]

Level of the country's economic development

The use of management consultants has become common practice in *industrialised countries*. In North America there are about 3,500 management consulting firms which thus constitute a major sector of the professional services. The figures are relatively lower in Europe, but in the United Kingdom and many other European countries the growth of management consultancy has been quite impressive in the last twenty years.

Consultants are closely associated with the design and diffusion of new management systems, methods and technologies, including the most advanced ones. A proper use of the consultant's knowledge and skills in order to complement those of the company's management has become a method of enhancing managerial effectiveness and competitive strength.

In *developing countries* the local consulting profession is a very young one. There is, however, a general trend towards a greater use of consultants. This is no doubt because management consulting can play a useful role in industrialisation and economic and social development generally. It can accelerate the transfer of management expertise and help to design and introduce management systems adjusted to the local setting. It helps thus to enhance the country's managerial competence—one of the key conditions of effective development.

The economic and political setting of the country

Management consulting had its origin in *free market economies*, where independent business companies now use consultants in many different ways at their own discretion. Over the years, however, consulting has spread from private business to government. At the present time the use of management consulting services by government administrations and by government-controlled public enterprises is common practice.

In *centrally planned socialist economies* consulting has had its own history. There was little scope for such special advisory services in the period when the planning and control of all important economic activities were still highly

---

[1] On specialisation of consultants see Chapter 23.

centralised, and enterprises had only restricted economic autonomy. This situation started changing in the late 1950s. In more and more cases, enterprise management became able to consider alternative courses of action to increase efficiency. Furthermore, the sectoral ministries and other central bodies started attaching more importance to economic and financial analysis, and to the evaluation of the effects of alternative technological, investment and other policies. As a result, various specialised professional institutions started providing advisory services both to enterprises and to ministries.

The economic reforms implemented in the last decade have stimulated a further growth of demand for management consulting services. These have developed as special services in research and development institutions, in educational and training establishments and, in some cases, as separate units where consulting is the main function.

Sectors of the economic and social activity

Most consulting assignments have traditionally been in industrial and commercial enterprises. But, from these sectors, consulting has spread to transport, catering, banking, insurance and so on. The growth of social organisations and services has led to demand for advice on their structuring and management. To give some examples, important management consulting assignments have been carried out for trade unions, sports and religious organisations, and international governmental organisations.

At the present time, management consultants are used in all sectors where management problems exist and have to be solved—and this applies to all organised sectors of human activity.

While some consultants have remained generalists, others have preferred to specialise sectorally, e.g. in the management of construction work, hospitals, transport or banking.

Size of organisations

Although *large organisations* possess considerable management experience and specialist staff in various management functions and techniques, they use consultants for reasons indicated in Section 1.2 above. Some large companies have their " permanent " consultants, available to provide help quickly if the need arises.

In a *small enterprise* the decision about the use of a management consultant may be a difficult one. The owner or manager may find such professional service too expensive, and he often does not see how in his particular situation he could co-operate with a man from outside. Nevertheless, a growing number of small enterprises in both industrialised and developing countries call for consultants' services, especially in matters of over-all business policy or for the introduction of specific management techniques. Some management consultants specialise in problems of smaller companies and there are countries (particularly developing ones) where subsidised consulting services are available to the smaller companies as part of small-enterprise promotion schemes.[1]

1.4 External and internal consulting

Consulting has developed as an external and internal service (seen from the viewpoint of an organisation using consultants).

An external consultant is administratively and legally fully independent of the organisations for which he works. An internal consultant is part of a particular organisational entity—a company, a group of companies, a government ministry or department, and so on. But precise limits between the two are difficult to draw—an autonomous consulting bureau reporting to an industrial ministry might be viewed as an internal unit since it is part of the government services, but may have the same working relationship to the public enterprises reporting to this ministry as have independent external consulting firms.

In the present-day practice of consulting, larger organisations in the public and private sectors use both external and internal consultants.[2]

Internal consulting services are often thought to be more appropriate for problems that require a deep knowledge of the highly complex internal relations, procedures and political factors in large organisations; and an awareness of the various functions of the organisation or of specific constraints affecting its operation. In government, they may be used for national security and interest reasons. If there is a steady demand for advice in special methods and techniques, an internal consulting service may be a cheaper and more productive arrangement. External consultants are preferred, even by organisations which have some internal consulting capability, in situations where an internal consultant would not meet the criteria of impartiality and confidentiality or would be short of particular expertise.

In some cases, complex assignments are entrusted jointly to external and internal consultants, or internal consultants may be requested to define precisely the assignment for an external consultant, and to collaborate with him in order to learn as much as possible from him during the assignment.

---

[1] On consulting in small-enterprise management see Chapter 22.

[2] Cf. H. R. Balls: " Use of external management consulting services " in *Interregional seminar on administration of management improvement services (Copenhagen, Denmark, 28.9-6.10.1970), Volume I: Report of the seminar and technical papers* (New York, United Nations, 1971; Sales No. E.71.II.4.9).

The basic principles and methods of consulting, which is the main subject of this guide, apply equally to the activities of external and internal consultants. Organisational differences will be examined in Part V dealing with the organisation of consulting.

RANGE, SCOPE AND CHARACTERISTICS OF CONSULTING WORK

2

2.1 Range of problems

As explained in Chapter 1, managers call in consultants if they seek help in problem solving. The term " problem " is used here to indicate a situation about which management is concerned (and which probably requires some managerial action) but is not quite clear what action to take, where to start and how to proceed. This, of course, is a very general definition of what a management problem is, but it corresponds to reality. Indeed, the range of problems entrusted to consultants is extremely broad.

Corrective, progressive and creative problems

Seen from the viewpoint of the quality or level of the situation, the consultant may be asked to rectify a deteriorated situation (corrective problem), improve an existing one (progressive problem) or create a totally new situation (creative problem).

In an enterprise, for example, difficulties may have arisen in marketing. The volume of sales of a product which has been manufactured and distributed successfully for several years suddenly drops and this starts causing serious financial difficulties. The reasons are not very clear. Everybody will agree that this is an urgent management problem which calls for immediate action. It is a *corrective problem*. This means that, with almost the same resources, a more satisfactory performance was achieved in the past than is the case now. The problem is clearly defined if it is accepted that restoration of the original condition is all that is required. This is " trouble-shooting ". The process of solution is the tracking back of the deviations that have taken place, and finding and correcting the reasons for them. But it is more than likely that, while doing this, opportunities are found for ending with something better than the original.

Progressive problems represent another group. They involve the very common task of taking an existing condition and improving it. They may concern partial elements of management, such as accounting techniques, administrative procedures or record keeping. For example, a company using historical costing feels that it should switch to standard costing to enhance the accuracy and efficiency of cost control and thus be in a better position to take cost-saving measures when these are needed. In such cases the consultant may have models or standards used elsewhere and his main job will be to examine the conditions of their application, decide on necessary adjustments and help to persuade and train the staff directly concerned by an improved procedure.

But many progressive problems are less structured. A client organisation may have a good potential for becoming more effective, but realistic targets have to be set and measures devised in various areas of management. It may involve a whole network of technological, administrative, financial and personnel changes.

Creative problems provide the consultant with the least amount of starting information. There may be little more than a few desires and some bright ideas.

This applies, for example, to an enterprise with no operational or financial difficulties and no particular need for interventions that would improve its performance in the short run. The business forecast indicates that for some time there should be no trouble either with marketing or with the supply of raw materials and other resources. In spite of that, management feels that the enterprise has a much greater potential for development than has been realised so far. But what should be done to anticipate future opportunities and be prepared to take them? Spend more on research and product development? Build a new plant to expand capacity for the existing products? What type of market research should be undertaken? Are there measures by which the enterprise itself could influence future demand for its products?

In such a case, the consultant may have to do a great deal of creative thinking and have recourse to unconventional ways of developing solutions to problems.

Needless to say many assignments will have elements of all three types of problem mentioned above. While working on an apparently progressive type, the consultant may discover that many corrective measures are needed first. Or, on the contrary, a corrective problem may require an entirely new, creative approach, since otherwise it would no longer be possible to stop the process of continuing deterioration.

The nature of consulting requires that any situation is seen in the perspective of future opportunities. If called on to deal with a corrective problem, the consultant will *always* ask whether a rectification of a deteriorated situation is really what is needed, or whether instead the organisation should not look for new ways of defining its purpose and objectives, and enhancing the effectiveness of its activities. A basically corrective problem may thus be turned into a progressive or creative one.

Management functions and techniques

As for the specific management functions and techniques with which consultants are concerned, the profession has passed through several stages of development. In the 1920s a number of consultants, in particular in the USA, started offering services primarily in the production area—in work study, production engineering and rationalisation. The next major area tackled was accounting. Some work in the personnel and human relations field was also done. Consulting in general management was confined to questions of structure and procedures. In the postwar period, consulting in marketing and also in various newer management techniques, operations research and systems design started expanding rapidly. At this point the profession could claim to provide a complete set of consulting services. This was followed by fairly quick expansion and by changes in the concepts of consulting in general management, embracing perspective problems of business strategy, long-range planning, decision making, and, more recently, organisation development.

The present situation is that there are consultants available for any type of management problem—functional, inter-functional, general—and for the application of any of the many management techniques, including the traditional techniques of method and time study, and the newer quantitative and behavioural science techniques.[1]

Technological and social aspects

Another aspect of the scope of management problems handled by consultants is the relationship of management to technology and the social sciences.

As a rule, management consultants are not equipped to deal with problems that are purely technological. But they must know something about the relationships between technology and management. In areas where technology and management are jointly involved, such as production engineering, problems of organisation have to be seen in relation to the technological aspects of methods study, plant layout, choice of machines, design and choice of tools and transport equipment, etc.

In practice management consultants with an engineering background can deal with certain problems that are both managerial and technological. But they turn problems of pure technology over to specialists in technological research, development and engineering.

The position is somewhat similar with regard to the social side of organisations. Good management consultants are aware of the importance and complexity of social and psychological problems in organisations and of their

---

[1] How this affects the specialisation and organisation of consulting units will be discussed in Chapter 23.

impact on management. Without some knowledge of the social sciences and their methodology, the consultant would be approaching in an amateurish way the difficult task of generating and monitoring change which affects people and requires their involvement. However, a management consultant may in certain cases have to apply for specialist help from a professional psychologist, sociologist, or other social scientist. This might be available within the same consulting unit (in the larger ones) or from specialised institutions.

2.2 The consultant's roles

The consultant, as an agent of change, can assume two basic roles—that of a resource consultant and that of a process consultant.[1]

Resource consultant

To bring about change this type of consultant provides expert information and service, or recommends a programme of action, thereby transferring knowledge to the individual, group or organisation. In turn the knowledge provided is expected to affect attitudes, subsequent individual behaviour and finally the performance of the organisation.

This approach depends for its success upon correct diagnoses of needs, effective communication between client and consultant, the consultant's expertise in providing the appropriate information or service and an understanding of the full consequences of gathering information and implementing recommended changes.

Process consultant

In this instance the consultant as the agent of change attempts to help the organisation to solve its own problems by making it aware of organisational processes, of their likely consequences and of techniques for accomplishing change. As opposed to the resource consultant, who is primarily concerned with passing on knowledge and solving problems, the process consultant is concerned with passing on his approach, methods and values so that the organisation itself can diagnose and remedy its own problems.

E. H. Schein has provided a detailed approach to process consultation which attempts to place the consultant in a truly professional setting. He defines process consulting as " a role of activities on the part of the consultant which help the client to perceive, understand, and act upon process events which occur in the client's environment ".[2]

---

[1] These roles are demonstrated in case histories given in Appendices 4 and 5.

[2] E. H. Schein: *Process consultation* (Reading, Mass., Addison-Wesley, 1969), p. 9.

In a modern concept of consulting, these two roles should be seen as mutually supportive. For example, a consultant may start his assignment as a resource consultant to acquaint himself with the problem and give evidence of his sound professional knowledge in a particular field. He will then endeavour to act more and more as a process consultant, but will switch temporarily back to his role of resource consultant if people in the client organisation get into situations where new knowledge has to be supplied if the process of change is not to stop. It would, therefore, be wrong to think that each of the two roles applies to different areas or functions of management.

2.3 Basic types of assignment

In practice it is most common to see the management consultant undertake the following assignments:

A management survey [1]

The consultant surveys the organisation's resources, results, management policies and patterns, with a view to identifying, or defining more precisely, its strengths and weaknesses and key problems that inhibit smooth operation or further growth. Some courses of action might be suggested. In most cases such a survey is undertaken as the first stage of a consulting assignment, which would continue once the conclusions of the survey were agreed between the consultant and the client. But an assignment may also consist of a survey only, the suggested action being left entirely to the client for detailed specification and implementation.

While a survey which is the first step in an assignment is usually very short (a few days), some complex surveys of large organisations whose performance is seen as unsatisfactory may take several months.

Special surveys and studies

Special surveys and studies may be commissioned from consultants in any management area. Examples are feasibility studies for new investment, market research studies, surveys of consumer attitudes to the company's products, collection and analysis of information for long-term planning or studies of trends in the supply of raw materials.

These studies might go into great detail and depth, both in the collection of information and in the analysis. The consultant completes his work by submitting the study report and discussing it with the client.

---

[1] Other terms used are management audit, consulting survey, diagnostic survey, diagnostic evaluation, business diagnosis, pilot study, company appraisal and so on.

Working out solutions to defined problems

In most cases the client wants more help than a survey of his problems. He asks the consultant to work out solutions to the problems—to draw up a new organisation for the company, redesign an information system, prepare a new wage scheme, devise a training programme for supervisors, propose a new plant layout and material flow, and so on. Again, some assignments will be completed at this stage if the client is sufficiently equipped to implement the solutions without further help from the consultant.

Assisting in implementation

The consultant may be requested to stay in the organisation while his proposals are being put into effect. He may be involved in implementation in many different ways, including selecting and training personnel, helping management to persuade people about the priorities of the new system and correcting the system on the basis of first experience with implementation.

Acting as an advisor

While every consultant is an advisor, here we have in mind a consultant acting in an advisory capacity in the narrow sense of the term, i.e. answering questions when asked and probably also expressing certain views on his own initiative, but not directly undertaking new systems development and application.

For example, top managers in many important firms like to sound out a consultant before launching new projects or presenting various proposals to the board of directors. Or management and workers' representatives may agree on the use of an expert in a dispute concerning norms and wages. However, in all instances such as this the consultant will need to exercise care that he does not slip inadvertently from his advisory role into the role of arbitrator in the course of presenting his findings forcefully.

In different assignments these activity types are combined in varying ways. Every client has the right to decide how far he wants the consultant to go—if he wants to receive a survey report with some criticism and recommendations, or detailed proposals for changes to be prepared, and if he wishes the consultant to participate in implementation and, if so, how. Experience shows that clarity on this point is vital for effectiveness in consulting. In preparing an assignment and the terms of reference for the consultant, it is essential to define precisely what is to be considered as the end result and at what stage management wants the consultant to leave the organisation. This helps to avoid misunderstanding—cases when consultants submit global reports while management was looking for detailed proposals for action, and situations where consultants are trying to see their proposals through the implementation phase while management would prefer to be left alone.

THE CONSULTANT-CLIENT RELATIONSHIP

3

Consultants help in solving the problems of other people and organisations. There are, therefore, " two major aspects to any consulting relationship: (1) the analysis and solution of the problem, and (2) the relationship between consultant and client. " [1] These aspects are interlinked and if the consultant-client relationship is not properly understood by both the parties, even the best scientific approach to problem solving will give no practical results. The history of consulting has seen thousands of assignments whose reports have been buried in managers' desks or which have caused a complete misunderstanding in the client organisations because the complementary roles of consultant and client were not defined or relations became distorted in the course of the assignment.

3.1 Who is the client?

The client, in the widest sense of the term, is the organisation which employs the services of a consulting unit. Here we have an institutional relationship. But there is also a client in a more narrow sense of the term—the person (or group of persons) in the client organisation who initiates the bringing in of the consultant, discusses the assignment with him, receives reports and so on. He is in a personal relationship with the consultant.

As a rule, consulting assignments are commissioned by managers in senior or top positions (in general or functional management) and are concerned with the areas of responsibility of these managers. The position of the assigner must be commensurate with the scope and importance of the problem to be tackled—for example, a marketing manager cannot really ask for a review of the organisation of the whole firm. But not all assignments have to be

---

[1] P. W. Shay: *How to get the best results from management consultants* (New York, Association of Consulting Management Engineers, 1974), p. 38.

commissioned directly by top management—there are numerous assignments at middle or lower management level and one of the middle managers (in a functional or production department) may then represent the client. As a rule, lower-level managers would not have the job of recruiting a consultant and officially representing the client organisation for this purpose.

In addition to the key person in the client organisation there may be further participants in the assignment, or people interested in the assignment in various ways:

— liaison officers (to maintain daily contacts with the consultant in current matters concerning the assignment);

— employees assigned to work on the assignment under the consultant's guidance;

— managers and other employees who will be interviewed, asked to supply documentation, consulted on various aspects of the assignment, etc.;

— managers and other employees who are not involved in the assignment, but would like to know about it;

— managers and other employees who will be somehow affected if the consultant's proposals are implemented (they may be in any group above).

There is no need to emphasise that these groups may differ in their attitudes to the consultant and that, as a result, a very complex relationship between individuals and groups in the organisation may evolve during the assignment.

3.2 Creating and maintaining sound relationships

Introducing the consultant

At the beginning of an assignment there is a need to dispel uncertainty and speculations about the purpose of the consultant's presence in the organisation. A convenient moment for this is when introducing the consultant, and explaining his terms of reference, to managers and employees. This is done both in writing (circular letters or announcements) and through meetings, including meetings at which the consultant is present. To avoid inaccuracies and misunderstanding, the consultant should co-operate in preparing the announcement jointly with the client and should see that it includes all information which, according to his experience, should be made available to people in the organisation.

Sound management practice and good industrial relations require that workers or their representatives be given full information on matters of interest to the workers, relating to the operation and future prospects of the undertaking and to the present and future situation of its employees. This will be of importance in many consulting assignments. Both the consultant and his client have to be particularly sensitive to such assignments which, because of their nature, may require more than information and on which consultation and even in some cases negotiations should take place between management and workers' representatives or their organisations, in accordance with the industrial relations practice of the given country.[1]

Joint problem definition

One of the basic rules for the use of management consultants concerns problem definition. Managers who want to call for consultants' help should not merely recognise a need for such help, but define the problem as they see it, as precisely as they can. In some organisations, public and private, top management will not even consider authorising the use of consultants unless it is presented with a clear description of the problem.

The consultant, before agreeing to accept the assignment, must be sure that he can subscribe to the client's definition of the problem. With the exception of the most simple and clear cases, he wants to be able to reach his own conclusion as to what the problem is and how difficult its solution might be. This is done in the management survey.[2]

There are many reasons why the consultant's definition of the problem might differ from the client's. Frequently managers are too deeply immersed in a particular situation or have created the problem themselves by their past action. They may not realise its magnitude and depth. They may see symptoms but not the real problem. Or they are reluctant to admit the existence of certain aspects of the problem and prefer the consultant to " discover " them.

Comparison of the client's and consultant's definitions of the problem is an operation which lays down the basis of sound working relations for the whole assignment. Such comparison requires discussion. In this discussion the consultant has to make full use of his communication and persuasion skills so that the client will find it possible to accept the consultant's definition of the problem without feeling embarrassed. But the consultant must also be prepared to make corrections in his problem definition. Both the consultant and

---

[1] Cf. ILO Recommendation (No. 94) concerning Consultation and Co-operation between Employers and Workers at the level of the Undertaking, and ILO Recommendation (No. 129) concerning Communications between Management and Workers within the Undertaking.

[2] See Chapter 6.

the client have to see the final definition of the problem as a common result of preparatory work for the assignment.

Working relations during the assignment

The working relations during the assignment, including the frequency and form of contacts between consultant and client, will depend on the way in which the consultant is used. One alternative is an independent study or project, with no participation by the client's staff. Another alternative, probably the most common one, is an assignment in which managers and employees participate by supplying information, preparing documentation, working out some proposals and so on, together with the consultant. In a third case the whole project is undertaken by the client's staff and the consultant acts as a catalyst and advisor. Despite these differences, there are certain general rules governing working relations.

The frequency of personal and written contacts (interim reports) needs to provide enough opportunity for the client to control the progress of the assignment and for the consultant to seek further guidance and feedback from the client. It is not reasonable to expect that the consultant, once the problem has been defined, will lock himself in an office and emerge with a perfect solution one month later. In addition to regular contacts which may have been planned in advance, the consultant needs an open door to people whose opinion may be useful to his work.

Access to information is a basic issue. If a client feels that consultants should not have access to some information for any reason, and if this information concerns the problems to be solved, external consultants should probably not be called in at all and management should try to solve the issue with internal resources. But clients sometimes merely forget to convey some information or consider it unimportant or unreliable, although the consultant may find it very helpful.

In assignments of longer duration, it may be useful to diffuse some interim information about the work undertaken by the consultant, or provisional results, to those members of the management staff and other employees who know about the purpose of the consultant's presence in the organisation and are curious to see the results—especially if these may affect their work. The consultant may himself make suggestions to the client about interim information suitable for diffusion, and at which point this should be done.

The consultant's behaviour during the whole assignment has a strong bearing on working relations and the help which he will be able to obtain from the client and his staff. After all, people may not immediately appreciate the presence of somebody who comes from outside to show that they (individually or collectively) could work better and be more efficient. The consultant gains confidence and support by listening, being patient and modest, showing competence without using gimmicks to impress people, and by working in a highly organised and disciplined manner.[1]

If the working relations are good and the client is fully satisfied with progress made by the consultant, there may be another danger: the temptation to associate the consultant so closely with the solution of management problems that the client actually delegates some of his decision-making responsibilities to him. In such a case the consultant decides what is to be done and who is to do it in order to implement the proposals. Experienced professional consultants generally agree that this is a danger to be avoided.

There are two reasons for this. The first is that if the proposals and their implementation turn out to be unsatisfactory because of poor performance on the part of the client's personnel, the blame will be laid on the consultant if he is too closely involved. The second and more fundamental reason is that the consultant's basic job is to improve the client's capability in handling problems, and this capability is in no way increased if the work is done by the consultant alone. To use an analogy, the consultant's function is that of a physiotherapist, not that of a crutch.

The main factor in the working relations between consultant and client is that of change. This may begin to be implemented at some point in the assignment, or the consultant's work may prepare the ground for changes that will follow. The consultant's function is that of a change agent, and management has to assume the main responsibility for the implementation of change, even if a consultant is involved. These problems require detailed examination, which will take place in the following chapter.

---

[1] See also Chapter 10, pp. 109-111.

CONSULTING AND CHANGE

4

Change is the " raison d'être " of management consulting. Change in organisations is linked with change in people and there are many influences which operate in both directions—organisations influence people and people influence the development of organisations. A competent management consultant needs to be aware of these complex relationships and, in particular, to know how to approach varying change situations. This chapter is, therefore, particularly important to the understanding of the nature and methods of consulting.

People are, of course, remarkably adaptable and if they have no choice they can cope for a long time with a change that they do not like at all. But this is not the purpose of consulting. Management consultants should aim at changes which make organisations more effective, and, at the same time, make work more interesting and satisfying to people.

4.1 The process of change

The three-step sequential model

A useful concept of the change process is the three-step sequential model [1]: *unfreezing* or thawing out of established behaviour patterns; *changing* or moving to a new pattern; and *refreezing* or development of the new pattern. Within each of these steps certain conditions are considered to exist and specific sub-processes required to operate.

Unfreezing requires a somewhat unsettling situation as it is assumed that a certain amount of anxiety or dissatisfaction is called for, i.e. there must be a need to search for new information if learning is to take place. Conditions

---

[1] Originally postulated by the social psychologist K. Lewin and developed by G. W. Dalton. See in G. W. Dalton, P. R. Lawrence and L. E. Greiner: *Organisational change and development* (Homewood, Ill., Irwin, 1970).

which enhance the unfreezing process usually include more than a normal amount of tension leading to a noticeable need for change: e.g. an absence of sources of information, removal of usual contacts and accustomed routines; and a lowering of self-esteem amongst people. In many, if not most, instances these pre-conditions for change are usually present before the consultant arrives on the scene.

Changing or the movement towards change underlines the role to be played by the change agent (consultant) in partnership with management and workers. The change event is said to occur with the advent of an influencing agent of repute and prestige (hence the need for the consultant to be both good at his job and acknowledged to be good).

The sub-processes of changing involve two elements:

— *identification*, where the people concerned recognise the authority of the change agent, adopt his external or generalised motive, test out the proposed changes and, hopefully, accept the general principles of change, and

— *internalisation*, where individuals translate the general principles advocated by the change agent into specific personal goals by means of adaption, experimentation or improvisation. The process of internalisation of new goals is often quite difficult, usually requiring a good deal of creativity on the part of the change agent in assisting the changee to convert the external (general), to internal (specific and personal) motives for accepting the change proposed.

Refreezing occurs when the changee verifies change through experience. The sub-processes involved require a conducive and supportive environment (e.g. approval by responsible management) and are usually accompanied by a heightening of self-esteem in the changees as a result of a sense of achievement derived from task accomplishment. During the initial stages of the refreezing step it is recommended that continuous reinforcement of the required behaviour (by means of rewards, praise etc.) be carried out to accelerate the learning process. At later stages intermittent or spaced reinforcement is recommended to prevent extinction of the newly acquired behavioural patterns. Eventually the new behaviour and attitudes are either reinforced and internalised, or rejected and abandoned.

Levels and cycles of change

Another useful model is that describing levels and cycles of change which consultants ought to consider when devising the appropriate strategy for implementing proposed change.

As set out in the following diagram Hersey and Blanchard [1] talk about four *levels of change*: (1) knowledge changes, (2) attitudinal changes, (3) individual behaviour changes, and (4) group or organisational performance changes. A hierachy of difficulty is experienced in effecting change when moving from level 1 through to level 4. The relative levels of difficulty and time relationship are set out in Figure 1.

Figure 1. Time span and level of difficulty involved for various levels of change

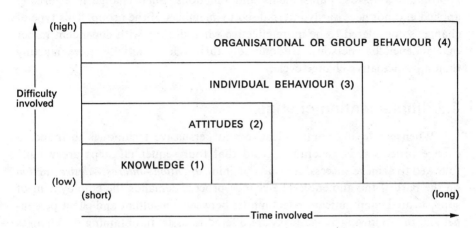

Using the above model the change agent may employ either a participative or a coercive *change cycle* or a blend of both.

Participative change commences with (1) the introduction of new knowledge which, it is hoped, (2) will influence and develop the appropriate attitude and (3) eventually shape individual behaviour by means of participation in goal-setting exercises leading (4) to formalised group participation in accepting the desired change.

Change of this participative nature requires a mature and relatively independent target audience because the goals set require personal achievement motivation in the changees. Additionally, the change agent requires a certain amount of personal prestige to influence the group. Although the cycle of change is slow and evolutionary in nature, it is considered to be long-lasting.

Coercive change is virtually the opposite of participative change. An authoritative source brings pressure to bear on the group behaviour (4) by

---

[1] See P. Hersey and K. H. Blanchard: *Management of organisational behaviour* (Englewood Cliffs, N.J., Prentice-Hall, 1972), p. 160.

issuing direct orders. As a consequence the individual's behaviour (3) can be expected to alter which should, in turn, influence both attitude (2) and knowledge (1). An extension of this change cycle is such that a return effect should come into operation where the knowledge (1) so gained should further confirm attitudes (2) individual (3) and group behaviour (4). Because the change is initiated from a position of power which imposes it, rather than from a personal source, the change introduced could be considered inherently volatile: it may disappear with removal of the power source able to apply the appropriate rewards, punishments and sanctions. Such change is externally applied and not necessarily internalised by members of the group. This type of change is considered to be more effective when dealing with dependent rather than independent persons. Undoubtedly this cycle is initially quicker acting than a participative change cycle.

4.2 Implementing change

When employing communicative and persuasive techniques to induce a change process it is generally agreed that four sequential steps are usually followed to achieve successful results: gaining *attention - interest - desire - action* on the part of the audience. The change process demands the employment of sophisticated communication techniques between consultant and client personnel and the following suggestions are offered to assist in obtaining the changes required.

Arousing attention to the need for change

Undeniably there must be unlimited methods of attracting attention of individuals and groups to new proposals. However, two proven methods are of particular interest to consultants.

The most effective manner of arousing immediate attention occurs when people become *anxious*. In special cases the introduction of a state of extreme anxiety is undeniably effective; e.g. a building will be cleared very promptly by reporting that a bomb has been placed in it. However, results show that the continued use of the heightened anxiety approach tends to be self-defeating. Recipients eventually ignore such threats especially if the alleged events do not occur.

Notwithstanding that, the use of minimal anxiety is effective as an attention-arousing device, which can be sustained over a long period. A particularly successful combination is to use an anxiety state to rouse attention to specific needs (i.e. the unfreezing process described above) and to follow up by providing a solution (from an accepted authority, e.g. the consultant) meeting these needs. Hence, the consultant should assess what will happen to the organisation, groups and individuals concerned if the new proposals are ignored, and draw attention to these possibly undesirable results. The logical follow-up suggesting a means of overcoming the problem ought to be the implementation of the new recommended course of action.

The second method is called *two-step information process*. The underlying idea is that the acceptance and effective introduction of change occurs as the result of a multiplier effect in the flow of information.

Detailed research findings suggest that people most likely to experiment and be influenced by new approaches possess certain characteristics. These persons, labelled as "isolates", are inclined to be highly technically oriented; to read widely on their chosen subjects; to attend frequently at meetings and conferences, to travel extensively in order to investigate new schemes. They may be considered by their reference-membership group to be something akin to "cranks". Surprisingly they are not likely to influence other members of their group directly.

Nevertheless, activities of these technically-oriented "isolates" are kept under constant observation by a second type who possess characteristics similar to those of "isolates" but, usually due to widespread interests in other fields, do not have the same amount of time available to experiment and test new methods in any considerable depth. This second type of person, identified as an "opinion-leader" does, however, have considerable influence over the reference group, and even beyond it. In addition to acknowledged technical expertise the person usually has considerable civic and social standing.

In tracing the life-cycle in the adoption of new procedures it seems that the new scheme is first investigated, along with other possible choices, by the "isolate" and is eventually chosen over other alternatives because of its proven technical superiority. At a later stage the "opinion-leader" adopts the new idea once he is convinced that the "isolate" has firmly decided on this new approach. Subsequently an "epidemic" phase erupts as the followers of the "opinion-leader" also adopt the new approach.

Therefore, when introducing change a strong case can usually be made for emphasising the highly technical aspects of the new approach in order to attract and convince the "isolates" and "opinion-leaders" who should under normal circumstances assist in influencing the other members of the group.

Creating interest in change

Once the consultant has attracted the attention of his target audience he is faced with the problem of creating further interest in his new proposal. Surveys dealing with reasons offered for the adoption of new schemes, approaches, etc., indicate the following breakdown (Table 1).

Table 1. Reasons for change

Reasons for change	Approximate % of response
Provides improved service (benefits)	50
Technical superiority over alternatives	20
Decision emotionally based	20
Mixed or uncertain reasons	10
Total	100

Most people claim that the change process adopted provides improved benefits to them. The consultant ought, therefore, always to make available ample information setting out the benefits to be accrued by all concerned if the new proposal is adopted.

A sizable group (20%) state that they are influenced by technical reasons when choosing a new approach (e.g. the " isolates "), and a similar sized group claim to be influenced for reasons that are emotionally based (they were persuaded by friends; everyone else is doing it; etc.). Some 10%, a minority group, often referred to as the " lunatic fringe ", represent a mixed section who are uncertain as to why they decided to change and, very often are highly critical of whatever scheme is employed. The consultant should realise that members of this minority can seldom be convinced, are downright difficult to deal with and, in many cases, do not know what they want.

Developing desire for change

Once the audience's attention has been aroused and interest in seeking change created, then comes the time to develop a desire for the consultant's proposal.

In presenting information to enhance the selection of a given proposal in preference to alternative schemes, it is often necessary to mention some negative aspects of the proposed scheme in addition to the more beneficial ones.

Similarly the positive and negative aspects of existing or alternative schemes should also be presented. This technique of providing all aspects of the case under review is referred to as an " innoculation " effect which weakens any counterproposals likely to arise at a later date. Experience has shown that an effective manner of presenting information where proposal B is intended to displace proposal A is to employ the following sequence:

(1) present a complete listing of the positive, beneficial aspects of proposal B;

(2)   mention the obvious and real drawbacks associated with proposal B;

(3)   describe a comprehensive listing of the deficiencies of proposal A;

(4)   indicate the most pertinent positive features of proposal A.

Following this presentation of the positive and negative features of the alternate proposals, the consultant should then draw conclusions as to why the favoured proposal (B) should be employed by listing the benefits to be accrued (i.e. service provided), the effectiveness of the new proposal (i.e. technical and economic superiority) and, if applicable, instances where such proposal has been successfully employed.

Commitment to action

It has been mentioned earlier [1] that the process of change involves: (i) identification with the change, and (ii) internalisation of the change. Whether these phases act in sequence, or simultaneously, is not very important. The essential point is to realise that they require commitment, involvement or participation by the person doing the changing. The change must be tested by the individual as he moves from the general (identification) to the specific (internalisation).

Therefore, as early as possible the people concerned in the change process require to be involved, so that these two vital elements can be comprehensively covered. However, a strong note of warning is offered concerning how participation might be achieved. Apart from attending brain-storming sessions employed for specific purposes such as to provide a data bank of ideas for the solution of creative problems [2], individuals should not be encouraged to seek their own methods of performing tasks if the general idea is to develop a best-method as recommended by the consultant. Results of studies show that where individuals are permitted to adopt their own approaches and the best-method or approved solution is later imposed, the individuals will exhibit some conformity to the new proposal, but will still diverge significantly from the approved method in following their own methods.

However, where persons in groups are provided with a best-method or approved approach in the first instance, it is found that subsequently individuals will vary only insignificantly from the set procedures. Diagrammatically, these results can be shown as in Figure 2.

In case 1 the end result is that individuals perform in a manner significantly different from the approved method although not quite as widely

---

[1] See p. 28.

[2] On brain-storming, see p. 148.

Figure 2. Comparison of two cases illustrating the effects on eventual performance when using individualised versus conformed initial approaches

Case 1 : *Subsequent behaviour diverges significantly from the conformed approach when individualised approaches are used prior to the introduction of the conformed approach*

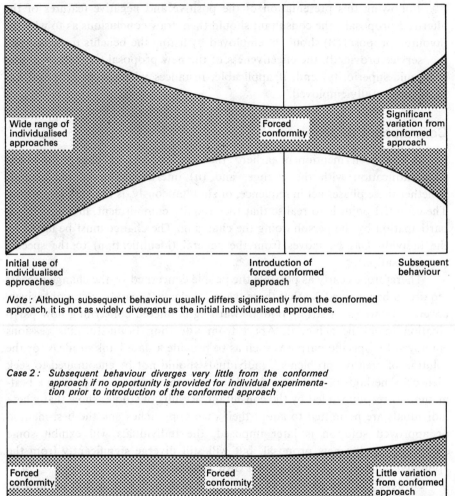

Initial use of
individualised
approaches

Introduction of
forced conformed
approach

Subsequent
behaviour

Note : Although subsequent behaviour usually differs significantly from the conformed approach, it is not as widely divergent as the initial individualised approaches.

Case 2 : *Subsequent behaviour diverges very little from the conformed approach if no opportunity is provided for individual experimentation prior to introduction of the conformed approach*

Conformed approach
used from the outset

Continuation of
conformed approach

Subsequent
behaviour

Note : Subsequent behaviour is significantly less divergent from the conformed approach in Case 2 when compared to Case 1.

different as during their initial trials. There is some tendency towards the norm. In case 2 there is much less divergence (significant in a statistical sense) in subsequent performance from the approved norm bcause individuals have not had an opportunity to rehearse in any manner other than in the approved one. Thus, where feasible, the consultant should attempt to introduce the approved method as a scheme applying to the whole group where individual differences can be kept to a minimum (often as a result of normal group pressures, coupled with the fact that no opportunity to develop individual ad hoc approaches is provided).

4.3 Techniques for assisting change

Consultants have access to a proliferation of behavioural-science based methods by which they are able to facilitate growth and change in individuals, groups and organisations. These methods include management by objectives, training (T) groups, transactional analysis, operations analysis, task group therapy, non-verbal communication techniques, organisation development, use of the managerial grid, achievement motivation, etc. It is knowledge and practice of skills in employing these techniques that set the consultant apart from the academic theoretician. The techniques may be acquired in part by studying research findings and publications but, more particularly, they will be developed by experience.

Organisation Development (OD) has been defined as " an effort (1) planned, (2) organisation wide, and (3) managed from the top, to (4) increase organisation effectiveness and health through (5) planned interventions in the organisation's ' processes ' using behavioural-science knowledge ".[1]

Organisation development is a matter for the whole organisation but involves contacts with individuals and groups with a view to assisting change in beliefs, attitudes, values and organisational structure to adapt to fit new situations. Examples of this technique which can be employed by the consultant to effect change are given below.[2]

Team development attempts to build up an effective management team by employing interviews, rating scales, discussions etc., to provide each member of the group with feedback about how others perceive the group in relation to himself and about how group effectiveness can be improved.

The inter-group-relationships approach endeavours to involve various departments, e.g. production and sales, in examining ways of increasing

---

[1] R. Beckhard: *Organisation development: strategies and models* (Reading, Mass., Addison-Wesley, 1969), p. 9.

[2] See also H. M. F. Rush: *Organisation development: a reconnaissance* (New York, The Conference Board, 1973).

collaboration. Techniques are used whereby the groups prepare descriptions of how other groups appear to them and how they think other groups feel about them. The purpose of the group work is to attempt to arrive at least at an understanding of other departments' points of view.

Confrontation meetings employ a highly structured approach in which selected staff are exposed to (1) historical and conceptual ideas about organisations, (2) preparation of a list of significant problem-areas in their own organisation, (3) classification of stated problems into categories, (4) development of plans of action to remedy problems, and (5) planning for implementation.

Goal-setting exercises require an individual and his line-boss to talk over the former's work-content and attempt to establish agreed targets for a scheduled period. This approach can be expanded to accommodate team goal-setting (management by objectives) and to include definition of the organisational structure by top-level management who set over-all major goals, and departments or other organisational units who set corresponding sub-goals, which can be discussed by all concerned at multi-level meetings.

4.4 Tactical guides for implementing change

An underlying key consideration when dealing with the phenomenon of change is that the achievement of change can only be verified by a change in behaviour. For example, a person may actually have learnt all that he is required to know about a new approach without it being possible to be sure that this is so, since there are no certain methods for measuring how much learning has taken place. We can, however, measure the change, if any, in the performance of the person under observation and thus, indirectly, gain some idea of the amount of learning that has occurred.

Tactic 1 : Spaced practice (quick and often)

Improvement in performance occurs more quickly, in greater depth, and lasts for a longer time (i.e. the decay or extinction curve is longer) if new approaches are introduced in relatively short periods with ample provision for rest periods, than if continuous or massed practice periods are employed.

A generalised improvement in performance noted where the " quick and often " tactic is employed (compared to a continuous practice scheme) is shown in Figure 3.

From the figure it can be seen that when a spaced practice approach is used and the results are compared with those of a continuous or massed practice approach for the same period:

Figure 3. Comparison of spaced practice with a continuous or massed practice approach in terms of performance

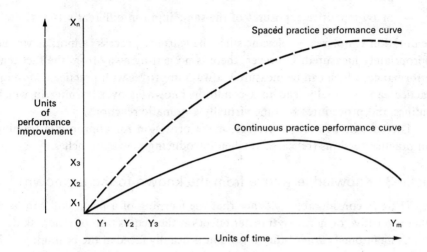

— improvement using spaced practice is quicker, i.e. the performance curve is sharper;

— improvement using spaced practice is greater, i.e. the performance curve is higher;

— improvement lasts longer, i.e. the decay or extinction curve is shallower.

These performance curves will almost invariably be obtained where improvement in skill can be measured as a result of practice or rehearsal. Thus the consultant is well advised to consider introducing change over time using relatively short practice sessions rather than rely on one large training input.

Tactic 2: Rehearsal (practice makes perfect)

It is a proven fact that where skill is involved results constantly improve with spaced practice providing, of course, that the correct procedures are practised.

As shown in Figure 3 performance constantly improves with continued practice until a ceiling level or plateau of performance is reached. Continued practice is then required to maintain this level of performance.

Although there may be grounds for debate as to whether or not learning (i.e. the cerebral functioning involved) of a new technique takes place

— as a sequential process, i.e. a little-by-little approach;

— as an all-or-none process (e.g. the "Eureka—I've-got-it" type of phenomenon);

— or by repetitive exposures of the same input in different settings,

the question is not really relevant since the learning process cannot, as yet, be appropriately measured. However, there is no getting away from the fact that performance, which can be measured, always improves with practice. Constant practice can eventually lead to a condition known as over-learning in which routines and procedures become virtually automatic reactions.

The consultant must, therefore, make provision for appropriate training and practice sessions (rehearsals) when introducing new approaches.

Tactic 3: Knowledge (move from the known to the unknown)

There is considerable evidence that the learning of a prior skill can have either a positive or negative transfer effect on the acquisition of a new skill.

As mentioned earlier,[1] the consultant is usually faced at the beginning with the need for an "unfreezing" phase; one designed to break down old habits. Surprising as it may seem, in order to be able to facilitate new learning it is usually more effective to have the learner in an "anxious" rather than "comfortable" state, because he is then more likely to seek, actively, information to reduce his level of anxiety. In a "comfortable" state, he is more likely to select information which will continue that state, i.e. to reinforce old habits rather than seek new approaches.

The consultant can use this attention-rousing device by referring to the present "known" procedures and showing that they are no longer suitable for present purposes. If he moves directly to introduce new approaches without first breaking down established practices, there is a grave risk of negative transfer effects taking place.

When introducing a totally new approach, however, there may be some benefit in building it on an appropriate existing procedure. In short, when introducing change, move from the known to the unknown (new approach).

Tactic 4: Goal setting (expect a little more)

According to S. W. Gellerman "stretching" is desirable when goals are being established. By this he means that targets should be set a little higher than would normally be expected to be attained.[2] D. C. McClelland supports this notion and adds that the goals should be realistic and be neither "too

---

[1] See p. 27.

[2] S. W. Gellerman: *Management by motivation* (New York, American Management Association, 1968).

easy " nor " impossible ", but such that a feeling of achievement can be experienced when they are reached.[1]

There is ample evidence to show that high expectations coupled with genuine confidence by a prestigious person often result in a changee attaining high performance and higher productivity. This effect can become cumulative, i.e. the improved performance encourages the individual to assume more responsibility and so creates in him greater opportunities for achievement, growth and development. Conversely, low expectations may lead to low performance which, in turn, leads to a situation in which credibility is lost and distrust and scepticism become the order of the day.

A further point is that, when introducing change, it has to be readily understood what this means in terms of goals. Such goals should be expressed in terms which are:

— quantitative (able to be measured in numerical terms);

— qualitative (able to be described specifically);

— time-phased (provision of commencement dates and expected duration before final attainment).

Tactic 5: Feedback (provide knowledge of results)

Successful introduction of change requires presentation of appropriate feedback information to permit necessary adjustments on the part of those undertaking the change process. The consultant must make provision for review and reporting sessions not merely as morale-boosting devices, but as a requisite for control and correction.

Tactic 6: Capacity (a little at a time)

People differ tremendously in their capacity to absorb new information and their ability to undertake new activities. Many writers have argued that there is a maximum number of " units of information " which an individual can absorb and process at any one time. In this connection G. W. Miller refers to the " magical number seven " (plus or minus two, to allow for variations in individual capacity).[2] By confining inputs to the lower end of the scale (viz: five), the consultant can avoid over-taxing any of his audience, although he may cause some degree of impatience among the most gifted.

---

[1] D. C. McClelland, D. G. Winter: *Motivating economic achievement* (New York, The Free Press, 1969).

[2] G. W. Miller: " The magical number seven, plus or minus two " in *Psychological Review*, Vol. 63, No. 2, March 1956.

The information can first be presented as a single whole and then be broken down into sub-units for more detailed study or, alternatively, it can be built up gradually by synthesis of the individual parts. The method chosen will depend on the nature of the problem, the composition of the audience and the consultant's personal preference.

During the introductory and concluding phases of an information session it is well to provide a summary of the total presentation. There is support for the idea that the attention of an audience reaches its highest level shortly after the commencement of a session and again shortly before its conclusion. At the outset the exposition probably has a novelty value, which begins to dissipate as physical and mental fatigue build up. Shortly before the conclusion is reached, however, the decrease in the level of attention accounted for by lack of concentration is usually removed as the audience begins to anticipate the end of this activity and the beginning of a new one. These high points in concentration are illustrated in Figure 4.

Figure 4. Generalised illustration of the high points in attention level of a captive audience

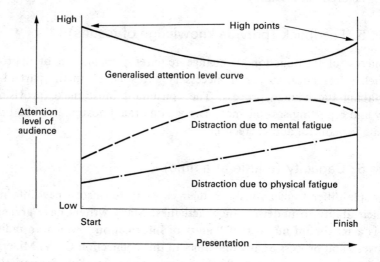

Tactic 7: Timing (allow enough time)

Attitude change and attendant behavioural change, except under unusual circumstances, need time. Because attitudes and habits take a long time to form, time must be allowed for them to be replaced by new ones.

In attitude change there is a so-called " sleeper " effect in which, regardless of the original source of new information, a time lapse (often in excess of four weeks) is required for attitude change to take effect. Unless there is a perceived dramatic need to institute a change it may take longer than has been deemed appropriate.

Tactic 8 : Evidence (words are not enough)

Verbal persuasion is inherently unstable and requires support in terms of behavioural change. The consultant must keep records of all performance improvements as support for the change process. For example, although daily output figures may decrease immediately following a change process, it is possible that errors or accident rates may decrease even more significantly at the same time.

4.5 Environmental factors bearing on the change process

Consultants attempting to effect change should be aware of environmental factors which may influence their work.

The perceived status of the change agent

To achieve immediate positive response in convincing people to accept change it is imperative that the change agent be considered trustworthy. This factor is not quite so important if long-term effects are to be achieved, as a " sleeper " or long-term delay effect may come into play in which there is separation between the content of the information and the original source of that information. It matters little if the change agent is seen as an individual who will gain personally from introducing change, providing it is not at the expense of those who are involved in the change. However, people involved in change are likely to be more affected by the alleged *attitude* of the change agent (e.g. ruthless cost-cutting) than by his *personality* (e.g. withdrawn, unfriendly).

The change agent should not only be an expert but he should, if possible, be introduced and recognised as one.

The informal communication network

Communications on a highly topical issue appear to produce greater and more rapid attitude change in an audience when the information is " accidently overheard ", or leaked via informal communication networks, than when delivered by the formal network. Rumours, which flourish in the absence of formal communications, are usually confined to the informal channels and can often be countered by appropriate use of the same network.

Objections to change

Resistance to change is not uncommon.[1] The consultant must learn, very early in his career, how to overcome objections. Broadly speaking, objectors can be classified as " sharpeners " or " levellers ". *Sharpeners* include those people who ask specific, detailed questions concerning the change process. Generally speaking, these types are genuine objectors who can be influenced more readily than other types by logical argument. *Levellers* are those who generalise and broaden the issue under review. These types are usually quite difficult to convince as they are often more interested in the form of their objections than in their content.

When the consultant has to *handle objections*, it is more useful to repeat the objection, put it in writing if possible, break it down into component parts and treat each component as a separate entity rather than attempt to deal with the problem as a whole. It is recommended to commence with those items on which agreement is most likely to be reached and move later to those items causing most disagreement. Should an issue reach a total impasse, it is better to reword the disagreement in objective terms relating to the new proposal rather than continue arguing in the, often, coloured and emotional words originally proposed by the objector. The consultant should frequently take the opportunity to recapitulate and to refer to parts of the original objection on which agreement has already been reached, before continuing with new points.

If a point is reached at which the consultant does not have the appropriate information on hand, this fact should be readily admitted and the objector advised that the information will be obtained and transmitted to him at a later date. The consultant should not fail to carry out this promise.

When objection to change becomes a matter of inter-group conflict, different problems requiring special treatment may arise. If a group sees itself threatened, there will be a closing of the ranks and more cohesive action, and the group will become more tolerant of authoritative rule by its chosen leaders. Hostility to " other " groups is likely to arise, especially if the situation is perceived as a " win-lose " encounter. Communication will become distorted and difficult, as each group will be prepared to admit only the positive aspects of its own argument and the negative aspects of the " enemy's ".

Basic strategies to reduce inter-group conflict require the establishment of goals upon which both groups can agree in order to restore valid inter-group communication. If possible a common " enemy " should be identified, thus setting up a superordinate goal. Emphasis should be placed on total goals rather than sub-group goals.

---

[1] Cf. J. G. Bensahel " How to overcome resistance to change " in *International Management*, September 1977, p. 66.

If possible, a reward system which encourages effective communication should be introduced. Groups should be exposed to a wide range of activities likely to enhance empathy and understanding.

Personality composition of the audience

To maintain control when dealing with a gathering or crowd of people is difficult at the best of times. When dealing with individuals or small groups there are sometimes opportunities to use group members as enhancers of the change process.

Individuals who are poised, confident and have a certain amount of self-esteem appear to be able to influence others who lack these characteristics. In turn, these individuals of relatively high self-esteem appear to be more influenced by information containing optimistic rather than pessimistic or negative connotations.

The consultant should use opportunities to enlist support for the change process from persons who possess such traits of high self-esteem by drawing attention to likely optimistic results. These persons are then in a position to support the consultant's proposals before the group.

MANAGEMENT CONSULTING AS A PROFESSION 5

The growth of management consulting has given ample evidence that at one time almost anyone could call himself a consultant and set up in practice. In its early years the business attracted the good, the bad and the indifferent. The word "business" is used deliberately: "professions" seldom start as such. Professional awareness and behaviour come when the early juggling with a little knowledge gives way to skilled application of a generally accepted body of knowledge according to acknowledged standards of integrity. The professions of medicine, law and the sciences all followed this path and management consulting is proceeding in the same direction.

The development of management consulting towards professionalism is part of a wider movement—that which aims at developing management into a profession. As advisors to managers on the application of the science and art of managing, consultants follow the major trends that affect management practice and theory. In many respects consulting can advance, and become more professional, only if the whole field of management is making headway towards professionalism. At the same time consultants constitute a specialised group, which has its own way of operating and has adopted a set of its own behavioural rules and working procedures. The problem of professionalising management consultancy is therefore not completely identical with professionalising management as such. It is even necessary to recognise that in most countries management consultants are aiming at professionalism with more vigour than the practising managers and that they play a pioneering role in professionalising management at large.

5.1 Key aspects of professionalism in consulting

Knowledge and skills

As consultants influence managerial decisions, of which some may be very important for the future life of organisations, it is fully justified to require them to possess the professional knowledge and skills needed for this role.

Some professional associations of management consultants try to define and continuously update a common body of knowledge for consultants [1], and consulting organisations that want to achieve a high professional reputation require a new consultant to possess a certain amount and depth of knowledge and complement this knowledge through initial and further training programmes. An individual engaged in consulting develops his knowledge by drawing lessons from new assignments and through further study.

Hitherto, however, the common body of knowledge for consultants has not been generally adopted and what associations of consultants have compiled is used rather for broad guidance of their members than as a binding standard.

The problem of consulting skills is quite delicate. While it is possible to define their scope in a general way together with the body of knowledge, to decide in a particular case whether a consultant has the skills needed to handle an assignment is a matter of professional judgement.[2]

As a general rule, and this is a major feature of professionalism, a consultant must be able and willing to critically examine his own knowledge and skills when considering new assignments. Quite often a potential client approaches a consultant with full confidence in his competence and he may even be unable to judge this competence. A professional consultant, however, would refrain from assignments that for any reasons do not lie in his field of competence. He may decline the assignment, suggest the use of specialists for some parts of the job, or try to propose another arrangement convenient to the client.

Objectivity

It is often stated that consultants are objective in their analysis, judgement and conclusions. This is certainly true in most cases as far as the consultant's will to avoid any bias is concerned. But consultants do not possess absolute, ideal skills of handling various situations and their attitudes have been moulded by their life experience, like attitudes of any other persons. Consciously or unconsciously, they develop not only certain work patterns, but also beliefs in certain types of methods and solutions—because they and their colleagues have applied such methods or solutions successfully in previous cases.

Occasionally this can go quite far. Some consultants even clearly favour one methodological approach which they consider as the most powerful tool for solving management problems. The same situation might be viewed by one consultant as a

---

[1] Cf. P. W. Shay: *The common body of knowledge for management consultants* (New York, Association of Consulting Management Engineers, 1974).

[2] Further aspects of consultants' knowledge and skills are discussed in Part VI " Developing Management Consultants ".

matter of diagnosing future business prospects and defining strategies, by another consultant as an organisation development, team-building exercise, and by a third one as a typical case for the introduction of management by objectives throughout the organisation. Some consultants are strong believers in the behavioural sciences and pay great attention to the psycho-sociological aspects of change, while others prefer the traditional approach using job analysis and time and methods study.

By emphasising that consultants may use very different approaches to the same problems we do not want to devalue their advice. But the word " objective " is to be used with extreme caution. If a consultant decides to approach his client's business and organisational problems in one particular way, although there may be other options, he should:

— inform his client about such a choice,

— give his reasons.

Chances of success of assignments

While most assignments may lead to improvements, there also are assignments that cannot produce any results for a variety of reasons and the money spent would be wasted.

For example, a client may want to make a change which is overdue and which cannot stop the over-all deterioration of the firm's situation. Or improvements are possible, but would require drastic personnel measures which the client is unable to consider. Or the benefits from tackling the problem may be so small that the consultancy fees are not justified.

If a professional consultant discovers such a situation in preparing the assignment, or even after he has started work, he informs the client candidly and suggests cancelling the contract.

Teaching people to work without consultants

No professional consultant would perpetuate his assignments by making the client dependent on his advice. " The only work that is really worth doing as a consultant is that which educates—which teaches clients and their staff to manage better for themselves ", said L. Urwick, one of the major contributors to the development of management consulting. The transmission of all information on methods used in the assignment, and the training of the client's staff so that they can repeat the same operations without consultants, is a key element in the consultant's professional approach.

This does not mean that the better the consultant teaches the client and his staff the less work he will have in the future. Clients will have new sorts of problems, and if the consultant continues to improve his competence he may be called again. Other clients will come and so on.

Length of assignments

Consulting services are not inexpensive and professional consultants do not try to stabilise their income by extending assignments beyond necessary time limits. For example, they do not suggest that they supervise the implementation of proposals if they can train the client's staff to do this without any external help.

Another case is that of urgent assignments, in which advice is needed very quickly so that serious financial or other trouble is avoided. A consultant must never take longer than the problem warrants, and make every effort to organise his work in accordance with the urgency of the situation.

Confidentiality

Management consultants engage themselves not to disclose any confidential information about clients, nor to make any use of this information to obtain benefits or advantages. The clients must be convinced that they can trust consultants, otherwise consulting cannot get off the ground.

In internal consulting the situation with regard to confidentiality is complicated. In certain cases consultants have an obligation, or a possibility, to disclose information on client organisations to a common superior (minister or other person). But under such circumstances managers are reluctant to use consultants. There has been, therefore, a tendency in a number of countries to apply confidentiality also to the public-sector consulting services.

For example, in organising its Bureau of Management Consulting, the Canadian Government has followed the following essential principles:
— studies are undertaken only upon request of the client department or agency;
— services are advisory in nature;
— services are confidential, and reports resulting from the assignment are made available only to the client.

In 1970 the Bureau of Management Consulting began to charge for its services and was thus put into competition with management consultants in the private sector.

Confidentiality is still an issue in many developing countries, where some local businessmen do not feel sure that information given to consultants coming from management or productivity centres will not be passed on to government-controlled bodies or tax collectors.

Social implications

Assignments undertaken by management consultants may affect the position and interests of people working in organisations and have important implications of a social nature for the environment in which a given organisation operates. This raises the very important issue of consultants' social responsibility. Are they responsible merely to the clients who pay them for the advice or is their responsibility broader?

The current trend is towards increased awareness of the social consequences of managerial decisions and the enhanced social responsibility of managers. Professional management consultants cannot stand aside. They have to make client managers sensitive to the social consequences of various decisions that may be taken as a result of consulting assignments. Whenever possible, the solution of social and environmental problems which arise from the envisaged technological and organisational measures should be embraced by the assignment, thus giving the consultant the opportunity to suggest measures that are not only technically or financially feasible, but also socially desirable.

It is fully justified to request consultants to warn managers strongly before decisions are taken whose social implications are likely to be negative—greater pollution, excessive physical or mental strain on the workers, more unemployment, etc.

5.2 Professional associations and codes of conduct

In a number of countries management consultants have established voluntary professional associations to represent their interests and regulate the activities of both individual consultants and consulting firms.[1] These associations have played a leading role in promoting professional standards of management consulting and helping this young profession to gain the confidence of the management circles and a good reputation in society.

By and large, associations of management consultants contribute to the development of the profession by

— developing and up-dating the common body of knowledge;

— determining minimum qualification criteria for new entrants to the profession (education, type and length of experience)[2];

— defining and adopting a code of professional conduct and practice for its members;

— examining various aspects of management consulting, organising an exchange of experience and making recommendations to members on

---

[1] Appendix 1 gives a list (with addresses) of associations of management consultants in various countries and of international associations of consulting engineers.

[2] For example, the Management Consultants Association in the United Kingdom requires member firms to have at least five years of consulting experience and at least 80% of the consulting staff has to hold degrees of recognised universities or equivalent qualifications. The bye-laws of the Association stipulate in detail a number of further conditions of membership.

improvements in consulting methods, organisation of units, selection, development and remuneration of consultants etc.;

— investigating complaints of violations of the code of conduct and taking disciplinary action.

The codes of professional conduct are basic instruments used by the consultants' associations to establish the profession and protect its integrity. They " signify voluntary assumption by members of the obligation of self-discipline above and beyond the requirements of law ".[1]

Above all, the codes include a definition of professional responsibility which is mandatory and serves as a basis for disciplinary action if a member infringes the agreed standards.

Thus, members of the associations engage themselves

— to place the client's interest ahead of their own;

— to keep information about the client confidential and take no advantage of its knowledge;

— to accept no commissions in connection with the supply of services to the client;

— to hold no directorship or controlling interest in any business competitor of the client without disclosing it;

— not to invite an employee of a client to consider or apply for suggested alternative employment;

— not to calculate remuneration on any other basis than a fixed fee agreed in advance, which may be on a time rate;

— to inform clients of any relationships and interests that might influence the consultant's judgement;

— to accept no assignment which exceeds the scope of their competence;

— not to work when their judgement might be impaired by illness, misfortune or any other cause;

— to refrain from seeking business by public advertising or by payment of commission for the introduction to clients.

There is a tendency in some codes of conduct to include a set of rules which define good professional practice and provide broad methodological guidance to members of the association. For example, the code promulgated by the Smaller Enterprise Consultants' Association of Japan in 1973 defines a

---

[1] " Standards of Professional Conduct and Practice " of the Association of Consulting Management Engineers (USA). The full text of this code is given in Appendix 2. Examples of other codes can be obtained from the associations listed in Appendix 1.

number of principles to be observed in consulting assignments. These principles emphasise, among others, the need to use the total approach to the client's problems, to examine each enterprise in a dynamic way, including its past history and future development prospects, to pay full attention to the individuality of the enterprise and to present proposals with their financial and other implications in a practical manner which will be easily understood by the client.

It is, of course, not the code of conduct itself, but its rigorous and intelligent application by all members of the association, which determines the real professional value and integrity of consulting services. Some codes even have a clause by which the consultants engage themselves to do nothing likely to lower the status of management consulting as a profession. This leaves much to the discretion of the consultants themselves.

5.3 The clients' contribution to consulting ethics

As management consulting is a partnership between consultant and client, it cannot become more professional and ethical without the clients' help. In particular, consultants can adopt and effectively apply such standards as will be seen to be realistic and sound in the management community that uses consultants. Members of the management community have then to observe these standards themselves and put no pressure on consultants in order to obtain confidential information on former clients, or reports and other services that are in contradiction with the adopted standards. Managers also help to promote professional standards by controlling the consultants' behaviour during assignments and conveying any dissatisfaction to the consultants' associations. To be able to do that, managers who intend to use consultants should be familiar with the code of conduct applied by consultants in a given country.

Of particular importance is the choice of consultants. By requesting and thoroughly examining information on consulting units whose use is envisaged, the client can eliminate those who do not meet the established professional criteria.[1]

---

[1] See P. W. Shay: *How to get the best results from management consultants* (New York, Association of Consulting Management Engineers, 1974).

LITERATURE TO PART I

Abramson R., Halset W.: *Planning for improved enterprise performance: a guide for managers and consultants* (Management Development Series No. 15) (Geneva, International Labour Office, 1979); 178 pp.

ACME: *Growth opportunities and trends in management consulting* (New York, Association of Consulting Management Engineers, 1977).

Albert K. J.: *How to be your own management consultant* (New York, McGraw-Hill, 1978); 256 pp.

APO: *Development of management consultancy in APO member countries* (Tokyo, Asian Productivity Organisation, 1978); 185 pp.

APO: *Productivity through consultancy in small industrial enterprises* (Tokyo, Asian Productivity Organisation, 1974); 500 pp.

Argyris Ch.: *Intervention theory and method: a behavioral science view* (Reading, Mass., Addison-Wesley, 1970); 374 pp.

Argyris Ch., Schön D. A.: *Organisational learning: a theory of action perspective* (Reading, Mass., Addison-Wesley, 1978); 344 pp.

Beckhart R., Harris R. T.: *Organisational transitions: managing complex change* (Reading, Mass., Addison-Wesley, 1977); 110 pp.

Bell Ch. R., Nadler L. (eds.): *The client-consultant handbook* (Houston, Gulf Publishing, 1979); 278 pp.

Bennis W.: *Organisation development: its nature, origins and prospects* (Reading, Mass., Addison-Wesley, 1969); 90 pp.

Blake R., Mouton J. S.: *Consultation* (Reading, Mass., Addison-Wesley, 1976); 484 pp.

Blake R., Mouton J. S.: *Making experience work: the grid approach to critique* (New York, McGraw-Hill, 1978); 125 pp.

Code of practice for the use of management consultants by government departments (London, Her Majesty's Stationery Office, 1975); 31 pp.

Dalton G. W., Lawrence P. R., Greiner L. E. (eds.): *Organizational change and development* (Homewood, Ill., Irwin, 1970); 390 pp.

Davis K.: *Human behaviour at work* (5th ed.) (New York, McGraw-Hill, 1977); 581 pp.

Fuchs J. H.: *Making the most of management consulting services* (New York, AMACOM, 1975); 214 pp.

Fuchs J. H.: *Management consultants in action* (New York, Hawthorn Books, 1975); 216 pp.

Gellerman S. W.: *Management by motivation* (New York, American Management Association, 1968); 286 pp.

Gowan V. Q.: *Consulting to government* (Cambridge, Mass., Infoscan, 1979); 368 pp.

Guttmann H. P.: *The international consultant* (New York, McGraw-Hill, 1976); 193 pp.

Hersey P., Blanchard K. H.: *Management of organisational behaviour: utilising human resources* (3rd ed.) (Englewood Cliffs, N. J., Prentice-Hall, 1977); 384 pp.

Hunt A.: *The management consultant* (New York, Ronald Press, 1977); 159 pp.

Interregional seminar on administration of management improvement services (Copenhagen, Denmark, 28.9-6.10.1970), Volume I: Report of the seminar and technical papers (New York, United Nations, 1971; Sales No.: E.71.II.4.9); 125 pp.

Katz D., Kahn R. L.: *Social psychology of organisations* (New York, Wiley, 1978); 838 pp.

Klein H. J.: *Other people's business (a primer on management consultant)* (New York, Mason-Charter, 1977); 202 pp.

Kuecken J. A.: *Starting and managing your own engineering practice* (New York, Van Norstrand Reinhold, 1978); 175 pp.

Leavitt H. J.: *Managerial psychology* (Chicago, The University of Chicago Press, 1978); 386 pp.

Lippitt G., Hoopes D. S. (eds.): *Helping across cultures* (Washington, International Consultants Foundation, 1978); 76 pp.

Lippitt G., Lippitt R.: *The consulting process in action* (La Jolla, Calif., University Associates, 1978); 130 pp.

Marlow H.: *Managing change—a strategy for our time* (London, Institute of Personnel Management, 1975); 170 pp.

McClelland D. C., Winter D. G.: *Motivating economic achievement* (New York, The Free Press, 1969); 410 pp.

Merry U., Allerhand M. E.: *Developing teams and organisations: a practical handbook for managers and consultants* (Reading, Mass., Addison-Wesley, 1977); 422 pp.

Rush H. M. F.: *Behavioral science: concepts and management application* (New York, National Industrial Conference Board, 1969); 180 pp.

Rush H. M. F.: *Organisation development: a reconnaissance* (New York, The Conference Board, 1973); 74 pp.

Schein E. H.: *Organisational psychology* (Englewood Cliffs, N. J., Prentice-Hall, 1965); 110 pp.

Schein E. H.: *Process consultation: its role in organisation development* (Reading, Mass., Addison-Wesley, 1969); 150 pp.

Shay P. W.: *How to get the best results from management consultants* (New York, Association of Consulting Management Engineers, 1974); 60 pp.

Shay P. W.: *Professional responsibilities of management consultants: ethics and professional conduct* (New York, Association of Consulting Management Engineers, 1973); 27 pp.

Shenson H. L.: *The consulting contract: strategies and sample contracts* (Woodland Hills, California, H. L. Shenson, 1977; mimeographed); 69 pp.

Sidney E., Brown M., Argyle M.: *Skills with people: a guide for managers* (London, Hutchinson, 1973); 230 pp.

Steele F.: *Consulting for organizational change* (Amherst, Mass., University of Massachusetts Press, 1975); 202 pp.

The consulting engineer and related professions (FIDIC Forum 1975) (The Hague, International Federation of Consulting Engineers, 1975); 67 pp.

UNIDO: *Manual on the use of consultants in developing countries* (New York, United Nations, 1972); 160 pp.

Walley B. H.: *Management services handbook* (London, Business Books, 1973); 448 pp.

Walsh J. E.: *Guidelines for management consultants in Asia* (Tokyo, Asian Productivity Organisation, 1973); 210 pp.

Periodicals:

Consultants News (Fitzwilliam, New Hampshire, Kennedy and Kennedy, monthly).

The Consulting Engineer (London, Northwood Publications, monthly).

The Howard L. Shenson Report (Woodland Hills, California, H. L. Shenson; monthly).

PART II

PREPARING AND CONTROLLING OPERATING ASSIGNMENTS

THE MANAGEMENT SURVEY

6

The management survey was defined in Chapter 2 as the first stage in most consulting assignments. Its purpose is to identify correctly the problem for which the consultant's help is required and prepare specific proposals for the client on the objectives, organisation and cost of the assignment.

6.1 Preparatory steps

Initial contacts

A management survey results from a contact between the consultant and a potential client. This may originate from one of the following events:

- direct inquiry (a potential client is looking for a consultant);
- spontaneous approach (the consultant approaches various organisations and offers his services to the management);
- lead (the consultant is recommended or introduced to a potential client by a colleague, a friend, a former client, etc.);
- former work with the client (the client turns again to a consultant whose work satisfied him in the past; this may be a direct extension of a recent assignment, or a new assignment suggested after the consultant's follow-up visit to the client organisation, etc.);

Further aspects of the promotional activities of consulting organisations will be discussed later.[1] It should, however, be noted at this stage that consulting organisations generally consider the spontaneous approach as the least productive, although most time-consuming. Former work with the client which led to good results, and recommendations based on results obtained in

---

[1] See Chapter 24, p. 251.

other organisations, are the references most likely to lead to new contacts and new assignments.

During the initial contact with the client the consultant usually arranges a preliminary meeting to discuss and obtain the client's agreement to a management survey.

Survey consultants

In many consulting organisations there is a special category of all-round consultants called *survey* or *diagnostic consultants*. These are senior members of the organisation, with broad knowledge of all management areas, experience in diagnosing the nature of difficulties in business and other types of organisation, and proven ability to discuss new assignments with senior people in client organisations.

As a rule, the consultant who would carry out the survey is the person delegated by the consulting unit to represent it at the preliminary survey meeting.

Preliminary survey meeting

The importance of the consultant's behaviour and performance in the preliminary survey meeting cannot be over-emphasised. Such a meeting is a short opportunity to gain the client's confidence and make a favourable impression on him. The consultant wants to make sure that he will meet the decision maker—the person who is not only interested in an assignment but also able to authorise a management survey, or submit a proposal for such a survey to a decision-making body. If a top executive (managing director, senior administrator, etc.) of an important organisation agrees to hold a preliminary survey meeting with consultants, the consulting unit should delegate a representative of equally high level.

The meeting requires thorough preparation by the consultant. Without going into irrelevant details, the consulting unit collects essential orientation facts [1] about the client organisation and its environment.

The meeting is a form of investigational interview in which each party seeks to learn about the other. The consultant should encourage the client to do most of the talking so that he hears about the circumstances which led to the meeting and why the client considered that consulting might help him. It is as well for the discussion to develop from the general situation to the particular and to focus eventually on the real issue.

---

[1] See p. 73.

While listening, and putting his own questions, the consultant assesses the client's needs in terms of sound management practice. He decides how best to describe the nature and scope of consulting as it applies to the client's problem. He must be absolutely sure the client understands and accepts his own role and responsibility in a consulting operation.

The client may be eager to proceed or may be reluctant to make a decision. The consultant should use care and patience in the exercise of persuasion, and keep mainly to the potential benefits to the client.

If the client is ready to agree to a preliminary survey, the discussion should move on to the arrangements for carrying it out, and cover:

— terms of reference for the survey;
— records and information to be made available, so that the client can start preparing them;
— identifying key people to be seen and setting up a timetable for interviews;
— how the survey will be announced to the client's staff and how the consultant will be introduced to them;
— attitudes of the staff to matters under survey;
— accommodation for the survey consultant (office space, typing facilities, etc.);
— availability of the client during the survey;
— dates for meetings with the client at the end of the survey, for presenting the proposals prepared.

Finally, the question of payment for the survey must be settled. Usually, short surveys are provided free of charge. Time spent on such surveys is included as overhead when calculating fee rates for consultations. Only where a survey is complex and likely to last more than five days will the client be expected to pay.[1]

The client may wish to discuss the proposed work with other clients of the consultant and may ask for references. This may happen before, during, or after the survey. In giving names, the consultant must remember the confidential relationship with his clients and cite only those who are willing to provide references.

6.2 The course of a management survey

At the beginning of the survey some definition of the problem is made by the client himself, who may also have certain thoughts about the style and cost

---

[1] In some countries management consultants also charge clients for short surveys.

of the consultant's work. During a management survey the consultant reaches an understanding with the client on:

— what the problem really is,

— terms of reference for the operating consultant or team.

The problem may be very clear to the client, or it may be very hazy or even unrecognised. In the case of a clear problem, discussion with the survey consultant ensures that he too has the same view. But the client may mistake the real cause of his difficulties, or may overlook some opportunities for improvement. If the problem is hazy, or even unrecognised by the client, discussion reveals it. As an example, the client may not realise that his published accounts disclose significant differences between his company and similar companies in the same field of operations. Discussions with the client on the reasons for such differences may reveal problems which the consultant can help to solve.

In addition to the specific problem, the client may have other areas of uncertainty. He may know very little about consultancy, or may have heard garbled tales of consultants and their methods of operating. In these cases he is almost always unsure of costs—and probably expects excessive fees. He may know little or nothing about the particular consulting unit and the professional expertise of its staff.

The consultant's experience (and that of his unit) in the industry or in similar situations will help him to understand the client's particular problem. The client becomes aware of the consulting organisation's professional competence as discussions demonstrate the survey consultant's knowledge and ability and disclose the work his organisation has done elsewhere and the specialists it can assign to introducing complex techniques. So far as cost is concerned, figures from other similar work are usually available, and provide a guide in the client's case. For example, the consultant may have ratios (e.g. operating weeks per numbers of client's staff) which enable him to make an initial estimate of cost. This estimate is extended and confirmed as more information becomes available during the survey.

The management survey includes the gathering and analysis of information on the client's activities. It also includes discussions with selected managers, supervisors and other key people, both inside and outside the client organisation. These discussions may indicate that there have been differences of opinion among managers on the nature of the problem and the best way of tackling it. They also provide an opportunity for the client's staff to judge the consultant and to appreciate that he intends to help them.

In summary, the purpose of the management survey is to review the resources of the client, examine the activities they generate, assess performance and identify opportunities for improving the results achieved. The client organisation's expansion potential is rapidly assessed, its strengths recognised, weaknesses that need to be remedied uncovered and underlying problems defined. At the end of the survey the consultant should have sufficient information to agree with the client on the terms of reference for an assignment.

Figure 5 shows the basic line of thought that the consultant has followed during the survey.

Figure 5. The consultant's approach to a management survey

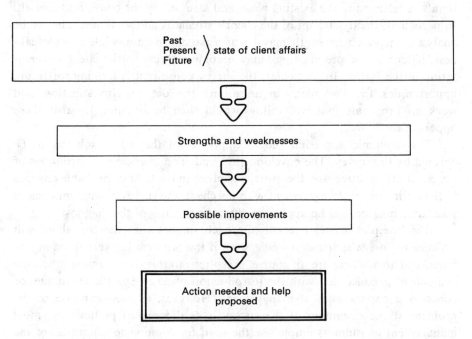

The end results of the management survey are summarised in two documents—the survey report and the survey notes—which are described in detail in Chapter 8.

6.3 Survey methodology

The methodological approach to the conduct of a management survey is determined by the following main considerations:

    (i) purpose (identification of the client's crucial problems, action needed, help proposed by the consultant);

(ii) time (time is usually short, which limits the possibility of collecting information and subjecting it to detailed analysis);

(iii) profile of the survey consultant (he may not know every industry and functional area in detail, but he has seen and examined many organisations before).

The essential approach is to take *a dynamic and comprehensive view* of the organisation, its environment, resources, goals, activities and achievements.

Dynamism in this context means that the consultant will examine key achievements and events in the life of the organisation, and probable future trends as reflected in the existing plans and assessed by the consultant himself. In particular, the dynamism of the client's strengths and weaknesses has to be analysed—a present strength may be of a passing nature, while a new weakness, hidden at the present time, may become a threat to the client's organisation in the future. In particular, the survey consultant is looking for future opportunities for the client organisation: the detailed investigation and work on proposals that will follow would then be oriented towards these opportunities.[1]

This dynamic approach should apply to all the major subjects to be covered by the survey. The development trends and changing opportunities of the client organisation are, therefore, examined in the light of probable changes in the environment. In agreement with his client, the survey consultant decides what time horizon will be applied in the various parts of the diagnosis.

The comprehensive, over-all approach implies that the consultant will *examine the organisation as a whole*, even if the problem is likely to be in one functional area. There are, of course, exceptions to this: for example, when the assignment is concerned with the introduction of a very specific technique, or concerns a narrow area of management. However, as the definition of the problem at the beginning of the survey is considered as preliminary, most management consultants emphasise the need for some wider appraisal of the organisation before confirming the existence even of a fairly narrow problem, and the feasibility of handling it in a consulting assignment of a certain size and duration.

It can be recommended that the consultant should proceed *from the general to the particular*: from over-all objectives and global indicators of performance to the reasons for lack of performance and thence into the examination in some detail of selected areas of the organisation's activities. An approach which started the other way round, by examining each management function (production, purchasing, marketing, etc.) in turn and hoping for a

---

[1] Useful guidance on such an approach can be found in P. Drucker: *Managing for results* (New York, Harper and Row, 1964).

balanced synthesis at the end, would entail much unnecessary work and might well prove misdirected. The approach from the general to the particular helps the consultant to limit the survey to matters of critical concern to the client organisation, or conversely may persuade him that the enquiry, to stand the best chance of achieving the results expected of it, must take into account every aspect of the enterprise's operation.

Such an approach implies that analysis will concentrate on *basic relationships and proportions* in the client organisation. This includes in particular:

— proportions between major functions and activity areas (e.g. allocation of human and financial resources to marketing, research and development, production, administration);

— relations between main inputs and outputs (e.g. sales related to materials consumed, the wage bill, or the number of employees);

— relationships between main indicators of efficiency and effectiveness (e.g. productivity, profitability, resource utilisation, growth);

— relationships between indicators of over-all results and principal factors that affect their magnitude in a positive and negative way (e.g. influence of excessively high work in progress on working capital and profitability).

The comprehensive, over-all approach is, however, combined with a functional approach wherever necessary. For example, if production turns out high-quality products at an acceptable cost, but the company's financial situation is precarious, the survey should point out whether the problem is likely to be in marketing, in excessive expenditure on research and development, in the shortage or high cost of financial resources, or something else. As a rule, if an assignment is likely to be exclusively or mainly in a specific functional area, this area will be examined in greater depth than other areas during a preliminary survey.

In his work, the survey consultant may use a variety of fact-finding and analytical techniques. These are discussed later, in connection with operating assignments.[1] In management surveys, however, emphasis will be on *comparison techniques*. In the absence of an exhaustive detailed analysis of data the consultant needs reference points which could guide him in his preliminary assessment of strength, weaknesses, and desirable improvements. He will find them mainly by making comparisons with:

— past achievements (especially if the organisation's performance has deteriorated);

---

[1] The reader may refer to Chapters 12 and 13.

— the client's own plans and standards (especially if real performance does not measure up to them);

— other comparable organisations (to assess what has been achieved elsewhere and whether the same thing would be possible in the client organisation);

— standards used by the consulting unit for this particular purpose.

The strength of experienced consultants lies particularly in making comparisons with other organisations and in the use of various standards that help them to assess the client's potential relatively quickly. The consultant would make extensive comparisons not only when he works with figures, e.g. with data on turnover or the utilisation of the firm's production capacity, but also in assessing qualitative information (e.g. the organisational structure or methods of work used can be compared with models from other companies).

In other words, the consultant's work is greatly facilitated if he can ask himself what levels of performance and what sorts of problems he would normally expect to find in that type of organisation to which the client organisation belongs. Such a question is meaningful if the consultant (or his unit) has some method of classifying organisations, developed by himself from experience or acquired from another source.[1] In such cases, organisations are classified by such criteria as size, nature of product or service and type of relationship to market, ownership and so on. For each type, there would be a listing of various attributes that are characteristic of it. To a survey consultant this is much more than a checklist, especially if some attributes are given in the form of quantitative data (e.g. values of ratios that should be found in a particular organisation type).

Well-established consulting firms try to supply their survey consultants with such information and guide them by means of manuals and checklists for management surveys and company appraisals. It is in the interest of the younger units in the profession to acquire or develop such materials and use them to improve their members' methods of work on the basis of common standards.[2]

Notwithstanding some general rules, senior consultants undertaking diagnostic surveys tend to have their personal priorities and specific approaches to surveys. Many of them start by examining the principal financial data, since these reflect the level and results of the activities of the enterprise in the most

---

[1] See, for example, ILO: *The enterprise and factors affecting its operation* (Geneva, International Labour Office, 1965), which includes a classification of enterprises into six basic types for inter-firm comparisons. Similar classifications, with empirical or recommended performance data, can be obtained from engineering consultants, suppliers of equipment, sectoral economic research institutes, centres for inter-firm comparison and other sources.

[2] On professional guidance see also Chapter 25, p. 261.

synthetic way. Some consultants emphasise the production scene: they believe
that a simple factory tour is most revealing and tells an experienced man a
great deal about the quality of the management. Still others prefer to analyse
the organisation's position and functions in the light of the external environment (market, government economic policy and plans, etc.) before turning to
financial appraisals and further investigations. As a rule, however, these are
just different starting points reflecting personal preferences and affected by
background experience of the survey consultant: eventually a systematic survey
has to embrace all areas needed for a comprehensive diagnosis of the
organisation.

6.4 Subjects for appraisal

The main subjects for appraisal in a global management survey are
grouped below in 11 subject areas (see Figure 6).

In addition to areas which concern the client organisation as a whole
(1 to 4, 10 and 11), there are subject areas covering the main functional aspects
of management—finance, marketing, production, research and development
and personnel (5 to 9).

As mentioned, in functional areas the survey consultant will look only for
facts that will help him to understand the nature of the client organisation,
appraise the level of performance, discover under-utilised resources and define
possible improvements. He will refrain from more detailed analysis, with the
exception perhaps of the area on which the assignment is to concentrate.

The paragraphs below are restricted to a summary view of each area.
Suggestions regarding more detailed investigations will be found in Chapter 7
concerning financial appraisal [1], in Part IV of this book dealing with consulting
in various areas of management [2], and in the ILO book " The enterprise and
factors affecting its operation ".[3]

Subject area 1—The client organisation

Under this heading the consultant will examine key information on the
nature, purpose, role and major characteristics of the client organisation. The
checklist in Table 2 indicates the scope of the subject. The consultant will be
particularly interested in historical events which may have shaped the client
organisation in a particular way and be the origin of various deeply-rooted
traditions and behavioural patterns.

---

[1] See p. 77.

[2] Chapters 16-22.

[3] See reference on p. 64. Appendix II of the book entitled " The attributes of an
enterprise and the effects produced by them " (pp. 159-190) is a useful checklist of effects
brought about by various changes in the attributes of an enterprise.

Figure 6.   Subject areas of a comprehensive management survey

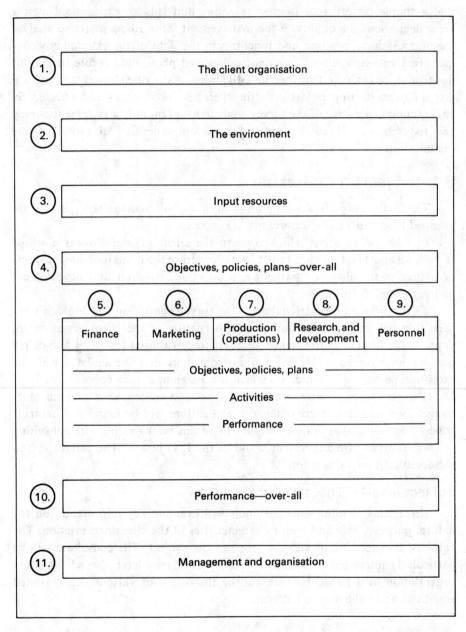

Table 2. Characteristics of the client organisation

Subject	Specification
Activity	Type (sector), purpose
	Main functions, products, services
	National or multi-national
History	When and how established
	Rate of growth
	Key events (acquisitions, mergers, technological breakthroughs, influence of wars or crises)
Importance	Volume of activity
	Volume of resources
	Position in country, sector, region, local community
	Goodwill, reputation
Ownership	Pattern (private, public, co-operative)
	Legal form (partnership, limited company, state enterprise)
Influences	Main owners
	Centres of control
	Social and political influences and pressure groups
Location	Where located
	Number and size of units
	Distances, communication

Subject area 2—The environment

The client organisation has to be seen in the context of a socio-economic environment with which it interacts in many ways. The checklist in Table 3 is very broad. In reality, it will be rather an exception for the consultant to review all aspects; in most cases only selected environmental considerations will apply. The subjects included in the checklist will be studied from the viewpoint of the needs and opportunities of the client organisation and not in a general all-embracing way.

Some of the environmental factors will be variables that the client organisation cannot influence. There are, however, assignments that may include proposals for changes in the environment—for example, a diagnostic survey of state import corporations may lead to a revision of the government system of import licences and customs tariffs. In another case, consumer taste may be influenced by education or advertising.

Table 3. Environmental factors

Subject	Specification
Economic	Broad economic setting
	Development level and trends
	Country's economic wealth
	Structure of market
	State of given industry in the country
	Financial system, availability of money
Natural resources	Raw materials
	Fuel and energy
	Water
	Land
	Impact of climate
People	Education
	Labour market
	Technical and business skills
	Training facilities
Socio-cultural	Structure of society (classes, ethnic groups, minorities, income distribution)
	Consumer taste
	Social, cultural and religious traditions
	Social security
	Social organisations (including workers' and employers' organisations), role, influence
Government	Profile, source of power, stability
	Economic policy, including regional development
	Planning, regulation and control of economy
	Taxation
	Government services and facilities
	Local government (functions in economic development)
Political	Structure of political life
	Impact of politics on management
Legal	Labour law
	Commercial law, etc.
Physical	Immediate physical environment
	Transportation
	Communications
	Housing
	Technical services
	Pollution

Subject area 3—Input resources

The input resources available to the client organisation (see Table 4) will be considered in a global way, without entering into questions concerning the organisation and management of resources that fall specifically under financial management, personnel management, etc. The main purpose will be to review the broad proportions between the principal resource groups from both the quantitative and the qualitative points of view, and to examine how far these resources are adequate for the purpose, the main objectives, and the development opportunities of the organisation.

Table 4. Input resources

Subject	Specification
Capital	Volume
	Structure
People	Main categories
	Skills, experience
	Motivation, integrity
Technical know-how	The organisation's own and purchased
Plant and equipment	Buildings, machines and other (volume, age, technical level, state)
	Productive capacity

Subject area 4—Objectives, policies, plans (over-all)

The study of the client organisation's objectives, policies and plans is a key element in management surveys, and is a basis for performance appraisal.

First, the consultant examines the methodology used by the client: he wants to know whether the organisation as a whole has formally defined objectives, what sorts of objectives are used and how they are determined. The same applies to management policies, i.e. the main rules (written and non-written) that the organisation and its units are bound to respect in taking decisions. Finally, the system of planning will be reviewed (long-term plans, operational plans, no plans at all, etc.).

Second, the consultant reviews the content and real values of the main indicators in this area. He needs to know what particular objectives, policies and strategic plans the organisation has and how they are inter-linked and harmonised. Special attention is paid to conflicting objectives and policies, and to blank areas in which the client operates without objectives or plans.

Subject area 5—Finance

This is a key area of any management survey because the financial strength and results of business organisations reflect the potential and results of almost all other areas and functions.

The *financial appraisal*, as the survey in this area is frequently called, concentrates on analysis of the client's financial reports for the preceding three to five years as a means of assessing strengths and weaknesses, measuring past performance and establishing upward or downward trends. The findings of the financial appraisal are used to orient further investigation and remedial activities in other functions and areas of management.

The importance of the financial appraisal warrants a detailed explanation of its scope and methods. This will be done in the following chapter.

Subject area 6—Marketing

In organisations that sell their products and services the marketing function provides an essential link with the environment. The survey consultant tries to get a picture of the market that is available and of the product-market strategy followed by the client. He will examine the effectiveness of marketing strategy and its impact on production, research and development, purchasing and other functions.

Various components of the marketing function, such as the organisation of sales, advertising, the location and turnover of stocks, warehousing, transport, etc., will be briefly reviewed if appropriate.

Subject area 7—Production (operations)

It is difficult to describe briefly the activities and problems that interest the survey consultant in the very large and diversified area of production. More than in other areas, the consultant's problem will be how to recognise essential information in the vast amount of data that production offers to him.

In essence, the consultant will concentrate his efforts on two issues:

(i) a general examination of the organisation of production and the layout of production departments, main material and product flows, relations between marketing and production, purchasing and production, and research and development and production;

(ii) an examination of key indicators of effectiveness of production activities (capacity utilisation, lead time of main products, volume and distribution of work in progress, equipment breakdown and stoppages, utilisation of working time of production workers, waste, quality of production, various losses in the production area).

In non-productive organisations (services, social organisations, government departments) the consultant will review, in an analogous way, the services or other operations that constitute the organisation's main " product ".

Subject area 8—Research and development

The first question on research and development (R and D) will be that of its role in the development of the client organisation. If the organisation is research-oriented and operates in a technologically advanced industry (such as electronics, telecommunications or petrochemicals), the management of its research function may have a considerably greater impact on over-all results than does production management. The consultant will examine relations in the total cycle of research - development - manufacturing - marketing. He will be interested in research and development expenditure and its utilisation, in the relationship of R and D management to general management of the firm, in the pace and problems of the transfer of R and D results to production, in the competence of key professional staff and the main achievements of the R and D department.

Even in organisations having little or no internal research and development some relationship to external research and development may exist, e.g. licences will be purchased, or new technologies bought in the form of equipment.

The organisation of investment (capital building) activities linked to the application of R and D results may require particular attention in organisations involved in extensive expansion or reconstruction.

Subject area 9—Personnel

The critical issue in the personnel area is the impact of personnel policy (i.e. criteria applied to selection, recruitment, promotion and remuneration) on the performance and development prospects of the client organisation. Although this may be difficult during a short survey, the consultant tries to get a true picture of how and by whom personnel decisions are made and how this affects the morale and motivation of people. Career planning and development, personnel performance appraisal and the role of staff training will then be briefly examined. In the field of remuneration and motivation, both financial instruments (wage policy, profit sharing) and other motivational factors (challenging work opportunities, employment security, social services) will be reviewed and their impact on the performance of the organisation assessed.

The consultant should in any case acquaint himself with industrial relations practices in the client organisation.

Subject area 10—Performance (over-all)

The examination of the client's (i) resources, (ii) objectives, policies and plans, and (iii) main activities and results in particular functional areas, enables the consultant to make some judgement on the over-all performance of the client organisation, assess whether this performance is fully satisfactory and point out necessary improvements. The indicators used for this purpose may include the rate of growth (of output, market share, sales, capital, employment, etc.), productivity, profitability, stability of employment, etc.

In planned economies, the fulfilment of planned quotas assigned to enterprises by controlling government departments, and the relationship between plan implementation and economic efficiency would be examined.

Table 5. Checklist for analysis of management and organisation

Subject	Specification
Top management	Boards, key positions
Organisational structure	Departments, divisions (including their relative importance)
	Relations between line and staff
	Centralisation and decentralisation
	Existence, quality and use of charts and manuals
Managers	Key personalities (professional and personal profiles, attitude to change)
Decision making	Practice applied to main decisions
Co-ordination	Methods, impact
Management information and controls	Information systems and control methods used, impact
Modern techniques	General policy, effectiveness
	What techniques preferred
	Use of computers
Communication	Channels, methods
Management style	Autocratic vs. democratic
	Use of collective bodies
	Attitude to participation
Employee participation	Organisation, methods, impact
Informal organisation	Causes, pattern, impact
External management services	Policy concerning use
	Use of consultants, experience

Subject area 11—Management and organisation

Step by step, the consultant will be extending and deepening his knowledge and understanding of the client organisation's management. He will try to determine the relationship between the weaknesses he has discovered and the ways in which decisions on important matters are prepared, taken, implemented and controlled. Special attention will be paid to the competence and personality of those who are in principal management posts. The checklist given in Table 5 indicates some points of interest.

6.5 Survey facts and figures

Nature of diagnostic information

A successful management survey is based on the rapid collection of information that reveals the type and extent of help that the consultant can give to the client. This information has to be selective; the reader already knows the reasons for this.

Diagnostic data tend to be global in nature. The survey consultant is interested in details only if they are indicative of some major problems and help to elucidate the problems for which he has been brought in. For example, detailed information on the work style of top management may help to diagnose over-all management patterns and practices that determine the atmosphere in the whole organisation.

Diagnostic information is to be collected in the subject areas described in Section 6.4. Both quantitative information (figures) and facts that cannot be quantified (verbal description of situations or problems) are needed.

Who collects and prepares information?

Before the preliminary survey meeting[1] the consultant, assisted by the information or documentation service of his consulting unit, collects some *orientation facts* about the client. These concern the environment in which the client operates and conditions within the client's organisation. The consultant starts by finding out which products or services his client provides. This information is easily obtained during the first contact with the client, or by asking him to supply sales literature. The nature of the products or services will place the client within a specific sector or trade, and the consultant will want to know its main characteristics and practices. Usually he will gather information on:

---

[1] See p. 58.

— terminology commonly used;

— nature and location of markets;

— names and location of main producers;

— types and sources of raw materials;

— weights and measures used in the industry;

— processes and equipment;

— business methods and practices peculiar to the industry;

— laws, rules and customs governing the industry;

— history and growth;

— present economic climate and main problems of the industry.

Trade journals and government publications will provide much of the above information, especially on economic trends. To gain a quick understanding of an unfamiliar manufacturing process the consultant can look at flow sheets of industrial processes, which summarise on one page a production process and its technical terms.[1]

As regards the position of the client's business, the consultant needs little information before he meets the client. He may be able to learn the client's financial position and recent operating results and immediate expectations and problems from published annual reports or returns filed in a public registry or credit service. He can also scan brief biographies of the top managers in a publication of the " Who's Who " type if one exists in the given country.

Between the preliminary survey meeting and the beginning of the survey the collection of information continues. The client prepares the information which he agreed at the survey meeting to give to the consultant; the consulting unit can pursue its search for information from public, governmental, business and other sources.

The bulk of the survey facts and figures is to be collected, classified and examined during the few days of the survey by the survey consultant himself and the client's staff assigned to help with the survey.

Sources of diagnostic information

The main sources of information for the management survey are:

— published information;

— the client's records and reports;

— files of the consulting unit;

---

[1] Available from Mechanical World (published by Model and Allied Publications Ltd., Hemel Hempstead, Herts, U.K.) and other sources.

— observation and interviewing by the survey consultant;

— contacts outside the client organisation.

Published information may be issued by the client, or by other interested organisations.

The client's publications usually include:

— annual financial and operating reports;

— financial, statistical, trade and customs returns to government, trade associations, credit organisations, and economic surveys;

— sales promotion material such as catalogues and advertising brochures;

— press releases.

Other sources may provide information on:

— conditions and trends in the client's economic sector, including technological developments;

— trade statistics and reports;

— regulations which the client must observe;

— management practices;

— labour-management relations.

The client's internal records and reports will provide information on his resources, objectives, plans and performance, including:

— information on plant and equipment;

— reports to managers on financial results and costs of activities, services and products;

— sales statistics;

— production performances;

— material movements;

— personnel appraisal.

The files of the consulting unit will contain information on the client if he is not a new one, and may also supply information on similar organisations.

Observing activities and interviewing key managers, supervisors and workers is vital to information gathering. Tours of the client's premises, seeing people in action and hearing their views, worries and suggestions, give first-hand knowledge of how the organisation works in practice, how it lives, the pace it sets and the relationships between its workers. These are invaluable insights, which records cannot convey, but extensive interviewing and observation of activities are beyond the possibilities of preliminary surveys.

Contacts with other organisations associated with the client may be made either by the consultant, or by the client himself.

During their work, consultants make contact with many organisations apart from their clients. These contacts not only assist the current assignment but also establish a relationship which can be used in future management surveys. For example, contacts may be established with trade unions, employers' associations, sectoral research and training institutions, or management associations where members of the clients' managerial staff meet.

The survey consultant informs his client of the purpose and nature of any contact made. The client himself may contact some outside bodies, e.g. employers' associations, and should know of any consultant contact.

FINANCIAL APPRAISAL

7

Financial statements and records are an essential source of information for assessing the soundness of a business.[1] As mentioned in Chapter 6, a management survey invariably includes a financial appraisal. For this reason it is essential for the consultant to understand accounting reports.

7.1 The balance sheet and the income statement

This chapter gives an example of a balance sheet and an income statement in modern form. These will serve to illustrate the explanation of financial analysis that follows.

The main items on the balance sheet have been lettered A to I, and the main items on the income statement lettered a to r for easy reference in the following discussions on the meaning of financial statements and the ratios which can be derived from them.

The *balance sheet* is a snapshot of the assets and liabilities of the firm on one particular day of the year, expressed in financial terms. It shows the sources of capital in terms of share capital, loan capital and retained earnings. It also shows how the resources are currently deployed in the form of land, buildings, machinery, plant, stocks and cash. It shows how much is owed to the company by debtors and what the company owes to creditors and the bank.

The *income statement* tells the story of the year's activities in terms of sales, costs and profit. It shows the sales revenue, the change in stock levels, the manufacturing cost of goods sold, the expenses of administration, selling and distribution and research and development, the operating profit, the interest expense, profit before tax, taxes and net profit after tax.[2]

---

[1] Some parts of this chapter, including Tables 6 and 7, are reproduced from E. G. Wood: *Bigger profits for the smaller firm* (London, Business Books, 1972), with kind permission of the publisher.

[2] The income statement of the XYZ Company in Table 7 does not give taxes and net profit after tax. Research and development expenses are not shown as a separate item.

Table 6. Balance Sheet of the XYZ Company Limited as at 31 December

		$
ASSETS	**FIXED ASSETS**	
	Land and buildings	51,000
	Machinery and plant	52,000
	Fixtures and fittings	3,000
	Vehicles	4,000
	A. TOTAL FIXED ASSETS	110,000
	CURRENT ASSETS	
	Stocks - raw materials	25,000
	- work in progress and finished products	62,000
	Debtors	80,000
	Cash	0
	B. TOTAL CURRENT ASSETS	167,000
	C. TOTAL ASSETS, FIXED AND CURRENT (*A+B*)	277,000
LIABILITIES	**CURRENT LIABILITIES**	
	Trade creditors	63,000
	Bank overdraft	45,000
	D. TOTAL CURRENT LIABILITIES	108,000
	DEFERRED LIABILITIES	
	E. MORTGAGE	7,000
	F. TOTAL EXTERNAL LIABILITIES, CURRENT AND DEFERRED (*D+E*)	115,000
	G. WORKING CAPITAL (*B−D*)	59,000
	H. FIXED CAPITAL (*A−E*)	103,000
	INTERNAL LIABILITIES	
	I. EQUITY CAPITAL (*G+H* or *C−F*)	162,000
	Ordinary shares	10,000
	Retained earnings	152,000
	SHAREHOLDERS' NET WORTH (INTERNAL LIABILITIES)	162,000

The assets side of the balance sheet

The assets side of the balance sheet is normally divided into two groups—fixed assets (line *A*) and current assets (line *B*). Fixed assets are those which the business intends to retain for the conduct of operations until such time as wear and tear and/or obsolescence render them inefficient. Current assets are those which the business acquires and realises rapidly in carrying out short-term

Table 7. Income statement of the XYZ Company Limited for the year ended 31 December

			$
a.	Sales		388,000
	Opening stock (finished products and work in progress)	48,000	
	Closing stock (finished products and work in progress)	62,000	
b.	Increase in stock		14,000
c.	Value of production		402,000
d.	Purchases		177,000
	Opening stock (raw materials)	22,000	
	Closing stock (raw materials)	25,000	
	Increase in stock		3,000
e.	Materials consumed		174,000
f.	Value added $(c-e)$		228,000
g.	Wages - direct	73,000	
	- indirect	20,900	
h.	Total wages		93,900
i.	Manufacturing expenses:		
	Social security	11,700	
	Power and water	4,200	
	Repairs	5,600	
	Consumable stores	1,400	
	Rent and rates	2,600	
	Insurance	1,100	
	Depreciation	8,000	
j.	Total manufacturing expenses		34,600
k.	Sales and distribution expenses:		
	Commissions	2,700	
	Travelling expenses	4,350	
	Advertising	2,850	
	Packing materials	1,300	
l.	Total sales and distribution expenses		11,200
m.	Administration expenses:		
	Salaries and benefits	40,200	
	Communications	2,250	
	Professional fees	450	
	Miscellaneous	600	
n.	Total administration expenses		43,500
o.	Total wages and expenses $(h+j+l+n)$		183,200
p.	Operating profit $(f-o)$		44,800
q.	Interest expense		4,100
r.	Profit before tax $(p-q)$		40,700

transactions. The fixed assets are usually valued at cost, less depreciation. The current assets are valued at cost or replacement cost, whichever is lower.

Fixed assets include land and buildings, plant and equipment, fixtures and fittings, and motor vehicles. Another asset usually included in the fixed category is long-term investments such as shareholdings in subsidiary and associated companies.

The theory of *depreciation* is that each asset should be depreciated at a rate which will reduce its value to zero at the end of its working life. It is simply a means of ensuring that the initial cost of an asset is not charged wholly against the income of the year of purchase. Instead, the charge is spread over a longer period to give a more true and fair picture. The depreciation shown in the balance sheet is not necessarily available as cash for replacement of the asset; in fact, the replacement cost may be considerably higher because of inflation and/or technical improvements. Depreciation is an accounting convention effected through book entries. Management must ensure, through long-range planning, that funds are available to replace worn-out assets.

The main categories of *current assets* are stocks, debtors and cash. Stocks may be separated into raw materials, work in progress and finished products. The figure for debtors represents the sum of money owed to the company by its customers for goods and services already supplied but not yet paid for. Cash in the balance sheet is usually cash at the bank plus a small amount in hand.

The liabilities side of the balance sheet

Liabilities can be classified into two main categories—external and internal. The external liabilities are moneys owed to suppliers, and any external loans such as bank overdraft. The internal liabilities are those to the shareholders, or, in other words, the total capital invested in the business.

The *external liabilities* may be further divided into two categories—*current* (line *D*) and *deferred* (line *E*). The main types of current liabilities are trade creditors and the bank overdrafts. The former type represents amounts owed to suppliers for goods and services already supplied but not yet paid for. The bank overdraft is, in theory, a short-term credit facility provided by the bank to help the company meet its day-to-day payments to suppliers and employees while awaiting payments from customers.

Common types of deferred liabilities are mortgages (loans secured against the land and buildings), long-term bank loans and hire-purchase loans. In every case the instalments or other amounts payable within one year should be included in current liabilities. Debentures, or bonds, are another type of deferred liability.

The *internal liabilities* also can be divided into two categories—capital originally provided by the shareholders, and the accumulated earnings not distributed to shareholders but retained for use in the business.

Many balance sheets show items called *capital reserves*, usually arising from revaluation of land and buildings. Although these items are a form of profit, they are not available for distribution and cannot be paid out as cash. Balance sheets may also show *revenue reserves*, which are simply retained earnings. The term " reserves ", both capital and revenue, can be misleading, as the reader may think that it represents cash funds; in fact, the reserves may be entirely locked up in fixed assets, stocks and debtors. The modern tendency is to confine the use of the term to retained earnings which are specifically earmarked for certain purposes, such as plant replacement, research and development, etc. The existence of such reserves is notice to the shareholders that management has decided, in the interest of the company, to retain a portion of earnings and not to distribute everything in the form of dividends.

The balance sheet can be summed up in the formula

$$\frac{\textit{Total external liabilities} + \textit{Shareholders' capital employed}}{\textit{Total assets}}$$

The income statement

The example (Table 7) on page 79 shows the modern presentation of the income statement. If the consultant is supplied with financial statements in the traditional layout, he will usually find it useful to redraft them along modern lines, showing comparative figures for five years. Although opinions differ, most accountants attempt to improve the usefulness of the income statement by making it easier to understand and by highlighting the following information.

Value of production (line *c*)

This figure is obtained by adjusting the sales revenue for any increase or decrease in the stock of finished products. A further refinement is to adjust the stock increase or decrease from cost to selling price; however, as the change in stock level is seldom very large, it is often an unnecessary elaboration. The concept of value of production is important for comparing one year with another. As the sales revenue can fluctuate from year to year, due to changes in the level of finished stock, the value of production is a more reliable measure of the activity of a company in manufacturing terms.

Materials consumed (line *e*)

The materials consumed figure is obtained by adjusting material purchases for changes in stocks of raw material. Again its importance is its value in comparing years. The ratio of purchases to sales may be meaningless if stocks have varied, but a change in the ratio of materials consumed to value of production is often significant.

Value added (line *f*)

Value added is simply the difference between the value of production and the materials consumed. It is far more significant than sales turnover or value of production. There is no point in boosting total sales turnover if the extra income is swallowed up in higher material costs; therefore management should aim at raising the value-added figure, since this is the sum available for paying wages and expenses, and is thus the figure which determines profit.

Analysis of expenses

In the modern format expenses are grouped under four main headings— manufacturing (line *j*), sales and distribution (line *l*), administration and financial (line *n*), and interest expense (line *q*). This grouping facilitates comparison with other years and also indicates the relative importance of the four groups in the particular business.

7.2 Interpretation of financial statements

What sort of thing should a consultant look for in studying a set of financial statements?

First, there is the over-all picture presented by the current year's figures. Is the company making enough profit? How strong is it in financial terms? Is it taking or giving too much credit? Are the stocks too high?

Secondly, there is the picture that emerges from studying trends over a period of years. Is the company becoming more profitable? Is it expanding too fast? Is productivity rising or falling? Is liquidity improving or deteriorating?

In both these pictures it is necessary to distinguish between two conflicting aspects of the company's operations—profitability and solvency. A business can be highly profitable yet financially weak. Another may be financially strong but not making enough profit. The method used to interpret financial statements is to calculate certain *ratios*. Cash figures alone are almost meaningless; an increase in profit from $10,000 to $15,000 may be good or bad, depending on the amount of extra resources used in generating the extra profit.

Many different ratios can be developed from a set of financial reports, but some of them are of little value or are simply variations of each other. There are 24 ratios which the survey consultant will find useful. They have been numbered 1 to 24 and may be classified as shown in Table 8.

Table 8. Key ratios

General ratios (1 to 3)	Show the performance of the whole company, i.e. including use of assets in investments external to the company's own operations.
Management performance ratios (4 to 9)	Show the performance of operating management, excluding effect of external investments.
Financial performance ratios (10 to 15)	Show the use of working capital and liquid assets.
Shareholders' ratios (16 to 18)	Show company's rating as an investment.
Cost breakdown ratios (19 to 24)	Give breakdown of main costs and indicate where control needs strengthening.

In the following formulae for calculating the above ratios, letters A to I refer to lines on the balance sheet (Table 6) and letters a to r to lines on the income statement (Table 7). The figures after each formula are taken from the same statements.

7.3 Use of ratios in financial analysis

General ratios

1. *Return on capital*
$$= \frac{profit\ before\ tax}{capital\ employed} = \frac{r}{A + G} = \frac{40,700}{169,000}$$

2. *Annual turnover of capital*
$$= \frac{sales}{capital\ employed} = \frac{a}{A + G} = \frac{388,000}{169,000}$$

3. *Profit margin*
$$= \frac{profit\ before\ tax}{sales} = \frac{r}{a} = \frac{40,700}{388,000}$$

Return on capital is the fundamental index of profitability. It indicates to the consultant whether the client's business generates outputs commensurate with the resources invested. Although profit is often expressed as a percentage of sales, the effect of turnover of capital is frequently overlooked; it is important that these two factors be considered together. Return on capital is a function of both profit to sales, and the rate of capital circulation in number of times per year:

$$\frac{Return\ on}{capital} = \frac{Profit}{margin} \times \frac{Annual\ turn\text{-}}{over\ of\ capital}, \text{ or } \frac{profit}{capital} = \frac{profit}{sales} \times \frac{sales}{capital}$$

Figure 7. Relationship of factors affecting return on capital employed

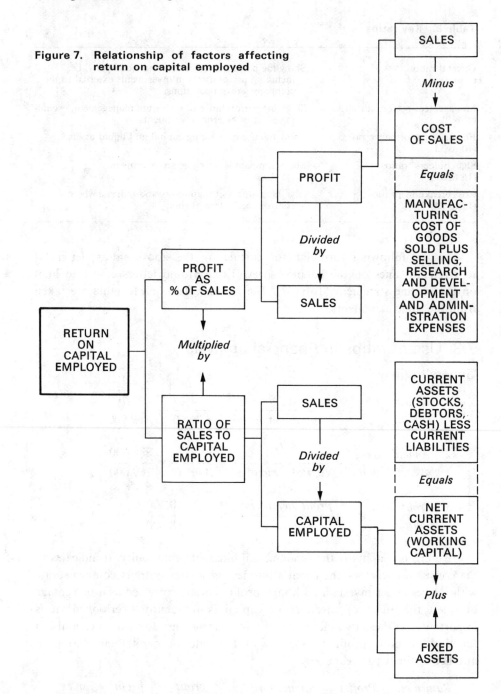

As the chart shows, capital employed is defined as the sum of fixed assets and net current assets (working capital). Fixed assets do not include the intangible assets, i.e. the book-value of goodwill, patents, copyrights, etc.

These ratios can be subdivided as shown in Figure 7. Where an adverse trend in return on capital employed is indicated, further analysis of the secondary ratios will help to isolate the reasons.

Management performance ratios

4. *Return on oper-*
    ating assets $= \dfrac{operating\ profit}{operating\ assets} = \dfrac{p}{C} = \dfrac{44,800}{277,000}$

This ratio gauges the effectiveness of all decisions on investment of funds and planning and control of activities made by all levels of management from shop foreman to managing director. Again, this ratio can be divided into its two components as follows:

$$\textit{Return on oper-} \atop \textit{ating assets} = \frac{operating\ profit}{sales} \times \frac{sales}{operating\ assets}$$

To illustrate, consider two companies in the same business:

	Jones Company	Smith Company
Sales	$5,000,000	$3,000,000
Operating profit	$ 400,000	$ 300,000
Operating assets used	$2,500,000	$6,000,000
Operating profit to sales	8%	10%
Turnover—sales to operating assets	2.0	0.5
Return on operating assets	16%	5%

Jones Company, although it earns a lower percentage of operating profit to sales than Smith Company, works its assets harder, and is much more effective. Efforts to improve the results of operations of Jones Company should concentrate on increasing the percentage of operating profit to sales. Smith Company should work for higher turnover.

This ratio is another way of looking at capital employed. Non-operating assets are excluded from the calculation in order to arrive at the figure for assets available to management.

The return-on-capital concept is an extremely useful method of problem diagnosis. Much can be learned about a company by following this simple analytical approach. As will be seen, many of the remaining 20 ratios are simply refinements of this basic theme.

5. *Added value per $*
    of operating assets $= \dfrac{added\ value}{operating\ assets} = \dfrac{f}{C} = \dfrac{228,000}{277,000}$

This ratio is a refinement of sales to operating assets. Growth in terms of sales turnover is not necessarily an indication of improvement, as the increase may be due to an increase in the cost of material used. Deducting the cost of materials from the sales figure has the advantage that it discounts any fluctuations in material costs.

6. $\dfrac{\text{Turnover}}{\text{of stocks}} = \dfrac{cost\ of\ sales}{stocks} = \dfrac{e\ +\ h + j - b}{stocks} =$

$$= \dfrac{174{,}000\ +\ 93{,}900\ +\ 34{,}600\ -\ 14{,}000}{25{,}000\ +\ 62{,}000}$$

The ratio of sales to stocks provides a very rough indication of stock turnover. It is better to subdivide the ratio into three parts, one relating stocks of finished goods to sales, another relating work in progress to value of production, and the third relating raw materials stocks to materials consumed. These ratios reveal whether stocks are higher than needed to keep activities going, thus tying up excessive capital, or too low, leading to stock-outs which hinder production or sales.

7. $\dfrac{\text{Utilisation of}}{\text{fixed assets}} = \dfrac{added\ value}{fixed\ assets} = \dfrac{f}{A} = \dfrac{228{,}000}{110{,}000}$

This is a refinement of the ratio of sales to fixed assets. The ratio is a breakdown of ratio 5 and should be used in conjunction with that ratio to determine whether a fall in asset utilisation denotes poor utilisation of fixed or of current assets.

8. $\dfrac{\text{Added value}}{\text{per employee}} = \dfrac{added\ value}{number\ of\ employees} = \dfrac{f}{number\ of\ employees}$

This is a broad indicator of productivity. Again, added value is preferable to sales. The latter can be misleading, since it can be influenced by changes in material costs. Another useful ratio is

$$\dfrac{Added\ value\ per\ \$}{of\ wages} = \dfrac{added\ value}{total\ wage\ bill}$$

An increase in productivity per employee can be offset by an increase in wage rates, resulting in no benefit to the company. By calculating and comparing the trend of both ratios, the true state of affairs can be determined.

9. $\dfrac{\text{Capital intensive}}{\text{indicator}} = \dfrac{fixed\ assets}{number\ of\ employees} = \dfrac{A}{number\ of\ employees}$

Examination of this ratio over a number of years will indicate a trend toward capital-intensive operations or otherwise. It is also useful in inter-firm comparison.

Financial performance ratios

10. $\dfrac{\text{Utilisation of}}{\text{working capital}} = \dfrac{sales}{working\ capital} = \dfrac{a}{G} = \dfrac{388,000}{59,000}$

From a performance point of view, the faster working capital is turned over, the better; for working capital is used to generate sales. However, if the turnover is too fast it can indicate inadequate working capital. A sudden drop in income or a slowing down in collections from debtors can leave the company very short of money.

11. $\dfrac{\text{Vulnerability}}{\text{of stocks}} = \dfrac{stocks}{working\ capital} = \dfrac{stocks}{G} = \dfrac{25,000 + 62,000}{59,000}$

If stock forms a large part of working capital, price falls may necessitate considerable write-offs from profits; thus the business is more vulnerable to trade fluctuations. A large investment in stocks can also result in cash shortages.

12. $\dfrac{\text{Collection}}{\text{period}} = \dfrac{trade\ debtors}{average\ daily\ sales} = \dfrac{trade\ debtors}{\dfrac{a}{365}} = \dfrac{80,000}{\dfrac{388,000}{365}}$

This ratio indicates the number of days' credit allowed to customers, and therefore whether excessive capital is tied up. If the company sells both for cash and on credit, a more accurate measurement is average daily sales on credit.

13. $\dfrac{\text{Current}}{\text{ratio}} = \dfrac{current\ assets}{current\ liabilities} = \dfrac{B}{D} = \dfrac{167,000}{108,000}$

The current ratio is widely used by banks and other leading institutions as a measure of the solvency of a company. It is commonly claimed that companies with a current ratio of 2 or more are safe, and therefore good risks for a loan from the bank. In practice, many companies operate quite satisfactorily on current ratios of 1.5 or even less. As with all ratio analysis, the significant consideration is the trend.

14. $\dfrac{Liquidity}{ratio} = \dfrac{liquid\ assets}{current\ liabilities} = \dfrac{debtors\ +\ cash}{D} = \dfrac{80,000\ +\ 0}{108,000}$

This ratio also measures the ability of the business to meet its current obligations, but it is a far more severe test than 13 since it concentrates on strictly liquid assets, the value of which is fairly certain. It is sometimes known as *the acid test ratio*. Liquid assets include cash and debtors but not stocks. A ratio of 1+ is generally considered satisfactory, but again the important point is the trend.

15. $\dfrac{Sales}{vulnerability} = \dfrac{fixed\ costs}{operating\ profit}$

Companies operating near their break-even points will have more volatile profits for a given percentage change in volume than those operating well above their break-even levels.

The example in Table 9 illustrates this (selling price = $100 per unit; variable costs = $50 per unit; fixed costs = $100,000).

Note that an increase in volume from 2,500 to 3,000 units, i.e. 20%, results in an increase in profit of 100%. Looking at it the other way, a decline in volume from 3,000 to 2,500 units, i.e. 17%, cuts profit in half. Thus the higher the ratio of fixed costs to operating profit, the more vulnerable the business is to a fall in sales volume.

Table 9. Sales vulnerability

Volume in units	2,000	2,500	3,000	3,500
Sales	$200,000	$250,000	$300,000	$350,000
Variable costs	100,000	125,000	150,000	175,000
Contribution	100,000	125,000	150,000	175,000
Fixed costs	100,000	100,000	100,000	100,000
Operating profit	0	25,000	50,000	75,000
Sales vulnerability	∞	4.0	2.0	1.33

Shareholders' ratios [1]

16. $\dfrac{Financial}{gearing} = \dfrac{fixed\text{-}interest\ capital}{capital\ employed} = \dfrac{E}{A\ +\ G} = \dfrac{7,000}{169,000}$

Fixed-interest capital includes loans, mortgages, debentures and preference shares. The term *gearing* signifies that portion of a company's long-term

---

[1] Also called investment-rating ratios.

capital on which it has to pay a fixed return, as opposed to that portion on which the return varies with profits. The ratio is a measure of the extent to which the business has used long-term loans and fixed-interest capital to purchase assets. Obviously if the ratio is higher than 0.5 the company could be forced out of business by the creditors. A safe target to aim for is no more than 0.4, but a slightly higher figure is not necessarily imprudent. There is always a conflict of interest between profit and survival; the more a business can use borrowed money to finance profitable operations, the better will be the return on its shareholders' investment, provided the rate of interest on the borrowed money is lower than the rate of profit being earned. If a business minimises its borrowings in the interest of survival, its profitability will be lower than if it borrows money on cheap terms. Gearing is also referred to as " financial leverage ", or " trading on the equity ".

17. $\dfrac{Dividend}{cover} = \dfrac{ordinary\ earnings}{ordinary\ dividend}$

This ratio simply shows the number of times that dividends paid to ordinary shareholders are covered by earnings accruing to the ordinary shareholders. As a rule of thumb, earnings should be about twice the dividend.

18. $\dfrac{Profitability\ of}{shareholders'\ capital} = \dfrac{net\ profit\ after\ tax}{net\ worth}$

This is a way of measuring the return to the owners of the business after all taxes and interest have been paid. It appraises the earning power of the ownership investment, which is crucial to the financial analyst interested in investigating equity funds.

Cost breakdown ratios

19. $\dfrac{materials\ and\ bought\text{-}out\ parts}{value\ of\ production} = \dfrac{e}{c} = \dfrac{174{,}000}{402{,}000}$

20. $\dfrac{wages}{value\ of\ production} = \dfrac{h}{c} = \dfrac{93{,}900}{402{,}000}$

21. $\dfrac{manufacturing\ expenses}{value\ of\ production} = \dfrac{j}{c} = \dfrac{34{,}600}{402{,}000}$

22. $\dfrac{research\ and\ development\ expenses\ [1]}{value\ of\ production}$

23. $\dfrac{sales\ and\ distribution\ expenses}{sales} = \dfrac{l}{a} = \dfrac{11{,}200}{388{,}000}$

24. $\dfrac{administration\ expenses}{value\ of\ production} = \dfrac{n}{c} = \dfrac{43{,}500}{402{,}000}$

One of the best starts to appraising the operations of a company can be made by tracing changes in material costs, labour costs, manufacturing expenses, research and development expenses, selling and distribution expenses, and administration expenses—all expressed as percentages of sales or value of production. Where adverse trends in the major classifications of costs are indicated, detailed analysis of the elements of these costs should be made.

Limitations of ratio analysis

A correct interpretation of the static picture presented by one year's figures requires considerable skill and care. For instance, if the fixed assets of land and buildings are undervalued in terms of the current market, a false impression may be given in the profit ratios. The comparison of one business with another should not be undertaken without the utmost care and unless the consultant is thoroughly familiar with both businesses. Different methods may be used to evaluate assets and calculate depreciation, policies on whether to capitalise expenditure or write it off against income may be different, the treatment of research and development costs may vary, changing price levels may invalidate attempts to compare and so on.

The main value of analysing ratios lies in studying the *trend* within one company over a period of years. Since this approach means comparing like with like, there is little risk of misinterpretation of the main trends.

Definitions used in calculating ratios

Liquid assets — Cash, debtors' accounts and other current assets readily convertible to cash.

Long-term liabilities — Debts payable more than one year from the date of the balance sheet.

---

[1] The income statement in Table 7 (p. 79) does not give a separate figure for research and development expenses.

Net assets	– Fixed assets, less depreciation, plus working capital.
Net profit	– Profit after interest and tax.
Net worth	– The balance sheet value of assets available for preference and ordinary shareholders.
Operating assets	– Total assets.
Operating profit	– Profit earned on the operating assets of the company, after depreciation, but before taxes and interest on long-term debts. Investment and other non-operating income is excluded.
Ordinary earnings	– The eventual profit available for ordinary dividends, after deduction of dividends on preference shares. Usually, only part of this amount will actually be distributed and the balance will be retained to provide growth capital.
Total assets	– Fixed assets, less depreciation, plus current assets.
Working capital	– Current assets less current liabilities.

SURVEY REPORT

8

The survey report confirms all the discussions between the survey consultant and the client and sets out the proposals for an assignment. Because the proposals have been developed in discussion with the client, the report contains no surprises. It does, however, provide a written proposal, and may sometimes be converted into a type of contract if the proposal is formally accepted by the client.

There is no rigid format for a survey report—much depends on the style of the consultant, the preferences of the client, and the scope of the survey and the proposed assignment. When the client needs extensive consulting services for a far-reaching overhaul of his business, the survey report can make this clear to him by summarising the findings of the over-all assessment and financial performance appraisal so that he receives a clear and comprehensive view of the situation, prospects, strengths and weaknesses of the business as a whole and its sections. If, on the other hand, he needs modest assistance to overcome a difficulty in one activity, he will probably expect a short survey report focusing on the specific problem, and be impatient of a lengthy study.

The survey report is the first written evidence to a new client of the consultant's work and great care should be taken in structuring, writing, reproducing and presenting it.[1]

8.1 Sections of the report

Whatever its length or structure, the report should deal with:

— present situation;

---

[1] Useful suggestions can be found in the *Guide to professional practice: suggestions for preparing proposals, interview report practice and survey report practice*, (New York, Association of Consulting Management Engineers, 1966). Further comments on consultant report writing are made in Appendix 7.

— proposals on how the consultant can assist;

— terms of reference for the assignment;

— benefits;

— fees and costs;

— consultant capability;

— terms of business.

Present situation

This part of the report describes the survey consultant's findings. They may briefly confirm anything the client already knows, then add at necessary length any new factors brought out by the survey. Points should be made in a way that leads naturally to the proposals without their becoming repetitious.

Proposals

This part describes possible solutions to the problems identified and courses of action recommended by the consultant. The proposals discuss, in general terms, the methods and techniques that would be used and the steps to be followed in developing and implementing the solution. It is essential to describe the part to be played by the client and the nature and degree of involvement of his staff.

Terms of reference

In this part the report sets out clearly what would be done during the assignment. The terms of reference establish a global programme for the operating team and would be used as a check on progress during the assignment. When the assignment has been completed the client can refer to them to satisfy himself that all the work has been done.

Benefits

Benefits are stated in quantified terms wherever possible, so that the client can measure what the assignment would achieve. Quantifications are usually conservative and may eventually be exceeded. Quantified benefits are, where possible, stated in money terms. Notional, or possible consequential benefits are avoided.

Monetary benefits are commented on to ensure that the client understands the implications. For example, a saving from reduced inventory of finished goods would only be achieved when stocks had been run down and this may require production to be cut back for some time. Benefits in other terms are stated as appropriate, e.g. output would increase from one level to a new level (in this case the client would be warned of the need for the orders to keep the factory occupied). Social and other benefits that may be difficult or impossible to quantify are described and carefully explained.

Fees and costs

The total consulting fees, method of invoicing and terms of payment are stated. The costs, shown separately, include those of client staff members who will work with the consultants and of purchase of any equipment that might be needed for the assignment.

Consultant capability

This section gives background information about the consultant organisation.[1] It is particularly important for a new client, or where the survey report is to be read by people whom the survey consultant has not met.

In some surveys, personal details or curricula vitae of the proposed operating team are included at the client's request or on the consulting unit's own initiative.

Terms of business

These concern the conditions of the contract that would be made between the client and the unit should an assignment be agreed. Legal aspects of contracts vary from country to country and should be thoroughly understood by both client and consulting unit. Terms of business are often given in a prepared document that can be attached to the survey report.[2] In most cases agreement requires no more than the client's written acceptance of the survey report.

8.2 Estimating fees and costs

The survey consultant calculates fees by estimating the time required to complete the assignment and converting it to money at a fee rate per man-day or man-week.[3] A time decision has to be carefully made. To overestimate might jeopardise the client's acceptance; to underestimate would place the operating consultants and the whole unit in a difficult position.

---

[1] The code of conduct adopted by the given consulting organisation may be enclosed as an appendix to the report.

[2] An example of terms of business is given in Appendix 3.

[3] Factors determining the consulting unit's standard fee per man-day are discussed in Chapter 25, pp. 263-268.

A well-established consulting unit has experience and records of times taken over a wide variety of industries, problems, application of techniques and client capability. Yardsticks are thus available for the comparative estimating of time in a new situation. Their use is in every case tempered by the survey consultant's judgement: the " difference " between clients and environments prohibits unconsidered transfer of data from one assignment to another.

The client's ability to pay the fees in time may be a constraint. This could involve either trimming the terms of reference or making the assignment intermittent over a longer period. Much would depend on the estimated return of cash benefits. If the survey consultant did not check the point beforehand, payment difficulty might lead to a revised survey report.[1]

A client may sometimes be anxious about the cost of the time his own staff would have to contribute. The consultant may usefully point out not only that the time is essential to the consultant-client alliance, but that it is cheaper than having to use more operating consultants' time to get through the work.

8.3 Presenting the report

The survey report is presented to the client at the end of the management survey and sets the scene for his acceptance and the subsequent assignment.

As a rule, consultants prefer not just to mail the report, but to hand it over to the client in a meeting which starts by a short oral (and visual, if appropriate) presentation of the report's summary. The report is transmitted at the end of the presentation, when it is subject to free discussion.

The consultant is ready to answer questions concerning the start of the proposed assignment. If the client is keen to start, there are obvious advantages in doing so while the enthusiasm is there and contacts established during the survey are fresh in people's minds. But an early date may not be easy to meet because of existing commitments of the best consultants suitable for the particular work.

The client's staff may also ask further questions about the consultant's organisation and the qualifications and experience of its men.

Though the consultant obviously would like to have a decision before the end of the meeting, the client may have good reasons for not wanting to give one. He should not be pressed. A professional consultant knows whether his performance was good enough and he can only exercise patience over the outcome.

The consultant should be flexible in choosing the most suitable way of presenting a survey report. For example, if the client wants to read the report

---

[1] The consultant should remind the client that fees may be deductable for taxation purposes.

prior to the oral presentation, the consultant should hand it over and agree that a meeting will follow. Also, if the client feels a need for another discussion after the survey report has been studied in his organisation, the consultant will accept the idea of a second meeting.

Organisations in the public sector are usually bound by rules which specify a minimum number of tenders before awarding any contract. But it is also becoming more and more common for industrial and commercial clients in the private sector to have surveys made by several consultants and to choose the one whose assignment proposals appear the most attractive. This does not make any difference to the way a survey is conducted and the report presented. In such cases, however, it may take several weeks or months before the client will be in a position to communicate his reaction to the report, and his decision on the choice of the consultants for the operating assignment.

8.4 Survey notes

This is an internal report for the use of the consulting unit, if its services are retained for the operating assignment. It includes documentation and information collected by the survey consultant, and his impressions of the organisation, management characteristics and methods of working.

Covered in particular are:

— names of managers met and any information collected on them;

— organisational features;

— analysis of the problem, including the consultant's thinking behind the proposed solution;

— other problems identified, potential problems, or areas of further work not tackled in the proposed assignment;

— personal comments on and assessments of the client, his attitude to consultants, and his likely reaction to the assignment;

— background information, including financial accounts, particularly any financial ratios used in the diagnosis;

— any other useful suggestions to the operating team.

The survey notes will be used mainly in defining assignment strategy, deciding on work plans, staffing the assignment and briefing the operating team.

PLANNING AND STAFFING THE ASSIGNMENT

9

9.1 Assignment strategy

Strategic considerations concern the optimum over-all approach to the planning and implementation of the operating assignment. To some extent, strategy is predetermined by the terms of the survey report, especially by the defined objectives and any requirements of the client. For example, the client may have set his own deadline for the completion of the assignment, which might be shorter than that which the consultant would usually allow; or the survey may have indicated that the receptivity to consultants is much better in some parts of the client organisation than in others. This may compel the consultants to adopt an assignment plan they would not normally choose. In other cases, the survey consultant may have come to some conclusions concerning the desirable pace of introducing change in the client organisation. This will be one of the key factors of assignment strategy, with many implications for planning and staffing.

By and large, strategy will determine:

— the starting points of the assignment;
— the pace of work;
— the sequence in which problems are to be tackled and partial proposals made;
— the time and way of presenting conclusions and solutions within the organisation;
— the time and way of implementing proposals;
— the profile and size of the consulting team;
— the profiles, numbers and ways of involvement of the co-operating client's staff.

An aspect of strategy is the need to keep a broad perspective in view all the time, and a willingness to look outside the limits of the diagnostic survey and the agreed definition of the assignment. A periodic review of strategy during the assignment is to be foreseen as well, including the subsequent review of the time scale and assignment plan if appropriate.

Strategy is based both on the survey report (which already includes some of its elements) and on internal recommendations to the consulting unit made by the survey consultant in his survey notes. It is then worked out in discussions between the survey consultant and his colleague who will be responsible for the operating assignment. The client is consulted on all aspects of assignment strategy, which needs to be harmonised with his views and priorities.

9.2 Staffing the assignment

Selecting the team

The staffing of a consulting assignment is a decision-making exercise in which the interests and desires of the client have to be reconciled with the possibilities and interests of the consulting organisation.

Obviously, every client would like to see the best consultants assigned to his organisation. So far he has been in contact with senior people—the survey consultant and, possibly, a member of the management team who came to preliminary survey meetings or was otherwise involved in negotiating the assignment. He will want consultants of this calibre to continue the work.

The practical solutions offered by consulting firms are usually the following.

Simple and relatively small assignments (as a rule in one or two functional areas) are carried out by one or several *operating* or *resident consultants*, specialists in particular management functions. Their supervision is entrusted to a *supervising consultant* (supervisor), who is an all-round senior consultant responsible for several operating assignments at the same time. This means that he is not present at the client's premises full time, but will regularly visit the operating consultant or team to control the progress of the assignment and provide advice.

This organisational pattern is, however, difficult to apply to extensive and complex assignments, to which clients look with considerable expectations. More and more client enterprises require that such assignments should be managed and implemented by the same person who did the preliminary survey and persuaded the client to use the services of his consulting unit.[1] In such a

---

[1] For example, large consulting firms were criticised for their assignment staffing practices by speakers from management circles at the 1971 conference of the FEACO (European Federation of Associations of Management Consultants).

case the survey consultant becomes a full-time team leader or project manager for the duration of the assignment.

Consulting organisations are well advised to consider very carefully to which assignments they should apply the first approach and to which the second. It is a subject that should be discussed with the client at an early stage after having established a contact with him. If the assignment is simple and does not warrant the full-time presence of a senior management consultant (their number in the consulting unit is limited and their time more expensive), this should be explained to the client.

There is, too, the factor of personalities: the correct matching of client and consultant personalities can make the difference between good, middling and poor assignments. Guidance on the client's characteristics, in terms of likes and dislikes, habits, interests and general way of life have been provided by the survey consultant in the survey notes. The consulting unit knows the personalities of its own staff.

The client and the consultant do not necessarily have to have everything in common. There are even advantages sometimes in complementing a client of one type by a consultant of another when a modifying influence appears desirable. The main thing for the consulting unit to avoid is putting two obvious incompatibles together.

Up to a point, it can be expected that every consultant will adapt to the normal and unavoidable differences, and the matching of people only becomes a matter of avoiding clashes at the more extreme points of human behaviour. An operating consultant has occasionally to be chosen for his ability to hold his own in a wide range of situations.

But it is equally important that the supervisor and operating consultants get on well with each other. Consultants do not see eye to eye in matters of individual preference any more than other people.

It is obvious that the choice of professional staff will vary according to the size of the consulting unit. The smaller units either have to work in a more limited field or employ highly versatile and adaptable men. In the extreme case, the problems for a consultant who is a sole-practitioner are plain to see.

Availability of suitable consultants

Before establishing assignment plans, the consulting unit needs to make sure that the consultants selected for the assignment will be available at the necessary point of time and for the periods required by the assignment.

To the consulting unit this is yet another piece in the jig-saw puzzle, to be placed within the total picture of its operations. There are obviously two conflicting criteria: the optimum scheduling of the given assignment and the regular and stable workload for all professional members of the consulting unit.[1] Occasionally, there may be two or more concurrent assignments in which the same consultant would be required at the same time.

The consulting unit tries to solve this conflict through proper planning of assignments. For example, the timing of the start may be quite arbitrary if the client does not need to start immediately. Furthermore, the pace of work and the presence of operating consultants in the client organisation may be adjusted to some extent; or it may be possible to persuade the client to wait until a fully competent operating consultant becomes available rather than require an immediate start at all costs. In another case, an early appointment of the team supervisor can be made so as to effect a bridging operation and arrange for preparatory work to be done by the client's staff.

In whatever way the situation is reconciled, it has to be in the best interest of the client. For example, the consulting unit must not suggest delays in assignments that are extremely urgent.

9.3   Over-all assignment plan

The over-all assignment plan covers the whole period of the assignment. It presents the operating team's main activities against a timetable (in weeks or days). It specifies the starting and final points of these activities, the volume of work (man/weeks or man/days) in every period in the timetable, and points of time for submission of reports (interim and final) and for progress control of the assignment.

Estimates of time in the over-all plan can be made:

— top down, when the consultant knows that he has a certain number of weeks and man/weeks available and tries to allocate them to a certain number of different activities;

— bottom up, when the consultant estimates the time needed for each particular activitiy and compares the total time thus obtained with the established deadlines and total estimates of man/weeks needed for the assignment.

Experience of the time for similar activities on previous assignments is useful in any case.

The length of assignments affects planning. A short assignment must obviously be planned in greater detail in order to complete it on time. A long assignment invites the temptation to neglect planning since there is no immediate time-pressure. If allowed to take this line, the consultants may

---

[1] On this problem see Chapter 25, pp. 263-268.

suddenly become aware that half the time has been used, and only one quarter of the programme accomplished. Long assignments may also tend to lose sight of ultimate objectives, particularly as the operating team becomes more accepted and part of the scene. A clear plan and its regular control avoid this.

A well-calculated over-all assignment plan allows for some contingencies and should only have to be altered when major events disturb the normal progress of the assignment.

The over-all assignment plan can be presented as a bar chart, a table giving numerical values, a network diagram (for long and complex assignments) or a combination of these.

It is useful to put down the client inputs and activities in the assignment plan in a way which enables a separate control of client and consultant inputs.

The plan is available for assignment control both to the consulting unit and the client organisation.

9.4 Short-term planning

Some parts of an over-all plan may refer to more detailed planning documents. There is a limit to how much of this is practicable and how far in advance it can be done, but there is always a good case for a detailed plan for the first three or four weeks of an assignment.

Sometimes, tactics of expediency in face of unpredictable occurrences might require the overlay of a short-term plan on the over-all plan, in order to break an impasse or show the way round a knotty problem.

A short-term work schedule may be used to plan a temporary increase in the number of operating consultants beyond the originally planned figures in order to accelerate some assignment activities. However, the option of injecting more consultants to complete the work in a shorter calendar time is not always given. The survey consultant has already agreed the time scale—calendar and consultant man/weeks. The addition of extra consultants does not reduce the time proportionally—as a rule, four consultants require more than one-quarter of the time that one would need. There are various reasons for this, one being the necessity to co-ordinate activities. Also, the capacity of the client to supply facts and figures and digest the consultants' ideas and proposals is limited, since they are extra to his normal load. Additional consultants may even hinder rather than help in such a situation.

One way of gaining time is to allocate junior or trainee consultants when an assignment suits the particular stage of their personal development. They can take over parts of the plan and save time at little or no extra cost to the client.

CONTROLLING THE ASSIGNMENT 10

Properly organised consulting assignments involve a number of preparatory, briefing and control arrangements and activities whose purpose is to make sure that the time of operating consultants is effectively used and their services meet the desired professional standards.

The description of assignment preparation and control procedures given in this chapter assumes that there are operating consultants (one or more) who are guided and controlled by a supervisor who visits them regularly at the client's premises. Clearly, appropriate adjustments will be made in the control of assignments where the senior all-round consultant who did the survey is also the full-time leader of the operating team, as discussed in Chapter 9.[1]

10.1 Pre-assignment arrangements

Appointment of liaison officer

It is usual for the client to appoint one or more of his staff members to provide close and continuous liaison with the consultants. The term "counterpart" is familiar in some situations. These people are of great assistance to, and time-savers for, operating consultants, especially during the early investigational stages. This may be full-time work. In some assignments consultants train the liaison men to maintain and develop the work after the end of the assignment.

Recruitment and training of client staff

The preliminary survey may have shown a problem caused by the shortage of competent people, with no prospect of finding suitable candidates inside the

---

[1] Cf. p. 100.

company. The client may do the recruitment and selection himself or may use the consulting unit's services. Either method will take some time.

Client staff—possibly including the liaison officer—may need preliminary training in certain techniques. The supervising consultant may assist in finding the most suitable courses for them to attend.[1]

Provision of equipment

Equipment may be for the purpose of expediting the assignment, for the client's continued use or both.

On one occasion the survey consultant knew of an inexpensive device for monitoring performance and analysing malfunctions in a production process. This not only saved the consultant many days of painstaking deductive investigation (and saved fees for the client) but became available to the client for permanent use. Equipment to be provided may include accounting machines, printing equipment, or anything to meet such needs as the survey consultant could diagnose with certainty.

Special training of operating consultants

An assignment may require certain skills in which the only available consultant is short of experience. He may get intensive coaching in the unit or gain direct experience by joining another assignment where the team is already practising the same methods.

Office accommodation

A consulting team should not have to hunt for offices when it starts an assignment. Either the survey consultant or the supervisor, when on a pre-assignment activity, should ensure that suitable accommodation is available.

Consultants need not have the best offices but they will not be highly regarded by the staff if they have only a small table in a corner of a general area. Without suitable office space, consultants cannot avoid losses of their expensive time.

Operating consultants on assignments need privacy for interviews, discussions with liaison officers, meetings with the supervisor, study of documents and writing. As a rule, meeting rooms are not suitable for use as consultants' offices.

10.2 Briefings

The final preparations for the start of an operating assignment are the briefings. These serve the purpose of:

---

[1] On training provided in connection with consulting assignments see Chapter 15, p. 161.

— giving the operating team all available information about the client and the assignment;

— ensuring that client staff are informed of the coming of the consultants.

Consultant briefing

One person likely to know little about the assignment before the briefing is the operating consultant, who has probably been very busy winding up his last assignment and in no position to give thought to a new one. If the supervisor has been involved with pre-assignment activity, he will know a great deal. Otherwise, the survey consultant will brief them both.

At the briefing meeting the team takes over the accumulated documentation from the preliminary survey. All matters pertaining to the start of the assignment are then discussed.

Table 10. Checklist of points for briefing

A. Hand over	1. survey report
	2. survey notes
	3. working papers borrowed from client
	4. published or other printed matter
B. Convey and discuss	1. terms of reference
	2. source of introduction to the client
	3. client experience of consultants
	4. client organisation's structure, personalities, general style of management, apparent centres of power and influence
	5. client's apparent needs and desires, real and imagined
	6. probable attitudes of staff
	7. basis of forecast results of the assignment
	8. assignment strategy and plan
	9. client's experience in the techniques the consultants intend to use
	10. key facts of the client's operation (see section 6.4 dealing with subjects for appraisal)
	11. production processes; trade jargon and terms particular to the business and the locality
	12. contacts made with trade unions and other bodies
	13. previous work in the sector (for the same client, competitors, etc.)
C. Inform on	1. commitments to the client in respect of various services of the consulting unit (training, recruitment, design, computing, etc.)
	2. arrangements for invoicing and payment of fees
	3. arrangements for starting date, time and place
	4. arrangements for office accommodation, staff liaison, secretarial and other support
	5. accommodation and meeting place of consultants before going to client organisation.

The typical checklist of points for the briefing given in Table 10 would guard against significant omissions.

Client briefing

Many of the points for final check with the client are covered in the list above. The remaining precautions in respect of the client may depend on how much time has passed since the assignment was agreed to and what the pre-assignment activities were. The main remaining checks are:

— that the client's views are still in accordance with the terms of the survey report;

— that he has adequately explained the nature and purpose of the assignment to all managers and other employees who will be in any way affected.

To ensure that this action is done properly the survey consultant or supervisor may offer to join in explanatory interviews and meetings.[1]

10.3   Starting the assignment

Introductions and tour of premises

The conduct of the first days of the assignment is of vital importance. The client has already met the survey consultant and possibly the supervisor, but may be meeting the operating consultants for the first time.

The members of the team new to the client are introduced to him, his main executives and other employees as already discussed.[2] These introductions should be comprehensive and should include all who might resent being missed. At the end, the consultants should ask tactfully if there are any others they should see. During introductions the consultants will sense whether the client's briefing of his staff was complete and understood. The team should be careful to remember names.

Introductions may be combined with a tour of the plant or offices. This gives a two-way opportunity—for the consultants to begin their orientation and the employees to get their first sight of them. The particular functional department for the assignment would be the major stopping place, but the first tour should be comprehensive. It could end with another tactful question—" Is there anywhere we have not been? ".

During introductions the team members should talk enough to show and arouse interest, but avoid any remarks that would suggest pre-judgement or over-confidence. This is the start of an exercise in patient listening.

---

[1] See Chapter 3, p. 22.
[2] Ibid.

Short-term programme

After introductions the team should make time to talk on their own and discuss impressions. They should re-check the over-all assignment plan. If there is not already a short-term plan, they should draw one up for the next week or two. The date of the supervisor's next visit is arranged and a copy of his own programme in the meantime is left with the operating team.

Starting work

With the departure of the seniors, the operating consultant is on his own for the first time in the new surroundings. This can be a ticklish time and if there is any stage fright this is when it happens. It is essential for the operating consultant immediately to *do* something and establish contacts with the client's people. Making the start is more important than what precisely is done first. The longer the delay, the harder it becomes. An experienced operating consultant soon overcomes any trepidation; for his experience shows him what initial steps would be effective in this new environment.

10.4 Operating consultants' self-discipline and self-control

The self-discipline of the operating consultants is a vital factor in assignment control. They are the full-time members of the team and often the consulting unit's sole representatives for 90% of the time of the assignment.

The consultants are constantly exposed in a situation where they are greatly outnumbered. They have to set an example for hard and high-quality work and intellectual integrity. It is primarily a matter of their own judgement to decide how the code of conduct and the unwritten rules of the consulting profession should be applied in the conditions of the client organisation—and from this viewpoint every organisation has its own behavioural patterns, habits, traditions, and also defects. Should questions arise, the senior consultant supervising the assignment has to help the operating team by his advice and guidance.

Assignment diary

At the end of the first day the operating consultant starts the assignment diary. This is an essential record of activity throughout the assignment. It is written up each evening with a summary of the day's significant events (or non-events) and of progress made. It is a necessary reference for the supervisor. Every paper or note written by the operating team should be recorded in the diary, and dated: sometimes the date proves to be its main value.

Time-keeping

The general rule is that the consultant on an assignment adjusts to the working hours of the client organisation. But the assignment programme is usually a heavy one and the operating consultant may need to work long hours to complete it on time. There may be both practical and tactical advantages in starting a little ahead of the rest in the morning and leaving a little later in the evening—so long as he does not appear to make a virtue of it.

The consultant's home may be far from the client's premises and he may occasionally need to travel on a working day. If this is foreseen, it should be discussed with the client before the start of the assignment. An agreement should be reached on how the working hours and days will be counted, and whether the consultant will be authorised to take time off for home travel if he has worked overtime.

When the assignment concerns departments working two or three shifts, the operating consultant must spend enough time on them all to find out all he needs. His reception on a night shift is often illuminating—workers may receive him warmly and appreciate that somebody is interested in their night-work.

Sensitivity, anticipation and reaction

The operating consultant has to be sensitive to all the points the supervisor would normally check. This sensitivity is allied to self-control. The operating consultant will encounter frustrations and must endure them with patience and good humour. Anger will only arouse opposition and the consultant may find himself being baited. At times people may put forward ill-considered views or provide incorrect information. In rejecting these the consultant must use tact and show tolerance, taking care to give reasoned explanations. There may be attempts to use him or involve him in intrigues. If he has his eyes and ears open, he may be sufficiently ahead of these games to sidestep them, and be respected the more for it. Genuine appeals must always be met with ready help: goodwill and co-operation do not come unless they are deserved.

Favours offered by client

Sometimes clients arrange for their staff to be able to purchase goods in local shops at a discount, or they may allow the purchase of the company's products at cost rather than at market price. The consultant is not a member of the client's staff, and should not expect to participate. If he is invited to join the scheme, he should consider the privilege with care and discretion.

The same rules apply to gifts from the client. There is perhaps no danger in accepting a parting gift, made as a personal gesture at the end of a satisfactory assignment, but at any other time discretion is necessary in deciding whether and how to accept gifts.

10.5 Control by supervising consultant and client

The supervisor visits the assignment as frequently as its circumstances warrant, usually at least twice a month. Visits are made more frequently when the operating consultant is new or when the assignment is going through a difficult period. Dates of visits should be known in advance to all parties so that appointments and other preparations may be made.

The supervisor spends time with the operating consultants and client together, to assess the development of the relationship between them, and separately, to find how each regards the other and the progress of the assignment. The supervisor also considers progress in relation to the wider policies and interests of both the client organisation and the consulting unit.

With the operating consultants, the supervisor may check some or all of the following points:

— that frequent and satisfactory contacts are being maintained with client personnel;

— that assignment progress is up to date and under control;

— that the assignment diary is in good order;

— that the operating consultants are not under stress from any form of harassment by the client;

— that in their anxiety to reach an early balance between financial benefits and fees, the members of the operating team are not tempted to go for a quick return from some potentially dangerous scheme;

— that the opportunities for putting in useful interim reports are used;

— that the operating consultants' morale is high, and their enthusiasm unflagging.

The supervisor is always ready to act as a sounding-board for the operating consultant's ideas and as an audience for rehearsal of presentations. He discusses the operating man's performance frankly and constructively with him, giving approval for work well done and guidance where improvement is necessary.

With the client the supervisor checks:

— whether he is satisfied with the over-all progress of the assignment, the contribution made by the operating team, and the relations that have developed between the consultants and the client's staff members;

— whether he has met all agreed obligations and inputs in the assignment.

To make control efficient, the client organisation has, on its side, to have its own procedure for examining progress of operating assignments. The scheduled interim reports submitted by consultants should be studied, views of staff members collaborating with consultants collected, and the consultants' working methods and behaviour observed. Any problem should be raised with the supervisor.

There are periods, particularly in the early stages of an assignment, when the work shows no tangible results. The supervisor may notice signs of fretting, impatience, lessening interest, or simply " cold feet ". The symptoms could be:

— people " too busy " to spend time with the consultants;

— defensive or reserved attitudes and a reluctance to talk;

— remarks like " your man is taking up a lot of our time ", or " you people are costing us a lot of money ".

The supervisor has to take these signs for what they are worth. They are not to be ignored, nor are they grounds for panic. They have to be countered by whatever overt or covert means are appropriate. It could be that in fact the client is not being sufficiently involved and does not know enough about what is going on.

From his sessions with the operating consultants, the supervisor might find that the assignment is in fact getting behind. If so, short-term measures may be agreed as discussed in Chapter 9.[1]

The supervisor, as a travelling representative of the consulting unit, would be informed if one of the clients were not paying the fees and would take this up during his visits. A tactful reminder may be all that is necessary.

If a client still does not pay, the consulting team may be withdrawn. No business can carry too many debtors but consulting organisations which are not subsidised are particularly sensitive to financial liquidity.

Supervisor's report

The supervisor keeps notes and gives reports to the management of the consulting unit in much the same way as the operating consultants keep the assignment diary. He may have five or so current assignments and cannot rely on his recollection of one control visit after making several others. These reports are for internal use only and can be hand-written.

It is useful to keep a duplicate book for each assignment. The bound pages are automatically filed; the tear-off pages go to inform headquarters about the assignment between the supervisor's meetings with his superiors.

---

[1] Cf. p. 103.

10.6 Further roles of the supervisor

The supervisor's view of the operating consultants goes beyond the terms and scope of a particular assignment. They are colleagues and continuing members of the same consulting unit. Support provided by supervisors, coupled with the over-all encouragement from headquarters, clearly affects the quality of every single assignment.

Liaison with the operating consultant

Whether the location of the assignment raises difficulties of communication depends on the type and size of the consulting unit and the geographical spread of its operations. Many operating consultants may be working a long way from their administrative centre for extensive periods.

Though the consulting unit may have a newsletter, hold regional staff meetings and perhaps an annual conference for everyone, an operating consultant may feel out on a limb for much of the time. The main line of communication between him and his organisation is through the supervisor.

The supervisor's visits are, therefore, important occasions for discussion of the consulting unit's news and results, interesting developments and other assignments, and for a bit of informal talk on what is going on. The operating consultant is made to feel he still belongs to an organisation. The worst complex a consultant could harbour is that so long as he is bringing in the fees nobody cares much about him. Supervisors thus have a responsibility to both the consulting unit and to their operating colleagues to keep the whole as close-knit as possible. Without it, an operating consultant on a long assignment may begin to identify himself too much with his client and lose his vital independence and objectivity.

Health and morale of operating consultants

A consultant's morale is unlikely to be high if his health is not good. Consultants on assignments tend to go on working when client staff would go on sick leave. Furthermore, a hotel is not usually the most sympathetic place for someone who is ill. The supervisor watches the operating consultants' health carefully; delaying a visit to a doctor could mean a serious illness.

A drop in morale can occur without a loss of physical health. Isolation from wife and family, frustrations of the assignment, or uninspiring surroundings all contribute. One of the telltale signs is that a consultant begins to hate the sight of the place he has to work in.

It should not be overlooked that consultants are—or become—somewhat different from people who work under the same roof and have a very close relationship with their colleagues. They are not " organisation men " [1], but are a collection of highly individual people who have to be managed as such. Their morale is mainly sustained by dedication to their profession and bolstered by success in it. The supervisor's role is to treat each one according to his present needs and future potential.

Personal development of operating consultants

Obviously, as a senior and more experienced member of the consulting unit and of the profession, the supervising consultant plays a key role in further training and development of colleagues who work in operating assignments. This will be discussed in detail in Chapter 28.[2]

---

[1] Cf. W. H. Whyte: *The organisation man* (Harmondsworth, Middx., Penguin Books, 1963).

[2] See pp. 303-307.

LITERATURE TO PART II

ACME: *Guide to professional practice (Suggestions for preparing proposals; interim report practice; survey report practice)* (New York, Association of Consulting Management Engineers, 1966); 35 pp.

ACME: *How to control the quality of a management consulting assignment* (New York, Association of Consulting Management Engineers, 1972); 30 pp.

ACME: *Professional practices in management consulting* (New York, Association of Consulting Management Engineers, 1966); 100 pp.

BIM: *Know your business! Vol. I: Business analysis; Vol. II: Managing the smaller company* (developed from the Swedish original) (London, British Institute of Management, 1973).

Boyce R. O., Eisen H.: *Management diagnosis* (Harlow, Essex, Longman, 1972); 282 pp.

Drucker P.: *Managing for results* (New York, Harper and Row, 1964); 240 pp.

Greenberg L.: *A practical guide to productivity measurement* (Washington D.C., Bureau of National Affairs, 1973); 77 pp.

ILO: *How to read a balance sheet.* An ILO programmed book (Geneva, International Labour Office, 11th impr. 1975); 124 pp.

ILO: *The enterprise and factors affecting its operation* (Geneva, International Labour Office, 1965); 200 pp.

Mitchell R. L.: *Reconnaissance: survey and assignment definition* (course material) (Turin, International Centre for Advanced Technical and Vocational Training, 1973; mimeographed); 30 pp.

Rosenberg S. L.: *Self-analysis of your organisation* (New York, AMACOM, 1974); 190 pp.

Shay P. W.: *How to get the best results from management consultants* (New York, Association of Consulting Management Engineers, 1974); 60 pp.

Stern J. M.: *Measuring corporate performance* (London, Financial Times, 1975); 74 pp.

Walsh J. E.: *Guidelines for management consultants in Asia* (Tokyo, Asian Productivity Organisation, 1973); 210 pp.

Wood E. G.: *Bigger profits for the smaller firm* (London, Business Books, 1972); 191 pp.

PART III

METHODS OF EXECUTING ASSIGNMENTS

FRAMEWORK OF AN OPERATING ASSIGNMENT

11

This chapter opens the third part of the book, in which the methodology of operating management consulting assignments will be examined step by step.

11.1 Basic steps in assignments

Although there is a wide range of assignment situations, there tends to be a common essential sequence of steps which the consultant takes in the process of the investigation and solution of the problem. Assuming that the scope of the assignment was defined at the end of the preliminary management survey, and that all pre-assignment arrangements have been made, the operating assignment would typically pass through the following four steps:

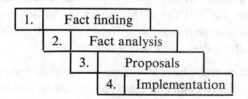

For the sake of clarity, these steps will be discussed as separate activities (each in one chapter). But in practice there will often be some overlapping in content and timing and a good deal of subdivision.

The monitoring of progress step by step is one of the key aspects of assignment control. For example, the length of the fact-finding phase must be kept in proportion not only to the importance of the problem but also to the time that will be available for the subsequent facts analysis and search for solutions. Quite frequently, partial conclusions reached in the course of the assignment will require the collection and analysis of further data, and the system will thus have to be recycled. In other words, assignment plans have to be adjusted if a new situation requires it.

11.2 Further refinements in problem diagnosis

An essential aim of assignment methodology is to achieve increasing accuracy and depth in the problem diagnosis.

The original definition of the problem made by the client will often receive a first revision as a result of discussion between the survey consultant and the client. It will then become the starting point for the operating consultant, and may well become further refined as he carries out his assignment. Very often the true nature of the main problem will not become apparent until various sub-problems in specific management areas have been examined.

It is even possible that the problem has changed somewhat during the time that has elapsed between the end of the preliminary survey and the commencement of the operating assignment.

The operating consultant will thus endeavour to avoid certain pitfalls in problem identification:

— he will not accept without question the definition made in the preliminary survey and follow it blindly without his own further diagnosis;

— he will be prepared to re-examine the definition of the problem (with all implications) at any point in the assignment, even if this will upset his strategies and plans, and require some new explanations and negotiations with the client;

— he will maintain a sense of proportion, see the difference between problems that require his and the client's action, and other problems that are cheaper to live with than to solve, or are not related to the essential issue for which the consultant was brought in;

— he will not gaze too long at a complex problem, but try to break it into partial problems small enough to be described and solved more easily;

— he will avoid tackling problems which are clearly beyond the scope of a consulting assignment.

In summary, it is a common feature of consulting in management that problem diagnosis is a process of gradual refinement.

The fact that the consultant's knowledge of the problem develops during the assignment has certain implications for assignment (operating) reports. Although there will be an agreed time schedule for submitting reports, any change in the definition of a problem, or a new agreement with the client to work on a newly discovered problem, warrants confirmation by a report (special or advance report, if necessary). In some circumstances (e.g. if the period between the survey and the operating assignment was long) it is as well to issue an early report even to confirm that the problem remains the same as accepted in the survey report, and to specify how the operating consultant intends to tackle it.

11.3 Matching methodology to problem nature

A correct understanding of the fundamental nature of the problem is essential if the consultant is to find the best approach to each step in the assignment and use the most appropriate methods.

For example, different work methods may apply to corrective, progressive and creative problems.[1] If the consultant deals with a problem that is essentially corrective, he will devote great attention to the examination of data on past developments, with particular regard to internal and external factors that may have caused an originally satisfactory condition to deteriorate. He may be able to find a great amount of data, and furthermore help from the client's staff will be relatively easy to obtain, especially if they are anxious to stop a downward trend. If the problem is progressive, a study of the past will still be made, but its importance may be smaller than in the case of corrective problems. Inter-firm comparison may be of great help, including the study of similar organisations in the sector which are attaining better results. It may be, however, that many people in the organisation will not understand why improvements are deemed necessary, and to obtain their support will require careful explanation. As mentioned earlier, creative problems provide the consultant with the least amount of starting information. The possibilities of collecting data and checking alternative solutions against standards may be limited. But creation is not the same as waiting until inspiration comes. The consultant will endeavour to imagine a feasible solution and work at its gradual improvement until something satisfactory emerges. He will try to use the principles of creative thinking and seek not mass collaboration on the part of the client's staff, but help from selected individuals known for their ability to conceive sensible new ideas. These principles can be applied to anything from setting up a new activity to laying out a new factory.

Similarly, the consultant has to consider whether the assignment involves predominantly administrative, technical, financial or human and social aspects. While complex management assignments will involve them all, in many assignments one aspect clearly predominates and this will determine the approach used. There is a link here with the functional areas in which the assignments are operating. For example, assignments aimed at important changes in company organisation can be expected to raise a number of psycho-sociological problems, while this is less likely to happen in

---

[1] See Chapter 2, p. 15.

assignments in financial management and accounting. Also, if the consultant works as a counsellor and catalyst trying to develop a team spirit and bring about a change in working relations between individuals and groups, the steps involved will differ from those used in a classical industrial engineering exercise.

Further comments on varying approaches used in assignments concerned with solving different types of management problems will be made in the following four chapters, and in Part IV dealing with consulting in various areas of management.

FACT FINDING

12

All sound consulting work is built on facts. Operating consultants need a considerable number of facts to have a clear picture of the situation, arrive at precise problem definition and relate their proposals to reality. Facts are needed also for assignments which try to develop something very new and involve a great deal of imagination and creative thinking. Facts may be difficult to obtain and in some cases fact finding may be the most tiring phase of the consultant's work, but there is no alternative.

12.1 Scope of assignment facts

The term " assignment facts " is sometimes used to indicate facts needed in executing assignments. Obviously many facts collected before and during the diagnostic survey, called " orientation " and " diagnostic " or " survey " facts in Part II of this book, will be of direct use to the consultant. He will obtain them from the survey report, the survey notes and the documents annexed to both. Many of these facts will become " assignment facts " and will be used and reviewed by the operating consultant.

The operating consultant will, however, go much further and in considerably greater detail in defining and collecting facts. He will also be able to use some other sources of information and methods of data gathering, e.g. arrange for special record keeping.

The kind of facts will depend on the area in which the assignment takes place and on the definition of the problem and assignment objectives. In particular, facts should enable the examination of processes, relations, causes and mutual influences, with special regard to under-utilised opportunities and possible improvements.

12.2 Defining necessary facts

Fact collecting has to be prepared for by thoroughly defining what facts are wanted. Experienced consultants will continue to apply the principle of selectivity, although they know that they need more detailed and precise facts than their colleagues who did the preliminary survey. They appreciate that virtually unlimited amounts of facts are available in any organisation, but that an excessive amount of them easily becomes unmanageable and cannot be fully utilised in the assignments. The cost of fact gathering cannot be ignored, especially if some data are not readily available and special schemes (observations, special record keeping) have to be established to obtain them.

But the definition of facts and their sources must not be too restrictive. If it is, this might exclude facts from which significant information on causes, effects or relationships might be drawn, and these are often found in unexpected places. At the beginning of the assignment, the consultant may well cast his net fairly wide, reject some data after preliminary examinations, but add others and so on.

The assignment facts have to be defined in closest collaboration with the client, especially with those members of the client organisation who know what records are kept, how reliable they are, and what data will have to be sought from other sources. This includes the definition of the content of data, degree of their detail, time period, extent of coverage and classification and tabulation criteria.

Every experienced consultant knows well that apparently identical types of data may have a different *meaning or content* in different organisations. For example " work in progress " may be defined in a number of different ways, it may or may not include certain items, and its financial value may be determined by various methods. The definition of categories of employees (technicians, middle managers, administrative personnel, production and auxiliary workers, etc.) is also subject to many variations. In old firms with established traditions this is complicated by the existence of their own terminology, which may differ from terminology that prevails in the industry to which they belong. The uniformity of data used in the management of various organisations will be higher in countries where some central planning and control exists, and where accounting and enterprise statistics have to observe certain official regulations. But even in these cases many differences will be found especially in the production area.

For *quantities*, the consultant specifies the units of measure, e.g. count of products, or their weight or volume, and sets the limits of accuracy, e.g. to the nearest 100 or to the last unit. Accuracy depends upon the purpose for which the data is to be used. Work study to set standard operating times may require accuracy to the nearest second with an error allowance of 5%. By contrast, a forecast of total volume of production for a year may approximate to the nearest thousand with an error allowance of 10%. If the consultant fails to set the limits of accuracy before data is collected, he may not obtain what he requires and have to repeat the recording process, e.g. operating times may be recorded in minutes or tenths or hundredths of minutes, when seconds are required.

The *degree of detail* of assignment facts will generally be higher than that of data used in diagnostic surveys. While general diagnosis stems from aggregate figures, e.g. total time spent by machines on productive work, change rests upon more detailed data, e.g. machining time for each operation, or time spent on productive work by certain types of machines, or in certain shops. The more detailed the facts the more time they will take to collect. At the start of an assignment the consultant may have difficulty in evaluating the advantages which detailed facts will yield. Before he collects the data he cannot know what weaknesses or opportunities for improvement they will reveal. He may obtain hints from the opinions of the client's managers. They will probably point out problems that deserve close examination. Otherwise the consultant may first collect data in broad categories, e.g. total number of days of sick leave taken by all workers. Analysis of this data will suggest more detail for certain categories, e.g. number of days of sick leave taken by each age group during the winter months. Data may thus be gathered in several steps before the consultant has a sufficiently detailed picture of the present situation and the ways to improve it.

Defining the *period of time* is equally important. For example, to design an inventory management system for finished ceramic products, the consultant must know the number of products sold. For how many years must he calculate the sales and at what intervals? The answer might be for each month in the last three years. In any case the period of time should be long enough to set a firm pattern of activity, indicate rates of growth or decline, and reveal fluctuation in activity due to seasonal variations or economic cycles. A considerably longer period will be chosen in enterprises that produce large capital goods, with a lead time of several years in product design and manufacturing, than in enterprises producing current consumer goods.

Periods of time need to be comparable: months or weeks have to include the same number of working days and so on. Periods when exceptional events occurred should be excluded, but recognised and accommodated in the new situation. Periods preceding major changes in operations, e.g. introduction of new products and dropping of old ones, have to be examined separately from periods of normal operation.

The choice of a period close to the start of the assignment recognises that the mere presence of the consultant may affect the results. In a particular instance, material wastage dropped substantially from the moment the consultant began to ask questions about it and before he actually did anything.

Obviously the choice of the period of time takes account of the availability of past records, and of changes that the client may have introduced in recording procedures.

Regarding the *extent of coverage*, the consultant must decide whether to collect total information (on all products, all employees, whole units and processes), or a selection only. As a rule, information will be collected for the vital few items that account for the bulk of activity in the current period, and for such items as are likely to become vital in the future (prospective new products, etc.). If the productive capacity is clearly limited by one group of machines which have become a *bottleneck*, the solution of the problems of this group may be a key to the solution of most other problems of the given department. In other cases, data will be collected for representative samples.

Finally, the preparatory work for fact collecting includes decisions on *organisation* and *tabulation* of data, which are made in the light of the end use of the data.

Typical groupings are:

  (i) *for events*—time, frequency, rate, trends, cause, effect (e.g. number of accidents according to causes that occurred each day of the week during the last year);

  (ii) *for people*—age, sex, nationality, family status, qualifications, occupation, length of service, earnings (e.g. average annual earnings of unmarried female employees with selected educational qualifications during each of the last five years);

  (iii) *for products and materials*—size, value, technical characteristics, source of origin (e.g. value of materials by type and size in the inventory at the end of the last twelve calendar quarters);

  (iv) *for resources, inputs, outputs, processes and procedures*—rates of activity (sale, consumption, production), location, control centre, geographical distribution, use of equipment (e.g. numbers of specified parts produced by selected processes during each of the last 24 months).

To arrange facts in digestible form the consultant plans how to tabulate them. Descriptions and narratives may be noted under selected headings on a separate sheet of paper or card for each heading, e.g. responsibilities of each manager. Processes and procedures may be represented by a chain of symbols, such as the activity symbols used by systems analysts or in work study.[1] Shapes are best shown on drawings. Figures are usually set out in tables.

---

[1] See, for example, A. Daniels and D. Yeates (ed.): *Basic training in systems analysis* (London, Pitman, 1969); ILO: *Introduction to work study,* Third revised edition (Geneva, International Labour Office, 1979) or H. B. Maynard (ed.): *Industrial engineering handbook* (New York, McGraw-Hill, 1971).

12.3 Sources and ways of obtaining facts

By and large, facts are available to consultants in three forms:

— records,

— events and conditions,

— memories.

Any of these sources may be internal (within the given organisation) or external (official publications, statistical reports, opinions of people outside the organisation).

Records are facts stored in forms that are readable or can be transcribed. They include documents (files, reports, publications), films, microfilms, tapes, drawings, pictures, charts, etc. Material stored in computer files and other data-processing equipment is also included under this heading. Facts from records are obtained by retrieval and study.

Events and conditions are actions, and circumstances surrounding them, which can be observed. Hence facts on events and conditions are obtained by observing, and recording the results of observations.

Memories are all the information stored in the minds of people who work in the client's organisation, are associated with it, or simply are able to provide information of use to the consultant (e.g. for comparison). This encyclopaedia of knowledge embraces hard proven facts, experiences, opinions, beliefs, impressions, prejudices and insights. The mind stores all this data in the form of words, numbers and pictures which the consultant cannot see, but can obtain from people by means of interviews, questionnaires, special reports, etc.

The co-operation between consultant and client at this stage will involve above all:

— joint consideration of and decisions on the sources of data to be used and in what way this will be done;

— the participation of the client's staff in collecting data (e.g. the use of client's junior staff for routine data gathering expedites the assignment and reduces its cost).

A skilful consultant will avoid having recourse to indirect and time-consuming ways of collecting information, if the same information can be obtained simply and directly. In many cases this means—go and ask people. People at all levels in industrial and other organisations possess an unbelievable amount of knowledge about their organisation and nearly everybody has some ideas on needed and feasible improvements. But they do not divulge this information if they are not asked.

Retrieval of recorded data

Records are a prolific source of information, and some records will be examined and studied in any management consulting assignment. Clearly, preference will be given to the use of information which is already available in records before looking to other ways of data collecting. There are, however, certain pitfalls to be avoided in retrieving recorded data:

- many records are not reliable and give in fact a distorted picture of reality. This is common in cases such as records on machine breakdowns and stoppages, or waste. Materials may be charged to products for which they were not used. Factory plans and layouts may be claimed to be up to date but seldom are. Organisational and operational manuals may include detailed descriptions of procedures which were abandoned a long time ago. If the consultant or the client himself has doubts, the validity of existing records should be verified before they are used;

- it is common in organisations in business and government that various departments have different records on the same activities, inputs or outputs. These records may differ both in the criteria used and in the magnitude of the recorded data;

- criteria and values used in recording are modified from time to time and the consultant must find out about all such modifications.

Special recording

Special recording can be arranged if information is not readily available in existing records, or cannot be relied upon. It may be established for a limited period, say a month or two, according to criteria proposed by the consultant. As a rule, the client's employees working in a given area will be asked to record data and pass them to the consultant. For economy reasons such recording should be kept simple and last no longer than necessary for reliability. Everyone should know at the start how long the period will be, and why special recording had to be introduced.

Observing

Observing is the method the consultant uses to obtain information which is not readily recorded. He is present while an event occurs, e.g. while a manager instructs his subordinates or while a worker performs a task, and uses his faculties of sight and hearing to note how the event occurs, in such a way that he will be able to suggest improved practices at a later date. Information which the consultant usually obtains by observation includes:

- layout of factory, warehouses and offices;
- flow of operations;
- methods of work;
- pace of work;
- working conditions (noise, light, temperature, ventilation, orderliness and cleanliness);
- attitudes and behaviour of managers, supervisors and workers.

Because most people feel uncomfortable under scrutiny, the consultant must take special care to put them at their ease before starting to observe their activities. First he should tell them what he is going to do. He should never start watching workers without warning. He should explain the purpose of his survey and make it clear that it is in no way critical but simply aimed at obtaining reliable information on how the activity is performed. An exchange of views with those under observation, allowing them an opportunity to point out all the factors influencing the activity and inviting their suggestions for improvement, will probably enlist their co-operation. As far as possible they should behave normally under observation and make no attempt to give a better or faster, or worse or slower performance than usual. If there is any unusual occurrence, the observation should be disregarded and repeated when conditions return to normal.

If procedures, operations and processes are observed, the consultant would choose one of the many methods that have been developed for that purpose.[1]

Where the assignment deals primarily with human problems and relations between individuals and groups, the consultant may explore the attitudes and behaviour of the client's staff in depth, through sociometric and attitude surveys and consultations.[2] In other assignments he probes less deeply into these aspects. Nevertheless he observes the inclinations, preferences and prejudices of staff to the extent necessary to understand how these affect the problems he is concerned with, and to enlist co-operation. Such observation continues throughout the assignment. It starts during the introductory meetings when he gains his first impressions. These he will verify during later encounters. To a considerable extent the consultant gathers information on attitudes and behaviour as a by-product of interviews to question memories, exchange ideas or develop improvements. However, during interviews not

---

[1] See references on p. 126.

[2] See, for example, J. Kelly: *Organisational behaviour* (Homewood, Irwin, 1969), W. J. Goode and P. H. Hatt: *Methods in social research* (New York, McGraw-Hill, 1952), or A. L. Edwards: *Techniques of attitude scale construction* (New York, Appleton Century Crofts, 1957).

directly concerned with personal traits, the consultant would distract both himself and his client by writing down his impressions. He should, therefore, make mental notes and put them into writing and classify them afterwards.

In doing this, the consultant will be interested in information such as:

— experience;
— beliefs;
— degree of self-confidence;
— strengths and weaknesses at work;
— likes and dislikes;
— special interests or motives;
— those the person respects and those he doesn't;
— sociability;
— willingness to co-operate;
— management style (autocratic, consultative, permissive);
— extent of original thinking and innovation;
— receptivity to new ideas.

By taking such personal traits and attitudes into account the consultant will increase his chances of understanding factors that affect change in the client organisation.

Special reports

Individuals or teams in the client organisation may be requested to help in the assignment by giving thought to particular aspects of the problem and putting suggestions on paper in the form of a special report. This would include any supporting information that the author might be able to supply. This method is selective—in co-operation with the client the consultant would choose those who are likely to have specific views on the problem in question, be aware of various pitfalls and know about past attempts to solve the problem. If, however, anybody in the client organisation offers to prepare a special report on his own initiative, this should be welcomed, although treated with some caution. The impact of special reports will be increased by defining their desirable outline in advance.

Questionnaires

In management consulting a questionnaire is useful for obtaining a limited number of straightforward facts from a large number of people (e.g. in a market survey), or from a small number of people widely separated from each other (e.g. reasons for equipment failure from users throughout a whole region). They are generally unsatisfactory for gathering all but simple facts.

The questionnaire may be distributed to correspondents with an explanatory note asking them to complete and return it, or canvassers may question people and note their answers on the questionnaire.

Either case calls for a full explanation telling the respondent:

— why he is being asked the questions;

— who is asking them;

— what the questioner will do with the replies;

— who else is being asked.

Before drawing up the questionnaire the consultant decides exactly what information is wanted, how it will be used and how the answers will be summarised and classified. Then precise, simple questions free from ambiguity are framed. As far as possible answers of " yes " and " no " or in figures should be invited. Where longer answers are required, it may be useful to provide a list of probable answers and ask for the right one to be marked. Questions should be arranged in logical order so that each answer leads to the next. It is advisable to group questions and lay out the questionnaire in such a way as to facilitate summarising and tabulating answers, particularly where mechanical or electronic sorters and tabulators will record the answers.

If there are some doubts about the respondents' ability to understand the questions and give clear answers, the questionnaire should be subject to preliminary tests.

Interviewing

One advantage that questioning during an interview has over the use of questionnaires is that every answer can be tested and elaborated. Questions supplement and support each other, confirming, correcting or contradicting previous replies. They also lead to related facts, often revealing unexpected relationships, influences and constraints. The interview is adaptable. If one line of questioning fails to produce required data, another can be tried. This may be suggested by the interviewee's answers. The consultant learns not only from the direct replies he receives but also from the inferences, comments, asides, opinions, anecdotes, attitudes and gestures that accompany them—provided he is alert and attentive.

In interviewing people the consultant is guided by general rules of effective interviewing, which have been described in various texts.[1] Some experiences and suggestions concerning more specifically the use of interviews in management consulting are given below.

---

[1] See, for example, in H. and Z. Roodman: *Management by communication* (Toronto, Methuen Publications, 1973), Chapter 5 " The Effective Interview ", or F. M. Lopez: *Personnel interviewing* (New York, McGraw-Hill, 1975).

In planning the interviews, the consultant determines *what* facts he wants to obtain, from *whom, when, where* and *how.*

What facts: In setting down the facts he wants the consultant takes account of the knowledge he can expect the interviewee to have; e.g. a production manager is unlikely to know precisely what terms of credit are extended to customers, while a district sales manager probably is not informed about the planned maintenance of machines. For background information a general discussion may suffice. On the other hand information that will help to solve problems or develop improvements needs to be thoroughly examined, probed and understood, e.g. workers' attitudes to simplifying working procedure in order to raise output.

Who should be interviewed: Obviously this should be those dealing with the activities under study, e.g. for billing procedures the invoice clerk should be the best source of information. To obtain full co-operation and avoid slighting anyone, however, the consultant should first approach the responsible manager and allow him to designate informants. Later he may refer to others to complement or confirm information. During initial interviews he can ask who will have supporting information.

When to interview: Information gathered from interviews makes more sense if it comes in logical order, e.g. if products are known it is easier to follow the operations for manufacturing them. Interviews should therefore follow a sequence so that each builds on the information of those preceding it. They should be preceded by a careful study of records so that time-consuming interviews would not be used to collect data available in another form. The interviewee's time possibilities and " mood " for an interview cannot be ignored.

Where to meet: Selection of a meeting place takes into account:
— proximity to the activity under study;
— the convenience of the interviewee;
— avoidance of noise and interruption.

Generally people are more relaxed and communicative in their own surroundings. They also have all information to hand there. Only if the interviewee's workplace has serious drawbacks such as noise, cramped space, or frequent interruptions should the consultant invite him elsewhere such as his own office.

How to proceed: Although the conduct of an interview varies according to the characters of the interviewee and the consultant, their relationship and the circumstances under which they meet, the following guidelines usually apply:

(i) *Before the interview:* The consultant prepares questions likely to reveal the required facts. The list will merely serve as a guide and a check that the interview covers all the necessary ground, and will not restrain discussion from exploring related topics. The consultant also informs himself about the interviewee's job and personality. When making an appointment, he informs the interviewee of the purpose of discussion.

(ii) *During the interview:* Further detailed explanations are given to the interviewee at the beginning. He is requested to help in solving the problem, encouraged to talk in an informal way and asked for agreement to note-taking. The questions asked should lead towards the required information. Nevertheless they should allow the informant to follow his own line of thought so long as it does not stray too far from the subject under review or become too trivial. He is likely to disclose more when free to express himself than when pinned down by insistent questions. Judicious comments supplementing his statements or relating them to required facts encourage communication and guide it. Except for such encouraging interjections, the consultant should not interrupt. Neither should he appear critical of the way things are now done, since this may antagonise the informant and dry him up. Arguing or jumping in with suggestions for improvement is to be avoided. The informant should rather be encouraged to point out possibilities for improvement. Taking careful notes of information and suggestions for improvement (but distinguishing between fact and opinion) ensures that nothing is forgotten, and also shows that views expressed are taken seriously. Suggestions for improvement are noted without commitment, but if they are used later this should be acknowledged. Before leaving, the consultant confirms what he has noted. He takes his leave pleasantly, thanking the informant for his help, thus leaving the way open for further interviews if necessary.

(iii) *After the interview:* The consultant reads over the notes of the interview, lists points to be checked and transcribes reliable information in the assignment's classified data record. In some cases it may be useful to send the interviewee a typed summary for verification. Information from one interview is used to prepare questions (e.g. cross-checking or tentative) for other interviews.

Estimates

An estimate is a makeshift and never fully replaces established data. Only when proved facts are not available, or for some reason are difficult to obtain, should the consultant consider estimates.

Estimates are best made by people working with the activity concerned, who have first-hand knowledge and who, in addition, will more readily accept proposals based on data they themselves have supplied. But wherever possible estimates should be obtained from more than one source and checked. If there are significant differences the informants themselves should try to resolve them. If they cannot do so, a test may be applied, observations taken or special recording installed.

The consultant may accept estimates:

— in respect of facts familiar to the client (e.g. frequent machine operations, or regular patterns of work);

— on aspects of the present situation that need not be precise (e.g. percentage of total costs represented by administrative overhead, in order to decide whether to control these costs closely);

— to indicate whether further observation would be rewarding (e.g. incidence of machine breakdowns, or stock-outs of finished products);

— to ascertain whether benefits from improvements are worth more accurate measurement (e.g. savings from material substitutes or change or product design);

— where the estimate can be tested (e.g. if estimates of operating times to be used for production planning and control would result in product costs permitting the client to sell at a fair profit).

The last example illustrates a sound use for estimates. Both for control of production and control of costs it is necessary to know for each product the quantity of each material used in production, and each manufacturing operation and the time taken to perform it. Obtaining all this information by observation and measurement is a lengthy and painstaking task which would cause long delay in installing controls. Supervisors, technicians and workers, however, can provide close estimates because they are familiar with the materials and operations. From their estimates a product cost can be calculated. If this permits the client to sell the product at a fair profit, estimates can be used to start the production control and cost control systems. Later, precise measurements can replace the estimates and improve controls.

Before using estimates the consultant *checks their validity* against proved experience. An effective way of doing this is to use a known total volume, quantity, or cost for a recent period, or a known capacity. This is compared with the measurement or capacity that results from multiplying an estimate for a single item by the total number of items. For example, the estimated quantity of material required to manufacture a product is multiplied by actual numbers produced during a recent period. This is compared with the quantity of material actually issued from store to production.

Another means of checking estimates is to compare them with data recorded elsewhere. Such comparison must be made with care and will only be valid if the data being compared relate to identical circumstances. Data for comparison may be found in trade or industry publications, or in the files of the consulting organisation.

In addition to checking the validity of estimates the consultant needs to consider the *degree of error* they entail and decide whether this is tolerable.

For example, suppose an estimated sales forecast was made with a 10% upper and lower limit of probable variation. It can be calculated how an error of 10% in the total estimate would affect the predicted profit.

Item	Total volume in $	% of total
Variable cost	60	60
Fixed cost	30	30
Profit	10	10
Sales	100	100

If the volume of sales drops by 10%, the result will be:

Item	Total volume in $	% of total
Variable cost	54	60
Fixed cost	30	33.3
Profit	6	6.7
Sales	90	100

The profit thus revised may be considered too low to give an acceptable return on capital employed. It may be decided to accept no more than a 5% decrease in sales below forecast, giving the following result:

Item	Total volume in $	% of total
Variable cost	57	60
Fixed cost	30	31.6
Profit	8	8.4
Sales	95	100

Where there is a strong probability that the error will remain within the limits of tolerance, the estimate will be used. For example, procedures can be installed to trigger remedial action by management when the limit is reached. In an opposite case the consultant has to devise ways of obtaining more precise and reliable data instead of using an estimate.

Screening the facts

A final remark on the use of the above-described ways of obtaining facts has to be made. It concerns the general need to verify and screen all data before subjecting them to one of the analytical operations in the next phase of the assignment.

The most obvious case is that of recording a production operation: if 19 recordings show a duration between 4 and 5 minutes, one recording indicating 12 minutes cannot be used for calculating an average figure. But this happens in quite different contexts, for example in accounting where overhead cost may be inaccurately distributed among various products, or accounts include items which belong to different accounts.

Cross-checking helps in some instances: e.g. in the case of information obtained in an interview, which can be verified by subsequent interviews. In other cases there is no possibility of cross-checking and it is the consultant's experience and judgement, plus advice sought from the client's staff, that help to " clean " the data prior to using them for various operations.

12.4 Notes, records and reports on fact finding

The consultant's early notes tend to be wordy and speculative while he is feeling his way and getting the situation into focus. As the course of the investigation becomes clearer, recording of the facts becomes more systematic. General note-taking may give way to charting and other analytical methods. The original decisions on tabulating and classifying data are verified and adjusted.

The orderly way the operating consultant keeps his papers, and files them for retrieval of information will help him to keep on course and provide for easy reference by the supervisor. The meaning of notes should be as clear months after the event as when they were written. No figure should be recorded without being qualified by its terms.

There is often a good case for submitting a progress report at what is ostensibly the end of the fact-finding step in an assignment. The period of obtaining facts may have been lengthy; many of the client's staff may have contributed but members of senior management may not have been involved very much. Meanwhile, the client has been paying the fees.

There is never any point in putting into a report the facts a client already knows. Nor should he be given a long list of shortcomings, if his awareness of them is the reason the consultant is there. But when the collected information contains factors that are genuine news to the client, or shows unsuspected links between effect and cause, it may well be useful to report on them. The nature and basis of the reference-period data may be an essential feature of a progress report.

If fact finding has indicated that the original problem definition is to be altered or redefined and assignment objectives amended accordingly, the consultant would use the opportunity provided by this report to make appropriate suggestions.

For the consultant, the salient facts, as " findings ", may have to be put in a report sometime and if done now would simplify the construction of a future report.

FACT ANALYSIS

13

Fact analysis is the second major step in operating assignments. The consultant has gathered a vast amount of data, but does not want to be submerged by it. He realises that data give a true picture of reality only to those who know how to work with them.

The purpose of fact analysis goes beyond an appraisal—the ultimate aim of an assignment is to bring about change and fact analysis is a further step towards this aim. It should indicate as precisely as possible:

— whether change is necessary;
— whether change is possible;
— what change is possible;
— what alternative is likely to be most effective.

There are, therefore, no clear-cut limits between *analysis* and *synthesis*. Synthesis, in the sense of building a whole from parts, drawing conclusions from fact analysis and developing action proposals, starts somewhere during fact analysis, which evolves towards synthesis. Indeed, to an experienced consultant analysis and synthesis are two sides of one coin, which he applies simultaneously. He does not have to discover new wholes by combining parts each time he undertakes an assignment—his theoretical knowledge and practical experience help him to synthesise while he is analysing. But he has to avoid traps that data and his past experience set for him—such as the temptation to draw hasty conclusions from superficially analysed facts and get fixed ideas before examining facts in depth (" This is exactly the same case I have seen many times before! ").

A simplified example can show the consultant's way of proceeding when he is examining facts. In a manufacturing enterprise production records and observations have indicated that an important share of productive capacity is wasted owing to machine breakdown and stoppages. Waiting for the arrival of qualified repairmen is given as a cause of the length of stoppages—in fact, the maintenance service is physically centralised in one place and organisationally in one unit reporting to the production manager, although the enterprise has a number of workshops located in various parts of a vast urban area. The consultant is tempted to suggest a decentralised organisation of maintenance, e.g. a repairman in every shop, or several centres, each located close to a group of shops. In this connection consideration would be given, among other things, to waiting times of repairmen—decentralisation would increase their number and a full utilisation of their time could not be guaranteed (this may be examined by the means of queuing theory). In a next step it is found that the production manager is opposed to decentralisation of technical services and generally prefers centralisation. For a while the consultant is tempted to see this fact as a major obstacle to solving the problem. But he hits on the idea of re-examining the technical causes of machine stoppages and the attitude of workers to machine breakdown. He collects more data and discovers that the wages of machine operators have no relationship to the effective working time of the machines. He also finds that most stoppages are caused by minor faults and that the operators could easily be trained to remove certain defects themselves. In his proposals, the consultant finally concentrates on changes in the wage system in order to motivate workers to keep machine stoppages to the minimum, on training operatives in minor maintenance and repairs, and on some adjustments in the functions of the central maintenance service.

13.1 Classification

The classification of data was started before the beginning of fact finding by establishing criteria for the organisation and tabulation of data.[1] Further classification, and adjustments in classification criteria, are made during fact finding (e.g. the consultant decides to use a more detailed breakdown of data than originally planned) and after it. If facts are recorded in a way which enables multiple classification (e.g. on punch cards), the consultant can try several possible classifications before deciding which one is most relevant to the purpose of the assignment.

Both quantified and other information needs to be classified. For example, if complaints about the shortage of training opportunities come only from certain departments, or from people in certain age groups, the classification must show this.

The main classification criteria used in management consulting are:

— time,

— place (unit),

— responsibility,

— structure,

— influencing factors.

Classification of data under *time* indicates trends, rates of change, random and periodic fluctuations.

---

[1] See p. 126.

Classification by *place* or *organisational unit* helps in examining problems of various parts of the organisation and devising solutions related to specific conditions of each unit.

Responsibility for facts and events is a different aspect—in many cases responsibility is not identical with the place (unit) where a fact has been identified.

Classification according to the *structure* of entities and processes is an essential one and uses a number of criteria. Employees, materials, products or plant and equipment can be classified from many different points of view. An important objective in this case is to define how changes in components affect the magnitude of the whole entity, and to direct action towards those components which have major influences on total results. For example, the total lead time of a steam turbine may be determined by the machining and assembly time of one component—the rotor.

Operations in a production process can be classified according to sequence in time and presented in a table or diagram, or on the plan of the workshop (which makes it possible to indicate the directions and distances of material movements in reduced real proportions).[1]

Organisational relations and informal relationships in organisations can be classified by the means of charts, diagrams, matrix tables, etc.

Classification by *influencing factors* is a preparatory step in functional and causal analysis. For example, machine stoppages may be classified by factors that cause them—lack of material, a break in energy supply, absence of worker, delay in scheduling, lack of spare parts, etc.

13.2 Analysis of relationships and causes

The purpose of this analysis is to examine whether a specific relationship exists between various factors and events and, if so, examine its nature. If possible, the relationship is quantified and defined as a *function*, where one or more dependent variables are in a specific relationship to one or more independent variables. The objective is to discover and define relationships which are substantial and not just accidental.

For example, the consultant may find out from data gathered in various firms that the cost of a major overhaul of machine tools is in some relationship to their purchase price. If such a relationship is defined as a function, he can forecast the cost of overhaul and its influence on production cost in other firms, if these use similar equipment.

---

[1] Various methods of representing classified elements of production processes are given in ILO: *Introduction to work study* (Geneva, International Labour Office, 1979).

Another way of expressing relationships is *ratios*. They may test whether inputs to an activity generate commensurate outputs, or examine whether resources and commitments are properly balanced.

As explained in Chapter 7, the use of ratios is very common in the financial appraisal of enterprises.[1] In the analytical phase of an operating assignment the ratios of global, aggregate data may be broken down into analytical ratios.

For example, a series of ratios can be used to measure labour productivity:

$$\frac{V}{E} = \frac{V}{DH} \times \frac{DH}{PW} \times \frac{PW}{W} \times \frac{W}{E}$$

where V = value of production,
          E = total number of employees,
      DH = total direct labour hours,
     PW = total number of production workers,
       W = total number of workers.

Causal analysis aims at discovering causal relationships between factors and events. Obviously, this is a key to proposals for change and to improvements. If causes which have brought about certain situations, results or problems are known it is possible to deal with these causes and influence them.

In highly complex systems, to which industrial and other economic organisations belong, events are rarely brought about by one single cause, but rather by a number of causes operating simultaneously. The analyst is looking for basic causes first of all. It is, too, a common feature of business organisations, well known to consultants, that in reality there are *chains of causes and consequences* (for example, workers' dissatisfaction is caused by lower earnings, which are caused by a reduced workload, which is the result of low demand, which is a consequence of stagnation in product development; this in turn results from mistakes in personnel policy within the design department, made because the chief designer is too conservative, and so on).

But how does the consultant discover that there is a causal relationship? As he has studied and practised management, and probably seen similar situations before, he approaches causal analysis with a certain amount of knowledge and experience. He has an idea about possible main causes—and for this he needs to have a comprehensive, synthetic view of the total process or system he is examining, and the whole organisation where this is happening. Only rarely would a consultant face situations in which unusual causal relationships would be discovered. But this happens as well; for example, a

---

[1] See Chapter 7, p. 82.

consultant from an industrial country working in a developing economy may discover causal relationships between social and cultural factors and the economic performance of an organisation which are unknown to him from his previous studies and work. In such circumstances he should verify that the relationships are of decisive importance.

13.3 Comparison

Comparison is closely interlinked with the methodological tools discussed above. Both classification and functional and causal analysis involve comparisons.

The principal alternatives for comparison which are commonly used in management surveys have already been mentioned.[1] In operating assignments, the same alternatives apply, but in addition to global appraisal comparison is used to examine operating details and develop solutions. The various bases for comparisons made within the client organisation are represented in Figure 8. The consultant can compare C with A, C with B, C with D, E with C and so on.

Figure 8. Various bases for comparison

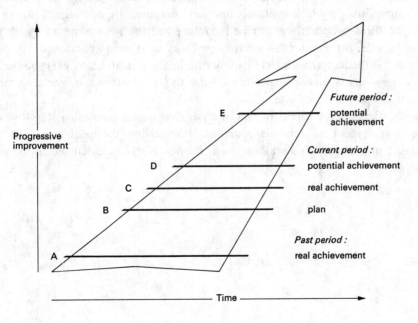

<hr>

[1] See Chapter 6, pp. 63-64.

Of special interest to operating consultants is comparison which helps to establish future standards (of potential achievement) and thus provide guidance for the development of proposals. It is particularly in this connection that comparison turns to examples, models and standards from *outside* the organisation and even outside the sector and country. The consultant considers whether the diversity of conditions permits such comparison, especially if this is to be used for more than general judgement—namely for specific suggestions to the client as to what to *do*.

13.4 Synthesis

As mentioned, to a management consultant the analytic method and the synthetic method are two sides of one coin. Notwithstanding that, as fact analysis is progressing the consultant's approach will be increasingly synthetic—he will be identifying basic relationships, trends and causes, differentiating between fundamental and marginal events and factors, and defining factors and elements that *have to be changed* if a whole process or organisation is to change.

In management and consulting practice synthesis is considerably more difficult than purely analytical work. Many bulky analytical reports are difficult to use, although they define tens of problems and suggest long lists of measures. But they lack synthesis and key measures are not identified. As all the measures proposed cannot be introduced at the same time and with the same vigour, action starts in a haphazard way or is soon abandoned.

A synthetic spirit and skill in synthesis are not given to everybody. To train new management consultants how to use synthesis is perhaps more essential than anything else.

Synthesis is the aspect of fact analysis that makes possible a step towards the development of realistic *proposals* for solving the problems that the consultant has identified and analysed. Proposals will be discussed in the next chapter.

DEVELOPING AND PRESENTING PROPOSALS 14

When the examination of facts has been completed and the main conclusions have been drawn, the operating assignment enters its principal phase, in which proposals for the solution of the defined problems are developed, evaluated and presented to the client. The rather long, patient and passive collecting, recording and examining of facts gives way to an active contribution which should bring about something new.

Developing and presenting proposals—Step 3 of operating assignments—can be further subdivided as follows:

3.1	Developing alternative proposals
3.2	Evaluating and choosing alternatives
3.3	Presenting proposals to the client

It is in this sequence that the consultant's work on proposals will be discussed in this chapter.

14.1 Developing alternative proposals

Why alternatives?

In most assignments the client expects the consultant to find and recommend the best solution. There are, however, valid reasons for drawing up alternatives.

First, alternatives are part of the very nature of management problems: nearly all such problems can be solved in several different ways. Another reason has to do with the consultant's professional conscience: he develops and evaluates alternatives in order to be confident that the one to be recommended is the best. Furthermore the client also may like to be presented with alternatives before making up his mind.

Time may be a constraint: in many assignments the time spent on collecting and examining facts is relatively long, and when it comes to the development of proposals there is a general desire to finish the project as soon as possible. The consultant is left with little time to prepare alternatives and develops only one solution. But even work on one proposal may have to be concluded somewhere short of perfection. The consultant may deplore this as a professional worker, and in many cases the difficulty can be avoided by properly scheduling the assignment and making sure that enough time is left for work on proposals. If, however, the time problem cannot be overcome, the consultant should consult the client and reach agreement on whether the time limit is to be maintained, or extended in order to arrive at a more complete solution.

Preliminary considerations

Before starting to change the present situation and spending time and effort on designing new solutions, the consultant wants to confirm that a change is necessary and clarify with the client what new conditions the change should establish. Once again questioning will bring about clarification.

Typical questions are grouped together in the checklist in Table 11.

Devising improvements

In devising ways of improving the client's situation, the consultant often draws on experience. He considers methods successfully used elsewhere, on the basis of knowledge derived from a variety of sources:

— the consultant's previous assignments;
— the consultant organisation's files and documentation;
— colleagues in the consultant organisation who have worked in similar conditions;
— professional literature;
— makers of the machinery, who may themselves have developed improvements;
— staff in other departments of the client organisation, who may have knowledge of the particular process;
— organisations which are prepared to communicate their experience.

All sources should be considered in the search for improvements. In simple cases, it may be possible to transfer a method used by another organisation—including forms, the system of coding, etc.[1] This, however, will

---

[1] It may first be necessary to obtain permission to use such methods and systems (see also Chapter 5).

Table 11. Checklist of preliminary considerations

I. What should the new arrangements achieve?
  - what level of performance,
  - what quality of output,
  - what new product, service or activity.

II. How will the new situation differ from the present?
  - different products, services or activities,
  - different method,
  - different equipment,
  - different location.

III. Are the effects likely to last?
  - is the client's business and his market changing so rapidly that before long there may not be a need for the new product, service or activity,
  - is there a possibility that people will revert to present practices.

IV. What difficulties will arise?
  - employee resistance,
  - work hazards,
  - over-production,
  - shortage of materials.

V. Who will be affected?
  - are employees receptive,
  - what should be done to prepare them,
  - do matching changes have to be made elsewhere.

VI. When is the best time to change?
  - at the end of a season,
  - during vacation time,
  - at the close of a financial period,
  - at the beginning of a new calendar year,
  - any time.

---

be easier if the problem to be solved is essentially of a corrective or progressive nature. In solving creative problems that require innovative solutions, the sources listed above may fail to suggest a suitable course of action and the consultant, in co-operation with the client's staff, will have to think out his own. In this connection, it might be useful to review some principles and methods in creative thinking.

Creative thinking

Creative thinking has been defined as the *relating of things or ideas which were previously unrelated*. The purpose is, of course, to discover or develop something new. The history of science and of business is full of examples of discovery based on creative thinking and there is no reason why the consultant could not approach many practical industrial and management problems by the same method.

There are *five stages* in the creative thinking process, and all need to be practised consciously to get the best results:

(1) PREPARATION: Getting all the known facts; applying convergent (analytical) thinking as far as possible; getting the problem defined in different ways, i.e. restating the problem.

(2) EFFORT: Divergent thinking, which will lead either to possible solutions or to frustration. (Frustration is an important feature in the effort stage and in the full creative thinking process. It is usually followed by production of the really good ideas.)

(3) INCUBATION: Leaving the problem in one's subconscious mind while one gets on with other things. This also gives time for inhibitions and emotional blocks to new ideas to weaken, and gives opportunities to pick up additional ideas from what one sees or hears in the meantime.

(4) INSIGHT: The flash of illumination that gives an answer and leads to possible solutions of the problem.

(5) EVALUATION: Analysing all the ideas obtained in the last three stages so as to find possible solutions.

Two of the stages—preparation and evaluation—require analytical thinking. The three central stages—effort, incubation and insight—require suspended judgement and free-wheeling. Wild ideas are deliberately fostered, the aim being quantity, not quality. Large numbers of ideas are obtained, new ideas being sparked off by earlier ideas. The key to successful creative thinking is the conscious and deliberate separation of idea-production and idea-evaluation.

Techniques of creative thinking include, among others:

Brainstorming. This is a means of getting a large number of ideas from a group of people in a short time. Typically a group of 8-12 people take a problem and produce ideas in a free-wheeling atmosphere. As mentioned, judgement is suspended and all ideas, particularly wild ideas, are encouraged. In fact the wildest ideas can often be stepping-stones to new, very practical, ones. Ideas are displayed on sheets of newsprint and are produced very quickly; a session may produce over 200 ideas in about an hour. Brainstorming is the best-known and most widely used of the techniques. Its main disadvantage lies in the fact that all ideas are evaluated. Many of them are foolish or totally irrelevant and have to be discarded to reach the few really good ideas.

Synectics. In this technique, which is similar to brainstorming, a group of about nine people take a problem. The " client ", whose problem it is, explains it, and participants put forward a suggestion for solving it. After a few minutes the client analyses the suggestion, saying what he likes about it before touching on the drawbacks. Then new suggestions are put forward and analysed until possible solutions are found.

Attribute listing. This technique lists the main attributes of the idea or object, and examines each one to see how it can be changed. It is normally used on tangible rather than intangible things. For example, a screwdriver has the following attributes:

— round steel shank;
— wooden handle;
— flat wedge end;
— manual operation;
— torque by twist.

Each attribute is questioned and changes are suggested. Some modern screwdrivers, i.e. with ratchets or a cruciform head instead of the wedge end, are examples of improvement.

Forced relationships. This technique takes objects or ideas and asks the question " In how many ways can these be combined to give a new object or idea? " For example, a manufacturer of furniture could take the items he makes and see if two or more could be combined to give a new piece of furniture.

Morphological analysis. This technique sets down all the variables in a matrix and tries to combine them in new ways. For example, if a new form of transport is required, the variables could be:

Type of vehicle	box, chair, sling
Travelling in	air, water, tunnels
Travelling on	rails, wheels, rollers, air
Driven by	steam, electricity, cable, petrol, gas

The combination of $3 \times 3 \times 4 \times 5$ variables gives 180 forms of transport, many of which exist; some have to be discarded, but some are worth considering.

Checklists may be used as *pointers to ideas.* Lists may be particular to the area (e.g. marketing, design) or general. Well known is Osborn's generalised checklist [1] in which the main headings are: Put to other uses?, Adapt?, Modify?, Minify?, Substitute?, Rearrange?, Reverse?, Combine? Checklists need to be used with care, as they can inhibit creativity by limiting the areas of enquiry.

In summary, no matter which technique is used, the following four guidelines apply:

SUSPEND JUDGEMENT—Rule out premature criticism of any idea.

FREEWHEEL—The wilder the ideas the better the results.

QUANTITY—The more ideas the better.

CROSS FERTILISE—Combine and improve on the ideas of others.

[1] A. F. Osborn: *Applied imagination* (New York, Charles Scribner's Sons, 1957).

In business and management practice, there is, however, a need to *struggle with barriers* to creative thinking. Most people are educated and trained to think analytically, but only a few are trained to use their creative ability. Creative thinking is also restricted by:

— self-imposed barriers;
— belief that there is always one right answer;
— conformity or giving the expected answer;
— lack of effort in challenging the obvious;
— evaluating too quickly;
— fear of looking a fool.

Awareness of the barriers to creative thinking, and a conscious effort to lower them in a creative situation, opens a vast area of new ideas, or ways of tackling problems. Suspending judgement is a particularly pertinent example of how a better understanding of the creative thinking process can help towards a fuller use of creative abilities in seeking solutions to difficult management problems.

14.2 Evaluating and choosing alternatives

The purpose of evaluating alternative proposals prepared by the consultant is to provide an objective basis for choice. This may have to be made from two or more new solutions, or between the new and the already existing arrangement (the consultant has to prove that the new alternative is more effective than the existing one).

The client usually expects that the consultant will prepare this evaluation and submit it to him. The consultant is also expected to suggest what alternative he would choose if he were in the client's place.

In most cases the client's professional staff will be closely associated with the evaluation process in all its stages, and the final choice will also be a joint affair. There are, however, assignments during which the client is less involved in analytical work. In such cases the evaluation and choice of alternatives submitted by the consultant could be a surprise to the client to some extent. It is probable that in such cases the client will wish to review the consultant's proposals very carefully.

The process of evaluation

Evaluation is not a one-off measure to be undertaken solely at a defined point of time in the assignment. When data are collected and examined, this should be done with due regard to the forthcoming evaluation excercise. At the beginning, the management consultant pays great attention to the definition on the ultimate benefits, but also on the effects of the client's policy, i.e. how much more money for wages he has to find, or how much more output he has to sell.

Example 2

The second example uses the method of *decision analysis*. The consultant has to evaluate two alternatives involved in erecting a new plant.

As a first step, the consultant examines whether both alternatives meet *essential needs* (see Table 15).

Table 15. Essential needs

Essential need	Criterion	Alternative A	Alternative B
Capital available— maximum cost (US$)	250,000	240,000	210,000
Minimum area of building (m^2)	3,000	3,000	3,000
Mains services	yes	yes	yes
Access to railway	yes	yes	yes
Maximum distance from existing works (km)	15	7	10
Latest occupation within (months)	12	8	10

As both schemes meet the essential needs, evaluation from the viewpoint of *desirable needs* will next be made.

The simplest way is to decide which alternative meets a higher number of desirable needs (see Table 16).

Table 16. Number of desirable needs met by each alternative

Desirable need	Alternative A	Alternative B
1. Lowest possible running cost	+	+
2. Under 10 minutes from shops	+	−
3. Served by public transport	+	+
4. Property appreciation prospects	+	+
5. Additional female labour available	−	+
6. Accessible to existing workforce	+	+
7. Maximum use of existing equipment	+	+
8. Lowest possible capital cost	+	+
9. Near low-priced housing	−	+
10. Space for further expansion	−	+
11. Park for 200-250 cars	+	+
Total	8 +	10 +

---

of the reference period for which data will be collected and used for comparison of the new solutions with the existing ones. In the course of fact analysis and work on solutions, the consultant continues to collect all factual data, opinions and suggestions and tabulates potential costs and benefits which may be of importance to evaluation and choice. He may even proceed to tentative and preliminary evaluations and make *preliminary choices* at an early stage. Unsuitable alternatives will thus be eliminated before more effort is spent on them. This concerns alternatives whose cost is prohibitive and those that are not practical in the given setting (external and internal environment).

Regarding evaluation criteria, there are some comparatively easy cases, such as the choice between two or three machine tools (of different technical level, productivity and price) for the same production operation. The number of criteria is limited and they can be quantified, especially if production records are reasonably good.

Let us, however, consider a case of major reorganisation in a manufacturing company—a frequent assignment in the general management field. There may be several alternatives, with varying degrees of decentralisation, different approaches to specialisation of major units within the company and different channels and techniques of communication. Personnel and training measures will be involved, and so on. In this case some criteria lend themselves to fairly exact calculation of costs—e.g. the training needed. Others do not—e.g. the higher effectiveness of decision making obtained thanks to decentralisation of authority and responsibility in marketing and product-policy matters.

In management consulting, the following situations prevail:

— the number of criteria is high; certain basic criteria are met by all alternatives and further criteria have to be examined;

— some important criteria (especially environmental, social and human criteria) are difficult, if not impossible, to quantify;

— the evaluation involves, therefore, some assessment of criteria which are not directly comparable (e.g. financial criteria are especially difficult to compare with social and human ones);

— this introduces a strong subjective element into evaluation—in the absence of hard data somebody has to decide how important various criteria are in the given case.

To overcome this last difficulty, and increase the element of objectivity in subjective evaluations, many attempts have been made in recent years to associate numerical values with adjectival scales. The principle is to use a group of experts (from the client organisation or other) to assign point values to particular criteria. The values thus obtained are then used in an evaluation model, e.g. in decision analysis.[1] The scale may be as follows:

Major improvement	=	10
Considerable improvement	=	7
Some improvement	=	4
No change	=	1
Some deterioration	=	−2
Considerable deterioration	=	−5

The *evaluation technique* used will be selected with regard to the nature and complexity of the particular case. It may be a simple break-even analysis, cost-benefit analysis, return on investment analysis, linear programming technique, decision analysis or other.[2] Broader social and environmental consequences of managerial decisions are particularly difficult to quantify and compare with economic and financial costs and benefits. Notwithstanding that, the number of techniques which attempt to account for these aspects in evaluation models and schemes is rapidly growing.[3]

Two examples of evaluation are given below.

Example 1

The first example is a simple calculation of the benefits from an assignment whose main objective was to increase productivity in a factory. The client has decided that wages will remain the same, but that only the normal hours will be worked, overtime being stopped. Incentive bonus is not paid, although the maintenance of wage levels, with a fall in hours worked (from no overtime) gives an increase in the hourly rate. The figures in one section are given in Table 12.

Table 12.   Data from one section

	Per week		
	Results during reference period	Results anticipated after change	Benefit from change (%)
Output of blanks (in thousands)	1,740	2,610	+ 50
Hours worked	450	410	− 9
Wages paid in $	920	920	None

Using the above figures, the results anticipated from implementing the change are as indicated in Table 13.

---

[1] See pp. 154-156.

[2] Some reference books will be found at the end of Part III.

[3] Cf. F. Hetman: *Society and the assessment of technology* (Paris, OECD, 1973).

Table 13.   Benefits from change

	Results during reference period	Results anticipated after change	Benefit from change (%)
Productivity			
Blanks per hour (in thousands)	3.86	6.36	+ 65
Earnings			
$ per hour	2.04	2.24	+ 10
Labour Cost			
$ per 1,000 blanks	0.529	0.352	− 33

The reduction in labour cost from $0.529 to $0.352 per 1,000 blanks will result in financial benefits, at the anticipated output, of:

$$(0.529 - 0.352) \times 2,610 = \$462 \text{ per week,}$$

or $23,100 per annum (50 weeks).

It should be noted that the benefits are calculated on labour cost only. As output has increased substantially, other benefits may arise from overhead recovery. Offsetting these benefits are the costs of the changes—in this case purchase of new machinery and re-layout. It should also be noted that two quite different costs are involved—capital (or once-off) costs in new equipment or re-layout in the section, and labour costs which continue.

In the figures quoted above output increased by 65%. This is a large increase which must be pointed out to the client who has to act: he must sell or tie up capital by storing it. The client may decide that the increase output is too high, and decide to limit the increase to say 30%, i.e. to 1,1 instead of 2,500 blanks per hour. In addition to altering the benefits considerably, such decision would change other figures, principally hours worked (and therefore the number of workpeople required).

The effect the consultant has to achieve depends on the policy the client adopts. This is shown in Table 14.

The table shows how the three aspects interact. Realiable data from reference period enable various alternative solutions to be evaluated, not c

Table 14.   Effect of alternative policies

POLICY	EFFECT ON		
To have the same —	Volume of work	Money spent	Labour required
Labour force	Up	Up	Same
Money spent	Up	Same	Down
Volume	Same	Down	Down

Table 17.   Decision analysis

Essential needs	Alternative A	Alternative B
Capital available: $250,000	Cost: $240,000	Cost: $210,000
Minimum area of building: 3,000 m²	3,000 m²	3,000 m²
Mains services	yes	yes
Access to railway	yes	yes
Within 15 km of existing works	7 km	10 km
Occupation within 12 months	8 months	10 months

Desirable needs	Weight	Alternative A			Alternative B		
		Detail	Points	Value	Detail	Points	Value
1. Lowest possible running costs	10	Est. $14,400 p.a.	9	90	Est. $13,200 p.a.	10	100
2. Additional female labour available	9	Few	2	18	Many	7	63
3. Accessible to existing workforce	8	7 km	9	72	10 km	6	48
4. Maximum use of existing equipment	8	Very good	10	80	Good	8	64
5. Lowest possible capital cost	7	$240,000	8	56	$210,000	10	70
6. Served by public transport	7	20 min. bus	7	49	15 min. bus	9	63
7. Park for 200-250 cars	6	210 cars	8	48	300 cars	10	60
8. Near low-priced housing	6	No	0	0	Two estates	10	60
9. Space for further expansion	5	Limited	5	25	Ample	9	45
10. Property appreciation prospects	4	Fair	5	20	Fair	5	20
11. Under 10 minutes from shops	3	8 minutes	10	30	15 minutes	0	0
Total value				488			593

Such a comparison may, however, be considered too primitive for a deep evaluation. Instead of marking alternatives by a positive (+) or negative (—) symbol, points may be assigned to them (e.g. from 1 to 9) and the alternative that has scored a higher total number of points will " win ". A third possibility, which is shown in Table 17 is to assign, first, a degree of importance (weight) (e.g. from 1 to 10) and, second, a number of points (e.g. from 0 to 10) to each desirable need. In Table 17 the desirable needs are re-ordered in accordance with their weight.

The importance of the subjective element in such evaluation is high, although a quantitative method is used. First, both the weight and the points assigned to each desirable need are a matter of soundness and objectivity of judgement in those who will be deciding on the respective importance of these criteria. For example, " space for further expansion " may be considered to be unimportant if no further expansion is foreseen and local labour resources will soon be exhausted. In another case, this may be a criterion with the highest weight. Second, the higher total number of points assigned to one alternative (B) does not automatically imply that this one must be adopted without further examination—this again will be based on individual judgement of experienced people, and may also reflect personal preferences and biases.

14.3 Presenting proposals to the client

When work on proposals and the evaluation of alternatives has reached an advanced stage, the consultant has to consider the time and form for the presentation to the client. This will depend mainly on the type of project undertaken and the working relationships between the consultant and the client's managerial and specialist staff.

In long and complex assignments involving strategic issues and costly investment or other measures, the client's staff is usually very much involved and keeps the senior management informed about progress. The consultant submits progress reports and seeks further guidance from the client at several points of the assignment. The presentation of final proposals does not bring, therefore, anything completely new. Essentially, information that the client has had from previous reports and other contacts with the consultant is summarised, confirmed and put up for decision.

In many other cases, however, the reporting which has preceded the presentation of proposals may have been limited. The scope of the assignment may not require reporting and discussions at each step; or, in assignments that will affect some vested interests (e.g. re-organisations), the client does not want to hold many meetings and have information circulated before the solutions have been defined and thoroughly examined by a restricted managerial group.

Hence the need for a well-prepared presentation which, in the latter case, may convey completely new information to a number of people.

Presentation

The presentation will normally be an oral one, with the backing of all the written evidence and audio-visual aids needed to support the case.[1] The degree of persuasion will depend on many factors and must be anticipated, prepared for and built into the presentation.

The objective of the presentation is, of course, to obtain the client's acceptance of the recommendations. The presentation meeting is held between the consulting team (including the supervisor), the client and those members of the staff chosen to attend. The client's liaison officer and other staff specialists may have an important role to play. Having taken a part in the investigation they may be informed about many details and should be in complete favour of the recommendations.

The consultant's presentation works through a logical series of steps, building up the case for the recommendations in so effective a manner that the client should have little or no hesitation in accepting them. At least, that is the idea. No presentation should be made unless the consultant believes that the probability of acceptance is high.

The presentation must never flood the client with analytical details or try to impress him by techniques that are normally the specialist's domain. However, the techniques used in evaluation should be mentioned. A clear picture of all solutions that have been envisaged is given and the choice proposed by the consultant is justified. The consultant must be absolutely honest with the client especially when he is explaining:

— *the risks involved* (the solution has never been used before; some category of professional staff will probably be against it; the real cost may be higher than foreseen);

— *the conditions that the client must create and maintain* (a high discipline in recording primary data is needed; some members of senior management will need to be transferred).

There may be circumstances known to both parties due to which acceptance at this point may be in principle only. There may be an agreed intention but a final decision may be contingent on a detailed study of written proposals by the client or on the recommendations being explained to and accepted by employees' representatives.

---

[1] See also Appendix 6 on " Person-to-person communication in consulting ". On details of consultant report writing see Appendix 7.

Where there have to be further presentations to representatives of trade unions, staff associations or other employee groups, the role of persuader and negotiator shifts to the client. Under no circumstances should the consultant take this on alone. He is, of course, ready to back up the client and help him to organise whatever explanatory campaign is necessary—and in this he should strongly advise against trying to get everything over at one mass meeting.

The decision

The client's decision on the consultant's proposals is subject to the same influences as any other managerial decision. Many research reports are available in which patterns of managerial decision making are examined. A. J. Rowe argues, for example, that rationality is eighth on the list of ten characteristics in order of importance to the decision maker. According to him " In any complex decision where personal or behavioural factors apply, the individual's preference will dominate the results ".[1]

We are not concerned here about the precise degree of probability with which this is likely to happen. What is essential is the consultant's awareness of the personal preferences and biases affecting decision making in the client organisation for which he is currently working. This awareness helps him to refrain from proposals which will not be accepted and to recognise again that consulting is much more than presenting optimum solutions: it also involves patient persuasion and explanation to the client and his people so that they will accept rational measures as their favourite personal choices.

The decision taken on the consultant's proposals may be the final point of an assignment seen from the consultant's point of view—if proposals are accepted for immediate or later implementation, but the client wants to do it by himself. It will, however, be an opening to the next step in an assignment if the client prefers further assistance.

---

[1] A. J. Rowe: " The myth of the rational decision maker " in *International Management*, August 1974, p. 38.

IMPLEMENTATION

15

Implementation is the final major step in carrying out management consulting assignments, and the basic purpose of the assignment from the client's point of view. The consultant, too, wants to see his proposals not only well received in meetings with the client, but implemented with good results. This does not mean, however, that the consultant expects to be involved in the implementation of his proposals in each case. If the client is technically strong enough—and the joint work with the consultant on proposals for solutions may have enhanced this strength—there may be no need for the consultant to take care of implementation. In many cases, however, it is understood from the beginning that the consultant will have to put into effect what he has put on paper.

15.1 The consultant's roles in implementation

As a rule, the consultant will participate in implementation in one or more of the following ways:

— by providing guidance and advice to the client staff responsible for implementation;

— by working out the details of proposals that have been accepted for implementation, and correcting them in the first stages of implementation;

— by training the client's staff.

Gradually the consultant will assume less and less and the client's staff more and more responsibility in the implementation of the project: the aim is to terminate the consultant's presence in the organisation as soon as the client can do everything by himself.

Detailing procedures

When a good deal of new methodology is involved, it is usual to prepare a manual for guidance in the procedures to be followed. Virtually all forms of re-organisation, irrespective of their functional or inter-functional aspects, require simple instructions on how to operate them. New paperwork has usually to be designed. The consultant may do this himself or may adopt part or all of some proprietary system.[1]

Programming implementation

Planning a campaign to introduce a new method or system is another instance of the usefulness of network planning or bar-charting techniques. The date of the " application day " will be rather more certain if planned for in this way. The time needed to obtain equipment and to design detailed procedures may be relatively easy to estimate. When there is a major physical move, as required by, say, a new factory or general office layout, a scheduled sequence of individual moves is necessary. When there has to be " business as usual " during the move, the schedule recognises the need for the minimum of upset. Sometimes a short, sharp campaign can take place during an annual shutdown. When it does, all employees are briefed on what they will find when they return so as to avoid some days of chaos.

Monitoring implementation

If the client so desires, the consultant will be his adviser in the first period of implementation, in the course of which a number of unforeseen problems may arise and first experiences with the new scheme may indicate the need for corrections.

When implementation is about to start, the consultant checks that all conditions have been fulfilled and all prerequisites are on hand.

At the moment of the start and after it, the consultant is available to answer any queries and help the client's staff to deal immediately with any problem that may arise. This is as much a question of tactics as of techniques, since little deficiencies and misunderstandings at the moment when something new is starting have a tendency to grow and turn into major difficulties if not dealt with immediately. In this the consultant may have more experience than the client.

It is not uncommon for decision makers, including the consultant, to experience uncomfortable after-thoughts once a decision has finally been reached, and implementation commences. This phenomenon is known as cognitive dissonance.

---

[1] In the latter event it has to be remembered that suppliers of such systems have a vested interest in selling stationery and that " standard " packages may not fit the given situation very well.

Prior to reaching a decision the decision makers usually spend an inordinate amount of time focusing on the benefits of the new scheme and the disadvantages of the present, or alternative, scheme. However, once a firm decision has been reached, the implementation process commences and the first problems inevitably appear, it seems that a good deal of time now becomes spent on reviewing the advantages of the previous, or displaced, scheme while comments are voiced on the drawbacks of the new scheme now being implemented.

It is readily conceded that it takes considerable talent to examine an existing scheme and, based on investigations and results obtained, devise a new, more effective one, but it also takes considerable courage to proceed with the implementation of the new scheme when problems, as is usually the case, are met with in the early stages of the implementation phase. When this happens the consultant would do well to take note of the maxim: " Take time to plan your work, then take time to work your plan. " The implementation phase should make adequate provision for a review of results and for carrying out required amendments. However, these activities must be planned well in advance and should not become ad hoc, blind panic events.

Jointly with the client, the consultant would make a regular and frequent *assessment of the progress of implementation*. Attention is paid to the pace of implementation and its broader consequences—e.g. whether the changes in plant layout and organisation of the production department are proceeding according to schedule and the delivery of any new product will start as promised.

The consultant's behaviour during this phase of the work affects the attitude of the client and his staff to implementation. He must be seen as an enthusiastic senior colleague who feels fully involved and co-responsible, and who would also be able to explain the roles and responsibilities of others engaged in the project.[1]

15.2 Training and development of client staff

The link between consulting and training is logical and natural. Both have the same ultimate objective—to do things better—and they support each other. In most operating assignments some training and development of client staff is foreseen in the work programme. It may take a variety of forms and its volume will differ from case to case.

Developing the co-operating team

Perhaps the most interesting and efficient, although the least formalised method, is the development of client personnel through direct co-operation

---

[1] In this connection the reader may refer to the change tactics explained in Chapter 4, pp. 36-41.

with the consultant on problem solving. This concerns the so-called liaison officer and other members of the team who are responsible for the project jointly with the consultant. If the consultant is a good one, he uses every opportunity not only to pass on routine jobs (such as data collection) to client staff, but increasingly to involve them in the more sophisticated operations demanding skills and experience and stimulating self-education. As this is an excellent learning opportunity, it is useful to assign to this job able people with good development potential, and not just those who can be spared from their normal duties for the period of the assignment.

Even managers in senior positions can develop, if the consultant knows how to communicate with them and if they are keen to find out what the consultant's work methods are and to learn something from him. That is why it is more interesting to a senior manager, if he gets a really good consultant, to interact with him frequently instead of just reading a final report at the end of the assignment.

Training for new methods and techniques

A common part of assignments is training of client staff in specific techniques. This concerns those staff members who are involved in the introduction and use of the technique (e.g. time measurement, statistical quality control, standard costing). A number of people may have to be trained; this may necessitate a precisely defined and scheduled training programme which precedes implementation and may continue during its first stages. A number of approaches are possible, such as:

— on-the-job training by the consultant;
— training of trainers by the consultant;
— training of experimental groups whose members will then train the remaining staff;
— formal in-company training courses (run by the consultant, special trainers brought in for this purpose, or the organisation's internal trainers);
— participation of selected staff in external training courses;
— appreciation programmes for those who are not directly involved, but should be informed.

Staff development in complex assignments

With the growth of sophistication and complexity of problems tackled by the consultant, the related training and development of people also becomes more difficult to design and organise. This is, for example, the case in assignments aimed at major change, such as extensive re-organisations, important changes in product and market strategies, or the putting up of new plant including the installation of a new management system. In addition to specific training in new techniques, which may also be needed, there is a case for a collective development effort which should bring about more substantial changes in management concepts, strategies, communication and styles.

In these situations, training in particular work techniques may have to be supplemented by programmes aimed at behavioural change. These may include seminars, working parties, discussion groups, special project teams, individual project work, exchange of roles, counselling by the consultant and by in-plant trainers, and so on.[1]

In addition to practicality, another important feature of training in connection with consulting assignments is that it generates interest in further training and self-development. Sound management stimulates and nurtures this interest, which may, in fact, be the main lasting contribution of many consulting assignments.

15.3 Maintenance and control of the new practice

If a new scheme is to survive and yield more in benefits than it costs, it has to be protected against a number of more or less natural hazards. Standards, systems and procedures are as prone to deterioration through wear and tear and neglect as are machines. Like machines, their performance may be reduced, eventually, to zero.

Maintenance and control should start while the consultant is still with the client organisation, but must continue after his departure.

Backsliding

A maintenance and control system has to guard against plain backsliding, which is able to occur for as long as people remember what they used to do before the change. Backsliding is not always reactionary. If a new method breaks down through trouble with equipment, supplies etc., work can only continue by doing something else. The most natural thing is to revert to the old practice if that is still possible. While the consultant is well advised:

— never to stop anyone working to the old method until it can be completely replaced,

he should also make sure that:

— after the new method has been proved it is impossible to revert to the old one.

---

[1] See Chapter 4, p. 35.

The way this is done will depend, as always, on the function of the assignment and the nature of its problems. A few examples are given below.

Paperwork: When a new paperwork procedure is installed, the stock of old forms is destroyed; so are the printing plates. Some official is made responsible for maintaining stocks of new forms and signing orders for reprints. The buyer does not pass orders for any printing signed by any other person.

Operating standards: The maintenance of factory work-standards requires similar vigilance. Working to standards must be made easier than working to non-standards. Any work outside the specification of the product or method should not be feasible within the standard paperwork. This is not to say that departures from standard are never allowed, but when they are, they are made self-evident.

Drawings: In an engineering drawing office it must not be easier to make a new drawing for a part than to find whether an existing part may be used. When a drawing is permanently changed, all old prints are tracked down and destroyed. An adequate control would prevent unauthorised prints being in circulation at any time.

All such measures are, of course, preventive. In their absence the alternative is often not a cure but a temporary expedient with a strong likelihood of recurrence.

Control procedures

A system of control, however, does not necessarily stop at maintenance in the narrow sense of keeping a scheme in the same state. After a time, any piece of reorganisation will begin to suffer from old age if nothing else. Other changing influences may render it less and less appropriate; the objective for which it was designed may be no longer there. Without a means of control, opportunities to modify and develop in line with changing circumstances may be lost.

It is, however, as easy to overdo control for its own sake as it is to become fascinated by any other technique. The consultant needs only to identify the key points at which significant departures will show up and choose the times at which they are to be checked. It is far from a matter of having to check everything every day: the criterion is usually how long it would take for anything serious to happen if it were not checked. More frequent checks are needed immediately after a change than later, when stability at a new level has been reached.

In financial areas, checks are part of budgetary control and made as often as the sensitivity of the situation demands. Labour performance checks may be built into weekly payroll/production analyses. Inventory controls may be in accordance with the main categories of stores.

Business companies accept the annual audit of their books as a matter of course but may forget that a periodic audit of their organisation and administrative methods is equally necessary. Apart from those detailed safeguards already mentioned, a periodic audit may be the only way of checking the whole system. Only an audit may reveal whether the total objectives are still being met, or are even still the same. It is failure to do this that allows the passage of time insidiously to erode the good work and its benefits.

Staff turnover is a common source of danger. If new staff members are not adequately briefed, they have little option but to act as they think fit, which may be towards surprisingly different objectives. The number of corrective problems the consultant has met in the client organisation may be an indicator of habitual neglect. If he does not change the client's basic attitudes to controls, his own work may get no better treatment.

15.4 Final assignment reports

Before and during the assignment the client has received several consulting reports:

— the survey report in which the assignment was proposed, based on a quick diagnostic survey;

— progress reports, whose number and scope varies, and in which modifications in problem definition and assignment plans may have been proposed;

— reports and documentation linked with the submission of proposals for the client's decision prior to implementation.

Whatever the pattern of interim reporting, there is a final assignment report issued at the time the consultant withdraws from the client organisation. Furthermore the consulting unit requires reports, which will be of help, above all, to its members who may be called upon to undertake similar assignments.

Report to the client

For a relatively short assignment this may be the only report and so has to be comprehensive. For longer assignments the final report may make passing reference to previous reports and go into detail only on the events since the last report was written. In all cases, as a closing report, it tidies up all the loose ends and covers the essential end-of-assignment facts and confirmations. It should be known before it is written whether the consulting unit is to provide a follow-up service.[1] If so, the report may not be quite as " final " as it otherwise would be.

In addition to a short comprehensive review of work performed, the final report should point out the benefits really obtained from implementation and make frank suggestions to the client on what he should undertake, or avoid, in the future.

Evaluation of benefits

This part is included in the final report if this is practical, i.e. if the consultant is leaving the client after a period of implementation which lends itself to evaluation. In other cases, it may be submitted later, if the client so desires.[2]

Through the evaluation of real benefits the consultant proves the correctness and accuracy of both the preliminary assessment (given in the survey report) and the evaluation of alternative solutions (presented to the client for decision prior to implementation).

Clearly, the implementation must have progressed enough and the conditions of operating with the new technique or system must have become normal and stabilised, if an evaluation of benefits is to give objective information. The consultant emphasises direct benefits obtained as a result of the assignment and leaves the consideration of indirect benefits (e.g. no increase in fixed costs) to the client.

It is not recommended practice in consulting to point out the savings: fee ratio. Again, such analysis is left entirely to the client, who appreciates that all benefits cannot be costed and that this ratio may be high in many simple, low-risk assignments, whose impact on over-all business results is limited.

Suggestions to the client

Although his job is completed, the consultant shows that he sees the client organisation in perspective if he points out possible further improvements, bottlenecks, risks, necessary action and so on. In any case he has to make suggestions on how the new system introduced with his help should be maintained, controlled and developed after his departure.

It is the policy of some consulting units to recommend a follow-up service to clients after the completion of operating assignments. An agreement reached on this question would be confirmed in the final report.

A good consulting report should be capable of commanding the respect of the client, who will consider it a source of further guidance. He will also

---

[1] See Chapter 24, p. 255.

[2] Consultants sometimes call it " savings report ".

be pleased to show them to friends and associates as the record of a worth-while achievement.[1]

Assignment reference report to the consulting unit

In addition to the final report to the client, the consultants compile an assignment reference report for their own organisation. This is usually on a one-page standard form and includes:

— client company name and address,
— assigner's name and title,
— nature and size of the organisation,
— operating function of the assignment,
— names of members of the consulting team,
— dates of start and finish,
— brief summary of objectives and results,
— references to all reports and documents that give details of the assignment.

In this short reference report, comments are made on the following questions:

(i) whether the value of the assignment for future reference is
> A: excellent,
> B: average,
> C: not to be used;

(ii) whether the client has agreed that the consulting unit may use him as a reference to prospective clients (the consulting unit is interested in this only if its rating under (i) was A or B);

(iii) whether the consulting unit rates the quality of the assignment as being
> above standard,
> standard,
> below standard (and if so, why).

These internal assignment reports are of great convenience and make it unnecessary to read the copies of client reports for simple facts on past assignments.

---

[1] Further details on writing and presenting consulting reports can be found in Appendix 7 " Consultant report writing ".

LITERATURE TO PART III

ACME: *Guide to professional practice (Suggestions for preparing proposals; interim report practice; survey report practice)* (New York, Association of Consulting Management Engineers, 1966); 35 pp.

ACME: *Professional practices in management consulting* (New York, Association of Consulting Management Engineers, 1966); 100 pp.

Barish N. N., Kaplan S.: *Economic analysis for engineering and managerial decision making* (New York, McGraw-Hill, 1978); 791 pp.

Bono de E.: *The use of lateral thinking* (Harmondsworth, Middx., Penguin Books, 1967).

Buffa E. S., Dyer J. S.: *Essentials of management science; operations research* (New York, Wiley, 1978); 528 pp.

Daniels A., Yeates D. (eds.): *Basic training in systems analysis* (London, Pitman, 1969).

Dawes R. M.: *Fundamentals of attitude measurement* (New York, Wiley, 1972); 165 pp.

Dunham R. B., Smith F. J.: *Organisational surveys: an internal assessment of organisational health* (Glenview, Ill., Scott, Foresman and Co., 1979); 179 pp.

Edwards A. L.: *Techniques of attitude scale construction* (New York, Appleton-Century-Crofts, 1957).

Emory C. W.: *Business research methods* (Homewood, Ill., Irwin, 1976); 483 pp.

Fuchs J. H.: *Making the most of management consulting services* (New York, AMACOM, 1975); 214 pp.

Goode W. J., Hatt P. H.: *Methods in social research* (New York, McGraw-Hill, 1952); 380 pp.

Greenberg L.: *A practical guide to productivity measurement* (Washington, Bureau of National Affairs, 1973); 77 pp.

Harrison I. W.: *Capital investment appraisal* (London, McGraw-Hill, 1973); 90 pp.

Hetman F.: *Society and the assessment of technology* (Paris, OECD, 1973); 420 pp.

Hice G. F., Turner W. S., Cashwell L. F.: *System development methodology* (Amsterdam, North Holland Publ. Co., 1974); 370 pp.

Horton F. W.: *Reference guide to advanced management methods* (New American Management Association, 1972); 330 pp.

ILO: *Introduction to work study* (Geneva, International Labour Office, 2nd edi 5th impr. 1977); 440 pp.

Ivey A. E.: *Microcounselling* (Springfield, Ill., Ch. C. Thomas, 1971); 306 pp.

Kepner Ch. H., Tregoe B. B.: *The rational manager (A systematic approach problem solving and decision making)* (New York, McGraw-Hill, 1965); 280 p

Lopez F. M.: *Personnel interviewing: theory and practice* (New York, McGraw-Hi 1975) 356 pp.

Maynard H. B.: *Industrial engineering handbook* (New York, McGraw-Hill, 1971) 1980 pp.

Morrell J. C.: *Preparing an organization manual* (London, British Institute of Management Foundation, 1977); 120 pp.

Osborn A. F.: *Applied imagination* (New York, Ch. Scribner's Sons, 1957).

Rickards T.: *Problem solving through creative analysis* (Epping, Essex, Gower Press, 1974); 198 pp.

Rothschild W. E.: *Putting it all together: a guide to strategic thinking* (New York, AMACOM, 1976); 262 pp.

Schein E. H.: *Process consultation: its role in organisation development* (Reading, Mass., Addison-Wesley, 1969); 150 pp.

Sidney E., Brown M., Argyle M.: *Skills with people: a guide for managers* (London, Hutchinson, 1973); 230 pp.

Starr M. K.: *Management: a modern approach* (New York, Harcourt Brace Jovanovich, 1971); 720 pp.

Wagner H. R.: *Principles of management science; with applications to executive decisions* (Englewood Cliffs, N. J., Prentice-Hall, 1975) 612 pp.

Weisslberg R. C., Cowley J. G.: *The executive strategist* (New York, McGraw-Hill, 1969); 250 pp.

White D. J.: *Decision methodology* (London, Wiley, 1975); 274 pp.

PART IV

CONSULTING IN VARIOUS AREAS
OF MANAGEMENT

CONSULTING IN GENERAL MANAGEMENT

16

This chapter is the first of a series of seven, each dealing with consulting in a specific area of management. The authors' intentions are not to describe the management techniques and practices of each area, but, in keeping with the spirit of the book, to provide basic guidelines to consulting. This chapter, and the following six chapters, can serve, therefore, as introductions to more detailed and deeper study of consulting in various techniques and areas of management, for which selected references are provided at the end of Part IV.[1]

16.1 Nature and scope of assignments in general management

There are three principal occasions on which consultants have to deal with problems of general management:

— during management (diagnostic) surveys;

— during assignments on specific functional areas of management, when it is found that certain changes in general management are required;

— during assignments dealing with one or more of the typical issues of general management.

These three instances are examined successively below.

Firstly, as explained in detail in Chapter 6, it is an established policy of most management consultants to carry out a brief survey of the whole organisation before proposing a specific problem-solving assignment.[2] Thus the first technical interaction between consultant and client is usually at the general management level.

---

[1] See pp. 237-241.

[2] See p. 57.

Secondly, in many cases the work agreed upon at the end of the initial survey will relate to a particular management function—and remain so for the duration of the assignment. It is not unusual, however, for consultants to have to tackle general management problems which are discovered, or defined with greater precision, in the course of functional assignments. In fact, any management problem seen as functional at the outset may turn out to be within the general management competence, if its importance reaches beyond the limits of a single function, or where existing decision-making procedures require the intervention of a general manager. There is a useful consultants' saying that " most shop-floor problems have their roots in the board-room "; experienced consultants are alert to any sign indicating that this applies to their particular case.

The third instance concerns assignments dealing with general management throughout their whole duration. They may take the form of extensive diagnostic surveys instead of short ones, especially if there is dissatisfaction at a high level with the way in which the organisation is managed (e.g. among the members of the company's board of directors, or in a ministry responsible for a public enterprise). Only a few management assignments extend beyond such extensive surveys and even these seldom develop into operating assignments in the orthodox sense. Such surveys occur particularly in large corporations and institutions equipped with internal services to assist implementation. It should also be noted that implementation of recommendations at the level of general management is likely to take considerable time with long waiting periods between events (e.g. the recruitment of a new executive may take six to nine months, or it may take a long time to obtain approval for a change in management of a public enterprise if this requires the consent of several government departments).

Nevertheless, there are operating assignments that may concern some specific aspect of general management (e.g. a company organisational structure) or even the total overhaul of general management policies and practices. The latter case would be found more often in small than in large enterprises [1]; if such an assignment should take place in a large organisation, it would be exceptionally complex and most demanding on consulting skills.

In many cases the general management consultant intervenes *at the highest level in the organisation,* namely, the top manager (who may be the person who has invited the consultant!) or the entire top management team. Clearly, this is not going to be an easy task. Even leaders keen to introduce change often do not realise that they must start by changing themselves. They often have a

---

[1] On consulting in small enterprises see Chapter 22.

particular self-image and the consultant may find that it is not necessarily shared by other people in the organisation. The consultant's problem then lies in explaining this to the top manager and persuading him of the need to change at the very top. Fortunately, it is not unusual to meet dynamic higher-level managers who are not only willing, but also able, to set good examples themselves.

A final remark has to do with the *style of consulting* to be used. In most cases process consulting [1] would be the appropriate approach—it is so much more effective to stimulate people in key positions to examine their attitudes and style of work rather than to present them with reports suggesting a range of measures thought out by somebody else on their behalf. In any case consulting in general management usually has little in common with assignments in which the consultant's aim is to introduce a well-defined technique. Its scope and objectives tend to be less precisely determined, and in some cases it may even be impossible to express ultimate objectives in clear terms at the time the work is initiated. Here the consultant's skill and art as a change agent are subjected to their most severe test; if he should fail, his report may well be accepted but certainly will not be implemented.

16.2   Basic choices

Modern approaches to management emphasise the determining role played by *basic choices* related to definition of: the sector or business in which the organisation is to operate; the social needs it is to satisfy and the market it is to serve; the long-term objectives and strategies that are to be followed; and the allocation of resources to the main activity areas.[2] If basic choices are wrong or nebulous, there is little point in aiming at perfection in organisation charts or endeavouring to reduce the cost of products which should probably not be produced at all.

The role of the general management consultant is in many ways analogous to that of a general manager in that he should avoid situations in which the basic choices are dominated by considerations of a single management function, irrespective of the needs and possibilities of other functions; and should ensure that specific contributions to strategy formulation will be mutually harmonised. A more detailed discussion of consulting in market, product and financial strategies is provided in other chapters of Part IV.

In the last few years, consulting in the basic functions and strategies of economic enterprises has helped to define new approaches to the question of

---

[1] See Chapter 2, p. 18.

[2] See e.g. H. I. Ansoff: *Corporate strategy* (New York, McGraw-Hill, 1965) and P. Drucker: *Managing for results* (New York, Harper and Row, 1964).

the *social responsibilities of business enterprises,* and to enhance the role of environmental considerations in business policy decisions. For example, some management consultants are able to undertake a " social audit " or " social responsibility audit " of their client organisations, which emphasises the social implications of important managerial decisions and endeavours to measure and appraise the client's social performance in addition to the economic and financial one.

Assignments in these areas tend to be *inter-disciplinary.* If management consultants are requested to deal with strategy and environmental issues, this will require their intensive direct interaction with higher management and with those functional units involved in business analysis, forecasting and long-range planning. As happens during the initial management survey, the organisation needs to examine its relationship to its external environment and the totality of its resources, functions and activities. However, in a full-scale assignment a considerably greater amount of data will be needed and the general management consultant may decide to call for help from specialist consultants in sectoral economic studies, market research, technological forecasting, surveys of labour markets, and like areas.

In centrally planned economies, or economies where governments have installed various controls over the activity of economic enterprises, the general management consultant will probably examine the basic choices concerning the client enterprise in the light of government development policies, plans and regulations which determine the authority and responsibility of enterprise management in this area. For example, the profitability of a product line may be affected by centrally controlled price policy, or the availability of raw materials for further expansion will need to be examined in connection with development plans which will increase the demand of other organisations for these raw materials. In many cases, basic studies of the enterprise's profile, development potential and strategies will have to be undertaken in agreement and in collaboration with the central body which supervises the client organisation.

Regardless of the manner in which they are determined, recommendations on basic choices usually have far-reaching consequences for the client's business. For example, a merger may be suggested, or even the discontinuation of important but old-fashioned products familiar to everybody in the firm for some considerable time. Large financial resources may be needed to implement new strategies, for example if a plant requires to be reconstructed. Before being submitted to the client, proposals of this nature must be studied and discussed in the consulting organisation by a team of senior members experienced in such matters.

16.3   The decision-making process

In addition to the basic choices—which are not made very often—there are literally hundreds of other choices that managers have to make in their decision-making capacity every day. In many organisations it may be the method and organisation of decision making (for both key and routine matters) which cause trouble. For example, excessive centralisation of operational decisions may deprive the organisation of the flexibility needed to react to new market opportunities. In another case, an autocratic owner may be taking decisions without conferring with professional experts on his own staff, who could easily prove that many of his decisions were based on wishful thinking rather than rational analysis.

The need to *examine and reform the total decision-making process* may be the very reason why the consultant has been brought in and may concern:

— the classification of decisions in groups by their nature, urgency, financial implications, degree of complexity, etc.;

— the ways in which typical decisions are taken (this may be quite difficult to find out);

— the respective decision-making roles played by specialists and line managers;

— the role of collective bodies in discussing and adopting decisions;

— the participation of workers' representatives in decision making;

— the decision-making and advisory roles of individuals in informal positions of influence;

— the responsibility for decisions, their implementation, and control of implementation;

— the use of decision-making techniques, models or formalised procedures.[1]

The possibilities of improvement are tremendous in this area and general management consultants are well advised to pay close attention to them.

16.4   Organisational structure

To examine and redesign the organisational structure used to be the " classical " assignment for general management consultants. When the basic structure was agreed, the consultant continued his work by producing detailed charts and job descriptions for each unit within the client organisation. The

---

[1] See e.g. C. H. Kepner and B. B. Tregoe: *The rational manager* (New York, McGraw-Hill, 1965).

end-product was often viewed as a set of organisational charts and instructions but, in fact, the principal benefit to the client was the effort and analysis that went into this job. Forgotten and " orphan " activities were often rediscovered, activities for which nobody seemed to be responsible were defined, and overlapping activities reassigned or done away with.

Many management consultants still continue to deal with organisational problems along these lines. The effective approach, however, neither starts with organisational structures, nor attaches greater importance to formal organisation than it really has in the total process of management. Structure, defined as the design of an organisation through which the enterprise is administered, follows strategy, and the most complex type of structure is the result of the concatenation of several basic strategies (such as expansion of volume of activity, geographical dispersion, vertical integration or diversification).[1]

Hence, if requested to assist in organisational matters, the consultant should examine whether the client has defined his objectives and strategies for future development and with what resources he is going to operate. No rigidity is advisable in questions such as what the span of control should be, or whether job descriptions can be adjusted to people or people should adjust to job descriptions.

A general trend is the *search for innovative and flexible organisational arrangements*, including arrangements that have not been considered by conventional organisational theory, but are likely to suit the particular situation. This may include a wider application of matrix and project organisation, the streamlining of communication channels and information flows (both horizontal and vertical)[2], or a complete revision of the centralisation and decentralisation of both decision making and particular operational activities in the organisation.

16.5 Management styles

In many assignments the consultants discover that the problem is not one of structure, procedures or plans, but rather one of the *style* in which the top manager, or top management team, fulfils the leading role in the organisation. Many psychological and sociological difficulties in organisations originate from the attitudes and behavioural patterns of top managers. The main reason for this lies in the very nature of management and leadership because the attitudes and behaviour of people at the top are under constant

---

[1] Cf. A. D. Chandler: *Strategy and structure* (New York, Anchor Books-Doubleday, 1966), pp. 16-17.

[2] On management information see Chapter 20.

observation by subordinate staff who have a tendency to adjust their attitudes and behaviour to models set by their leaders. Certain behavioural patterns thus spread over the whole organisation and may become very deeply rooted indeed. In this way a particular *climate* is created, which may determine to a large degree how people will act or react in various situations.

The practical problems in this area may fall into one or more of the following three groups.

A first group of problems concerns the manager's personality, as reflected in his behaviour in contacts with colleagues (especially subordinates) and his individual work methods and habits.

For example, if a top manager issues instructions but never controls their application, if he has the tendency to delay decisions as long as possible, or makes quick decisions without bothering about problem analysis, it is likely that a similar pattern will be adopted by many people in the organisation and those who would act differently might even run into difficulties. Another example might be that of a general manager who worked in production earlier in his career but has, in fact, never stopped being a production manager, and is happiest when detailed production problems arrive on his desk so that he can devote most of his time to workshop and supply problems. This, unfortunately, tends to bring about a distorted general management style, in which the various functions of management are handled in a very unbalanced manner.

The second group includes elements and features of the general manager's or management's value system. We cannot list all possible instances of values or priorities, which management may express in a certain way and thus, intentionally or not, set the tone for the thinking and action of people in the organisation.

Nevertheless, the following examples illustrate what we have in mind:
— reluctance to consider proposals for change, if they are made by the rank-and-file employees;
— prejudices against women managers and individuals from particular ethnic or social groups;
— preference for tale-bearing rather than open discussion;
— various forms of favouritism, nepotism or cliques in the organisation.

By providing these examples we do not intend to suggest that in his investigations the consultant will only be confronted with situations where negative attitudes on the part of the managers prevail. This is certainly not so, however such attitudes may be met in organisations that are clearly mismanaged. But consultants are called in to deal with problems and these problems may often be in the managers' attitudes and values systems. It is perhaps needless to add that the consultant is equally interested in positive attitudes, which represent the client's strength, and tries to develop and reinforce them, especially if this can ease the acceptance and implementation of his proposals.

The third group embraces elements of managerial style adopted and followed in the general management activity throughout the organisation. For example, McGregor analyses the difference between Theory X (the traditional view of direction and control) and Theory Y (the integration of individual and organisational goals in a way enabling the members of the organisation to achieve their own goals best by directing their efforts toward the success of the enterprise).[1] In similar vein Likert [2] proposes a fourfold classification of management systems, viz: (1) authoritative exploitative (2) authoritative benevolent (3) consultative and (4) participative.

A related key element of the general management style is *communication within the organisation*. There is a great difference between, on the one hand, organisations in which communication is very restricted, most people are deprived even of information which directly concerns them and higher management shows no interest in the views of the rank-and-file employee, and, on the other hand, organisations using communication to enlist people's co-operation and support and thus enhance their feeling of belonging to the organisation.[3]

The aspects of management style given above do not attempt to exhaust this essential component of general management. Our purpose is to bring them to the consultant's attention and suggest that in many cases he cannot avoid tackling such issues, however delicate and full of pitfalls they may look. Since many behavioural scientists have started practical consulting work in these aspects of management, some general management consultants prefer to leave this domain strictly to them in order " not to burn their fingers ". This is in direct contradiction to the comprehensive approach to management. While there is no need for a general management consultant to convert himself into a behavioural scientist, he should know enough about practical problems and theories to accept his responsibility for providing advice on the " less visible and less tangible " problems of management style and climate.

---

[1] D. McGregor: *The human side of the enterprise* (New York, McGraw-Hill, 1960).

[2] R. Likert: *New patterns of management* (New York, McGraw-Hill, 1961).

[3] ILO Recommendation No. 129 emphasises the importance of communication between management and workers within the undertaking.

CONSULTING IN FINANCIAL MANAGEMENT 17

17.1 Nature and purpose of financial consultations

By its very nature finance enters into every realm of business: it is a means of procuring resources to carry out business operations and it measures business performance and results, both in detail and globally.

Because of its all-pervading nature finance enters into many management consultations. As already explained in detail, a financial appraisal is an essential component of diagnostic surveys of business or other economic organisations.[1] In operating assignments, the financial consultant may collaborate with consultants in other fields, particularly production and marketing, measuring the financial implications of their proposals, or working on issues such as price setting, in which both financial and marketing considerations apply.[2] He may, however, undertake an assignment concerned with financial matters only, such as planning financial structures, finding funds, and designing accounting systems. Sometimes financial consulting arises from the clients' awareness of problems such as cash shortages. At other times surveys of clients' businesses, particularly financial appraisals, may reveal weaknesses in financial structures, systems or controls. Often consultants in other fields require the help of financial consultants to evaluate the financial feasibility of their proposals. If an operating assignment is in the area of business strategy and long-range planning it will invariably include consulting on financial implications of alternative strategies, and on strategies in the financial field itself, including the sources of new funds and an optimum use of funds. Such consulting will require the involvement of a financial specialist, or the general management consultant will need to have a good background in finance.

---

[1] See Chapters 6 and 7.
[2] See also Chapter 18, p. 190.

For the purpose of examining the nature of financial consultations five groupings are convenient:
— enterprise development,
— capital management,
— least cost operational alternatives,
— accounting systems,
— inflation accounting.

17.2   Enterprise development

This group includes *feasibility studies* of new developments. New ventures commonly considered include setting up new factories, adding new product lines, changing production processes, installing new equipment, entering new markets, setting up new storage and distribution centres and expanding existing operations. In each of these instances the consultant measures the resources required and the income and costs that will follow. Where the venture is new and distinct, such as building a new plant in a foreign country, the consultant works on total investment, income and costs. For extensions or additions to existing operations, incremental investment, income and costs are more reliable. The object of an assignment is to assess whether expected benefits justify the resources which the client must commit to the new venture. Financial estimates are merely the money values of labour, material, machines and installations to be assembled and the outputs and activities they generate. Before he can express expectations in money units, the consultant needs such basic information from marketing, production and personnel specialists. Feasibility studies are, therefore, usually undertaken by teams of consultants.

A simple example illustrates how consultants work as a team on a feasibility study. A manufacturer of leather shoes who wishes to enter the market for rubber footwear may request a consultant to conduct a feasibility study. A marketing consultant might start by measuring the demand for various types of rubber footwear such as gym shoes, gumboots and galoshes in markets open to the manufacturer. After investigation he selects the most promising types and fixes likely prices and volume of sales. In addition he proposes a marketing campaign and sales organisation. All his proposals will have to be translated into estimates of income and expenditure by a financial consultant. If the market seems to justify the venture, a production consultant plans the production facilities and labour force to be added to existing capacity, and estimates the material, labour and services required to produce the footwear to be sold. Again the information is turned over to the financial consultant who determines the amount of capital required for the additional facilities and calculates the addition to present production costs. He finalises the study by deducting expected costs from forecast income to see whether the resulting profit offers a favourable return on the new capital to be invested. He concludes by proposing the most appropriate method of raising the capital for the new venture.

If a client plans to *expand by acquisition or merger* he may engage a consultant to evaluate the financial consequences. He and the consultant together foresee the effect on outputs, income and costs of combining two or more enterprises. Product lines may complement each other and increase combined sales, or, conversely, may overlap so that some should be dropped. Production and marketing facilities and administration can usually be streamlined so that the combined investment and costs are less than those of the two separate enterprises. Taking such considerations into account the consultant advises whether the contemplated acquisitions or merger will benefit his client, e.g. whether two international airlines might merge and use one chain of reservation offices, service facilities and maintenance installations throughout the world instead of the two operated separately.

17.3 Capital management

The consultant has two main concerns under capital management. The first relates to sources of funds, and the second to the best use of funds. An assignment may consider only one of these aspects, or may combine the two when the client wants an assessment of the amount of capital he requires and recommendations on where and how to procure the estimated amount.

When advising on *procurement of funds* the consultant examines the client's capital structure and suggests appropriate balancing of owners' equity against loans, and sound gearing of long-term to short-term borrowing. He also considers conditions in the money markets, the prospects for obtaining risk capital or loans, and the relative costs of different sources of finance both in the short and long term. If his client has a stock exchange quotation the consultant should advise on a market strategy to attract capital and meet legal and stock exchange regulations. The client's dividend policy also comes under review to ensure sound reinvestment of profits consistent with inducement to investors to buy equities and sustain stock exchange values.

A typical problem is that of a manganese producer who wishes to add a new smelter, but needs a substantial amount of new capital for this. The new smelter will not come into full production for some four years. If the producer raises the capital by an issue of new shares he will probably depress the present market price of his stock because he will be unable to continue the present rate of dividend on the increased capital before the new smelter reaches full output. One solution may be to borrow the new capital by means of bonds bearing a fixed rate of interest. The interest could be treated as a capital charge against the cost of the new smelter. This would allow the enterprise to maintain its present dividend, or even to increase it by good management, dynamic marketing and raising productivity of present smelting capacity. With such a programme the bonds could carry an option to convert to common stock in five to ten years' time at a price above the present market level. By this means the new capital would cost less than a straight issue of shares now. A financial consultant with experience of transactions of this nature could give invaluable advice on the best financial strategy and act as an authoritative guide in negotiations with bankers, underwriters, revenue officials, issue houses, stockbrokers and stock exchange authorities.

The financial consultant frequently advises on the proper *use of funds*. His guidance is invaluable on the correct balance between fixed and current assets and the maintenance of liquidity. In this area he points out the disadvantages of either under or over trading and gives the client an understanding of cost-volume-profit relationships. He can also help his client to appreciate the importance of rapid turnover of working capital and the maintenance of economic levels of inventories, accounts receivable and accounts payable.

In many countries business companies face problems in managing the credit they give their customers. They also face various problems, financial and ethical, in deciding when and how they should pay their debts to suppliers. Financial consultants and commercial banks can provide managers with useful advice on these issues and help them to maintain the cash flow at a sound level.[1]

Often the financial consultant stresses the need for sound depreciation and replacement policies to ensure continuous renewal and upgrading of installations and equipment, a burning issue in many businesses in developing countries.

17.4 Least-cost operational alternatives

In any case where a manager, or a management consultant, can choose between two or more ways of carrying out an activity, a financial consultant may be called to evaluate which is the most favourable. The range of such consultations is wide and may involve choices in any area of management (such as repair or renew equipment, use overtime work or multiple shifts, purchase or lease equipment, make or buy certain parts, develop a new product or purchase a licence and so on).

Essentially the consultant's approach is similar in all of these examples. For each alternative he evaluates the amount of resources to be invested, the income or output that will result and the costs that will arise. He compares one alternative with another to find out which promises the most favourable return on investment over the expected life of the operation. Since he is dealing with extensions to or modifications of existing operations, he should base his decisions on incremental investment, income and cost, i.e. the investment, income and cost to be added to existing levels.

In many cases the value of the consultant's help will be enhanced by devising an evaluation methodology suitable to the particular conditions of the client's organisation and passing it over to the client, so that further routine

---

[1] See for example P. Chambers: "Stop sleeping on cash" in *International Management*, Volume 30, Number 11, November 1975.

evaluations of operational alternatives could be undertaken by the client's personnel.

17.5 Accounting systems

The financial consultant receives many requests for the design and development of accounting systems. Clients expect him to have extensive knowledge and experience to put at their disposal in developing systems for

— management information,
— financial accounting,
— billing customers,
— credit control,
— inventory control,
— payroll compilation,
— budgetary control,
— cost accounting,
— asset accounting and safeguarding,
— information processing, including mechanical and electronic data processing.[1]

In setting up one or more of these systems, managers try to ensure that they have adequate means to carry out some part of their tasks of committing resources and planning and controlling operations. Before he starts to design an accounting system the consultant has to determine what support managers expect, what the objective of the system is, the information it should provide, who will receive that information and how he will use it. To ensure that the system will serve the intended purpose, the consultant has to

— create an appropriate organisation,
— prescribe procedures for gathering, storing and analysing data and disseminating information,
— design forms to match the procedures,
— select suitable equipment,
— incorporate checks and controls.

Since the client's staff will have to operate the system, the consultant prefers to win their confidence and understanding by teaming up with them to design the system. He follows this with training for those who are going to carry out the procedures and guides them during the early stages of implementation.

---

[1] On consulting in data processing see Chapter 20.

17.6   Inflation accounting

Accounting systems usually record historical costs; the resulting information therefore ignores changes in the value of money. But the combination of costs in different years corresponding to different price levels has no more meaning than the addition of dollars, pounds, kwatchas, yen, francs, won and marks without conversion to a common currency. In a number of countries inflation has recently re-emphasised this defect.

Accountants and consultants have been looking for a remedy for some time; to this effect a proposal was recently made to introduce current cost accounting (CCA) [1].

CCA charges materials, supplies, services and the usage of fixed assets at replacement costs at the time of consumption. It also reflects up-to-date values of assets, liabilities and capital. By recording transactions in current values it takes account of inflation in all cost and financial information. It is not limited to a mere conversion of year-end financial statements from historical to current values, which is inadequate for managers' needs. In developing CCA a major concern is the determination of current values. As far as possible they should reflect actual replacement costs and present money values. A different conversion factor may apply to each element of cost and each category of asset and liability.

However, professional accountants do not give full support to CCA and, in many cases, prefer other solutions such as supplementary statements to company accounts. This was the tone of a July 1977 meeting of the Institute of Chartered Accountants in England and Wales, at which the idea of making CCA mandatory was rejected.

As yet accountants and financial management consultants have little experience of inflation accounting. Principles and procedures will have to be refined in practice. However, "the introduction of such a system should not be delayed by the search for an elusive and probably unattainable degree of perfection".[2]

---

[1] Detailed proposals can be found in *The Inflation Accounting Steering Group's guidance manual on current cost accounting* prepared by the Institute of Chartered Accountants in England and Wales and several other professional associations of accountants. The manual includes the so-called *Exposure Draft 18 (ED 18)*, which is a proposed statement of standard accounting practice on current cost accounting. The main ideas of ED 18 are referred to here with kind permission of the publisher.

On other techniques of inflation accounting see e.g. W. Chippindale and P. L. Defliese: *Current value accounting; a practical guide for business* (New York, AMACOM, 1977), T. D. Flynn: "Why we should account for inflation", in *Harvard Business Review,* September-October 1977, or R. K. Mautz: "Inflation accounting: which method is best?", in *Management Review,* November 1977.

[2] Op. cit., Appendix A, p. (ii).

CONSULTING IN MARKETING MANAGEMENT

18

18.1   General considerations

Consulting work involving the client's marketing activities differs in several ways from that dealing with the other functions. It is in its marketing that the firm finds itself in contact with external entities (competitors and clients) which have an independent existence. The firm's very survival depends upon how well it manages to adapt to the market conditions influenced by the activities of these entities.

One of the paradoxes of the marketing function is that when it is looked at closely it tends to disappear, like a stream going underground. It surfaces again in two forms—strategy formulation, and the organisation and management of the various market-related activities of sales, advertising, product and market research, physical distribution, etc. This leaves a definite gap in the organisation chart. Matters concerning the firm's over-all strategy, of which marketing strategy is an important part, can only be decided at the topmost level of the organisation, while running the various activities is a middle-management function.

Thus a consulting assignment that embraces the marketing function will usually develop into two quite separate tasks, one at the *strategy-formulating level* and one at the *activities level*. These two tasks are treated separately below. It is convenient here, however, to note briefly a third type of consulting activity.

This third type of activity is that of *marketing research*. It supplies analysed information to the client, leaving him to take any necessary action. In many cases, marketing research would be handled by consultants who have fully specialised in this field. There is a wide range of these, from large units which provide firms with data about their market shares on a subscription basis, down to individuals, frequently but not always university professors, who are often engaged to investigate the possible reactions of the public to change in package design, or do a market research study as part of a feasibility study for a new industrial project.

For example, a manufacturer of cooking oils was considering introducing rape-seed oil, or rape oil, into eastern Canada. This product was widely used in western Canada, but the manufacturer was worried lest its rather startling name should have negative connotations amongst the largely urbanised eastern housewives. Since his budget for research was puny he had no option but to entrust the investigation of this particular hazard to one of the small consultants. This firm, by ingeniously applying a technique involving measurement of the pupil dilations [1] of a small sample of housewives, was able to keep within this budget and yet establish, with a high degree of confidence, that the name of the product would not be a handicap to its marketing.

The consultant working on a client's marketing activities, unless he belongs to an organisation large enough to have its own marketing research division (and this is rare indeed), will often need to call upon one or more of these market research organisations for help. It will usually be cheaper to sub-contract such work than to start upon it from scratch. Therefore consultants should know that such special organisations exist, and what they can do. Good quality marketing research is surprisingly widely available, even in the developing countries (also some advertising agencies maintain research facilities of this type). To a marketing consultant market research specialists are not competitors, but professionals who complement his own work.

18.2 The marketing strategy level

Strategic decisions in marketing have far-reaching implications for the enterprise as a whole and for the management of particular functions, such as production, product development or financial control. No wonder, therefore, that even minor proposals may meet with strong objections from production or other parts of the firm and will require the intervention of a higher level of management. Major changes, such as dropping or adding product lines or changing over-all pricing policies are clearly general management decisions to be taken at top level.

A useful starting point is to classify the client's orientation towards the market. Three classifications are recognised: *product-oriented, production-oriented*, and *market-oriented*. In a product-oriented firm the emphasis is on the product itself, while in the production-oriented firm the dominant considerations in product design or modification are those of ease or cheapness of

---

[1] Measurement of pupil dilation is an advanced research technique for the assessment of consumer preference or rejection of normal presentations by measurement of expansion or contraction of pupil size. The major advantage of the technique is that it requires little or no instructions to administer; its major disadvantage, however, is the relatively high cost and technical operation of the instruments required.

production. In either case market considerations are ignored or de-emphasised. In a marketing-oriented firm the decisions are based upon the analysis of market needs and demands. The objective is to take the opportunities the market offers. This approach can produce any of the good effects of the other two orientations, and avoids their drawbacks. More important, it can identify new opportunities. Figuratively speaking, the management of the firm asks itself the following questions:

- what problems do our customers have that our products (or services) can solve more cheaply or better than any other products from other manufacturers?

- who has these problems?

- what are the particular circumstances of our customers, actual or potential, which would suggest modifications in our products, conditions of delivery, etc.?

The idea of thinking in terms of providing solutions to problems is a very useful one in marketing. It helps considerably in identifying new markets, finding new products for existing customers, finding new customers for existing products, and, very importantly, discovering potential and possibly unsuspected competition.

As a very simple case, consider a manufacturer of nuts and bolts. This enterprise probably thinks of itself as being in the metal-working business, and looks for new business on this basis. But what about its customers? Their problem is joining things together. So the firm could meet competition from firms making welders, rivets, cotter pins, or glues. This threat is also an opportunity, since the firm's sales force and distributors are already in touch with people who form a potential market for these items, which suggests that they could profitably be added to the firm's product line. The costs of marketing are high, so that anything that can add to the effectiveness of the various marketing functions (i.e. reduce the unit costs of marketing activities) can be surprisingly profitable. Such help can come from selling more items per sales visit, sending out shipments with more items, and turning small, unprofitable accounts into at least medium-sized ones.

The whole product line of the client should be analysed in this way, looking for what Standt and Taylor [1] call " congruence " (i.e. products which are mutually supportive). This congruence can be in either production or sales or both. Often it will be found that some products are in the line solely because they fit in with the production facilities (they are easy to make), without regard being paid to the demands of the customers, and with consequent dissipation of marketing resources amongst too many potential customers. It is also possible for the reverse to happen, production facilities

---

[1] T. Staudt and D. A. Taylor: *A managerial introduction to marketing* (Englewood Cliffs, N. J., Prentice-Hall, 1965).

being dispersed excessively to try and meet all possible demands of existing customers.

Next, the product line may be reviewed according to the criteria set out by Drucker, especially from the viewpoint of future opportunities offered by various products, and the cost related to the use of these opportunities.[1]

Such analysis should provide a sound basis for the consultant's recommendations concerning product additions or deletions. Sometimes it will indicate areas which need further investigation. For example, the marketing manager might insist that some sizes in a product line, although very small sellers, are necessary because the firm's distributors demand a " full " line from their suppliers. This should be investigated (sometimes " demand " means simply a mild preference), as should the possibility of " buying-in " the more extreme sizes.

In many enterprises *pricing* is regarded as the special province of accountants who determine at what prices the marketing people must sell. Yet this is an area in which both marketing considerations and cost criteria apply. If a marketing consultant finds that prices are set by unilateral decisions of accountants, he will be interested in reviewing how this affects marketing and the volume of sales. This may lead to a revision of pricing policy, including the establishment of new procedures for price-setting in the client organisation. The ultimate objective would be to make better use of prices as a marketing tool, but without running the risk that an increased volume of sales of underpriced products will cause a financial loss.

Credit to customers can be another common source of conflict between the marketing manager and the finance manager, especially in times of tight money.[2] It is probably the case that, more often than not, the marketing manager attaches too much importance to the use of credit. This is understandable, because his information on this matter comes from his salesmen, who like to have such a tool in their selling kit. When this conflict is encountered it is advisable to undertake some market research in order to find what the situation really is.

Another problem area for top management consideration is the question of the firm's *public image*, i.e. the opinion that customers, actual and, more importantly, potential, have of the firm. This should be broadly consistent with the image the firm has about itself, and which its salesmen are expected to create.

This problem can be illustrated by the results of research into the public image of three department stores in a North American town, carried out by the local business school. When the students interviewed the store managers, one manager said his

---

[1] P. Drucker: *Managing for results* (New York, Harper and Row, 1964).

[2] See also Chapter 17, p. 184.

store's image was built on quality, the second said his was built on prices, and the third said his store's strength lay in service. The research on consumer attitudes revealed that the same three images, of price, quality and service, indeed existed, but that each of the three managers was wrong about the image attributed to his own store. Thus, each manager was, and for some years had been,

(a) wasting most of his advertising expenditure,

(b) wasting most of the effort expended in training his salespeople,

(c) failing to give his customers the type of treatment they expected from his store.

It was extremely fortunate for each of these managers that the other two had misread the market as badly as he himself had. In the meantime the smaller stores in town were profiting from the way the three big ones were failing to cash in on their advantages.

When the consultant suspects that such a clash between his client's internal and external images exists he should investigate this possibility thoroughly. How to approach this is a question of consulting strategy. To change the firm's image is a difficult decision to take; the case for change must therefore be very strong. For example, the marketing consultant may call for the help of an independent market research consultant of good reputation, familiar with attitude research techniques. In any case, the relevant evidence should be collected and presented by a disinterested party, so that the client is assured of the objectiveness of the recommendation.

18.3   Marketing operations

Different firms have different ideas about which operations are part of the marketing function and which are not. Selling, advertising, promotion, dealing with distributors and market research are considered by almost all firms to be the responsibility of the marketing manager, but the situation with respect to new-product development, package design, or transportation and storage of finished goods (physical distribution) is usually far less clear.

For example, the case has been reported of a Canadian firm which for over two years deferred action on a consultant's report which recommended building an intermediate storage and distribution warehouse, with expected savings to the firm of about two million dollars a year. The simple reason was that no one could arrive at a decision about which department was to operate the proposed warehouse. While this degree of organisational futility is rare, the case nevertheless shows that top managements have difficulty making positive decisions concerning the administration of activities that cross departmental boundaries.

This situation, if it existed in the client's case, would have been observed at the diagnostic stage of the assignment, and appropriate recommendations made. If the operating marketing consultant detects such a case, he would be well advised to consult his supervisor, because organisational fuzziness in these areas could slow the progress of the assignment very substantially.

Sales management

The consulting activities in this field are straightforward. Proper training and motivation of salesmen are key items to be checked, as is the way that salesmen share their effective selling time between existing and potential customers and among large, medium, and small accounts. Another point to check is whether the client's advertising is being used to increase salesmen's effectiveness by generating curiosity and interest in the minds of customers. Such interest makes it easier to obtain appointments and helps interviews get off to good starts. This aspect of advertising is important principally in marketing industrial goods.

Advertising and promotion

Usually the client can obtain good advice in these activities from his advertising agency, but occasionally the situation can arise in which they are in the hands of lacklustre people, both at the client's end and at the agency's. A common but undesirable practice is that of setting advertising expenditures purely as an arbitrary percentage of sales, either past sales or forecast sales. It is much sounder to plan advertising campaigns in terms of objectives and then calculate the money needed to attain these objectives. This amount may be quite out of line with the resources available, in which case the objectives will have to be redefined on a more modest scale. Using this method has the advantage of giving the client some idea of what he can expect to achieve with his advertising expenditure.

Physical distribution

The analysis of the physical distribution function falls into two types. The first type deals with large complex systems involving multiple shipment origins and destinations, intermediate storage or trans-shipment points, etc. This type of analysis is extremely complex: the advantages of long production runs have to be balanced against storage costs at the various points in the system, service standards have to be balanced against the number of intermediate storage points, the optimisation of the location of these storage points requires very extensive computations, and quite elaborate procedures have to be developed to design schedules that maximise vehicle utilisation. This is definitely a job for specialists who know what suitable computer packages exist and have plenty of experience in using them.

The second type of analysis, by far the more common, boils down to deciding how much distribution should be done in company-owned vehicles and how much should be contracted outside. This sort of analysis is quite straightforward in principle, although it can often be very difficult to find the necessary costing data. Generally, and especially in the developing countries, too much transportation is done in the client's vehicles and not enough is contracted out.

Distribution channels

The main weakness in this respect is a tendency to bypass wholesalers and deal direct with retailers, a tendency which again is particularly pronounced in developing countries. This entails maintaining excessively large sales forces, with associated extra costs. Oddly enough, marketing managers under these circumstances often regard these large sales forces as a key competitive advantage, a surprising naïvety to find in firms which in many other respects can be quite sophisticated in management matters. The reason is that many manufacturers view wholesalers as poor distributors, who give inadequate support to the manufacturers' goods. But substantial savings can often be obtained by giving local distributorships to people who show entrepreneurial ability, even if this means setting them up in business. Appropriately designed incentive schemes can also be effective in obtaining better co-operation from distributors. The consultant who expects to do a significant amount of work for manufacturers of consumer goods will find it a good investment to spend some time in studying problems and needs of the wholesale and retail trade.

Packaging and new-product development

These two activities share the characteristic that, while the actual work is usually done by other departments, it is desirable and often vital that the marketing department be actively involved. Here the consultant has to consider two things. First, the marketing department should have the capability to become involved constructively, which means having the will and the resources to carry out or subcontract the required market and consumer research. Second, organisational arrangements have to be devised which will ensure that the marketing department's involvement will come about at a suitably early stage, and not, as often happens, after the designs have been finalised. These arrangements may take the form of a " new-products committee " or equivalent, whose approval is required before further funds can be allocated to new-product development.

18.4 Consulting in commercial enterprises

In this sector stock turnover (stock rotation) is one of the key issues. In a well-run firm this forms the focal point of all activities; purchasing and stock-level planning are based on target stock rotation objectives.

The consultant's first task in such enterprises is to check *the stock-control procedures*. Often these will be found to be unsatisfactory and suitable procedures will have to be established. Different types of goods need different stock-control systems. There are four main systems, suitable for groceries, general merchandise, fashion goods, and " big-ticket " goods (i.e. furniture, refrigerators, expensive cameras) respectively. Many enterprises, however, will need to use two or more of these systems, depending on the variety of goods carried.

The establishment of stock-control procedures comes first, because further work will need the data such procedures will produce. Indeed, very often the assignment need consist of no more than installing good stock-control procedures and training management in using stock-control data in planning and administration.

Some assignments, however, will also have various general management aspects (for example, setting up management-by-objectives schemes in multi-department firms), and sometimes training in specialised techniques will have to be arranged.

The above activities account for the bulk of what might be called corrective or remedial consulting in commercial entreprises. But there are firms that get themselves into more serious troubles through unsound policies. In these cases the remedies are usually obvious, if drastic, and the consultant's main function is to provide management with the moral support needed to make disagreeable or unpalatable decisions.

For example, a retailer of luxury goods (watches, sports goods, etc.) might have been seduced into giving extended credit terms because it is so much easier to sell such goods in this way (especially to irresponsible consumers), and then find himself with accounts receivable equal to six-months' sales or more, largely uncollectable.

Quite often retailers will pick store locations unsuitable for the goods they handle, trying to sell shopping goods in a convenience store site or vice versa. A variation of this situation is the case of the real-estate developer, innocent of all knowledge of retailing or consumer behaviour, who builds a shopping centre and then leases space to retailers of inappropriate type. Problems of this kind appear, and consultants are called to deal with them, soon after the shopping-centre " boom " starts in any area. They are quite common in many developing countries.

CONSULTING IN PRODUCTION MANAGEMENT

19

Production is essentially a process of transforming certain inputs into some required outputs in the form of goods or services. As such, a production function does not only apply strictly to manufacturing operations but also to other activities, such as construction and transport operations, health or even office services.

This process of transformation requires decision making on the part of the production manager with a view to getting an output of the desired quantity and quality delivered by the required date and at a minimum cost. The consultant's task is to advise management whenever necessary on the best means of achieving such an objective. In the performance of his functions, a production management consultant in most cases is able to measure and assess the fruits of his work quite tangibly. In this sense he is probably in a more fortunate situation than his colleagues in other areas, such as general or personnel management.

The production management consultant can approach his assignment in a systematic way looking at aspects relating to:

— the product or products,
— the methods and organisation of work,
— people.

In the production area, problems submitted to the consultant may have very different degrees of importance to the client organisation.

At one end of the scale there are problems which belong to the group of " basic choices ".[1] A production consultant may have an important say in a team which is examining the client's total strategy: for example, a marketing consultant may suggest that certain products are complementary as they are

---

[1] See Chapter 16, p. 175.

intended for the same customers and are marketed in the same way, but the production consultant may prove that the same products are not complementary from the manufacturing point of view.

At the opposite end of the scale there are a myriad of problems whose common denominator is the need to meet certain criteria with regard to productivity, cost or job satisfaction in specific production tasks. Such problems tend to be operational in nature. But the consultant will be well advised not to lose from sight the broader needs of the client organisation, as it is not unusual for assignments in very specific production fields to disclose problems that are much more profound and lie outside the production departments.

A case history of a specific consulting assignment in production management is given in Appendix 4.[1]

19.1 The product

Although the production management consultant is not a product designer and nobody can expect that he will know every product in all its details, certain aspects of the product may predetermine production effectiveness to a large degree and the consultant has to deal with them. For this he will need to enlist the full co-operation of the product-design and other special technical departments.

In respect of the *product, parts and accessories design*, the consultant may have to examine:

— how many parts the product is composed of; whether some parts can be eliminated through better design, or have any unnecessary features removed;

— if certain parts can be standardised to match parts of other products and so enable the use of the same machines, tools, jigs or fixtures;

— whether some components can be replaced by cheaper ones which would yet perform the same function (for example in the chemical or cosmetic industries some fillers can easily be replaced by others);

— whether the design lends itself to easy handling.

The consultant knows that products have to be matched with the equipment on which they are manufactured (e.g. with its dimensions, precision, productivity and cost), and vice versa. In a number of cases he may have to examine this relationship and make recommendations to the client concerning either the product, or the equipment used, or both.

---

[1] See p. 325.

The *utilisation of materials* is another important aspect. Its examination includes not only the main materials used in making a product but also other items such as packaging materials, fuel, paints and lubricants.

The consultant needs to look at the possibilities of minimising waste and improving the yield of various materials. He may also look at the possibility of reworking waste, utilising by-products and selling waste and scrap.

In enterprises which use and store a very extensive range of materials, the consultant may achieve improvements by helping to reduce this range or even introducing some standards in this area.

By enquiring about certain aspects of *product quality*, the consultant may be able to improve on the control of quality and even achieve savings. He may examine:

— the appropriateness of the established tolerance level from both the marketing and cost points of view (in some cases unnecessarily tight quality standards are established which can be quite costly);

— the position and frequency of inspection points, the need to establish new points or abolish others;

— the method of sampling used and its adequacy;

— the quality-consciousness of the workers and the influence of training on quality.

19.2 Methods and organisation of production

Flow of work and layout

Several symptoms can indicate the need for improving the layout:

— is bulky or heavy material moved further than smaller or lighter material?

— does the working place appear to be cramped because of machinery or equipment which is either inaccessible or too large for the available space?

— is there frequent backtracking of work in progress or cross flow with other products?

— are there signs of congestion in some areas, while others appear quite spacious?

— is housekeeping in order, and are premises tidy without much material lying about and blocking the flow?

— by the same token are aisles well marked and clear?

— is space utilisation adequate, particularly in the stores, and are overhead areas utilised?

Once the need for tackling a layout assignment becomes apparent, a consultant must collect information on the space requirements for machinery, storage, work in progress, auxiliary services (canteens, washrooms, telephone installations, etc.), calculate the space required, determine and plot the flow of work and then integrate the space needs with the flow so plotted.[1]

An important consideration, however, is that of making cost estimates of the proposed layout by comparing savings in space, equipment and labour costs with the cost of additional space, handling or storage equipment.

Materials handling

Through better handling of materials, a consultant can achieve lower costs arising out of larger unit loads, reduced waste and more even distribution of productive capacity. In his survey, a consultant may observe the following phenomena:

— too much manual loading and unloading, particularly of heavy materials, which can be hazardous;

— excessive temporary and disorderly storage;

— frequent damage or breakage during transport.

He can then make a diagram showing the movement of material in the area under investigation, and examine the type of handling equipment used, as regards speed, depreciated value, load, flexibility of use and maintenance needs.

In choosing substitute equipment, some guidelines are useful:

— economy in handling can be achieved as the size of the unit and speed of transportation are increased;

— equipment and methods that are versatile and can be used for several products are to be preferred to those that are mainly designed for one product;

— gravity should be used as much as possible rather than horizontal movements.

Catalogues of manufacturers, as well as materials-handling associations' literature, can be consulted for the choice of equipment. In this area, however, cost estimation of alternative means of handling should be balanced by value judgements.

---

[1] See, for example, ILO: *Introduction to work study* (Geneva, International Labour Office, 1979) or H. B. Maynard: *Industrial engineering handbook* (New York, McGraw-Hill, 1971).

Maintenance

The consultant should enquire about the methods used for maintaining and repairing equipment and machinery. In particular, he should find out:

— how normal greasing and lubrication is done and whose responsibility it is;

— if a preventive maintenance scheme exists, whether it is justified and how it is implemented;

— whether a proper inspection schedule exists;

— if a cost estimate of repairs is made and kept for each machine.

He should also enquire about emergency repairs and consider whether increasing the size of the maintenance crew could pay off in terms of less machine down time. In addition, a consultant can examine whether the life of certain individual components of equipment or machines could be prolonged through either redesign or change of lubricant. Finally, he should study machine replacement problems in relation to maintenance costs.

If major equipment is to be overhauled, especially in process industries, the consultant can help the client to achieve considerable savings by introducing scheduling for such operations (applying network planning techniques if necessary).

Job and work methods

Traditionally this has been an area where a good deal of a production consultant's time is spent. But as production operations become highly mechanised or automated, the scope for doing work in this area becomes more limited.

A consultant working in this field examines the way a certain operation is being performed and attempts to develop an easier and a more effective method. He utilises a number of well-known charts such as the operation chart, the flow chart, and man/machine and activity charts. He should also understand ergonomics, an essential element of job design.

While numerous jobs lend themselves to methods improvement, a consultant should give priority to those that are critical, because they either constitute a bottleneck or are repeated by a number of operators.

A consultant will find it most useful to invite workers', foremen's and managers' suggestions, to get them involved in the working out of a new method. In many cases, production workers and technicians will be able to point to improvements that can well escape the consultant.

Setting performance standards

This is probably one of the most intricate problems that faces a production consultant. Performance standards are needed for a variety of reasons including the determination of labour costs and hence the ability to decide in matters of pricing and bidding; in " make or buy " questions; in machine replacement problems and so on. Such standards are essential for production planning, wages and incentive schemes. Invariably a certain standard exists for every piece of work performed, though it may be a formal recorded standard or a perceived informal standard which a foreman or a worker estimates for a given job. The consultant is called upon in this area either to review a formal standard or to establish one. A crucial point is the need to perform the assignment with the knowledge and approval of the persons whose performance is to be assessed and of the trade unions.

Generally speaking, a consultant can use one of three methods: work sampling, a stop-watch time study or predetermined time standards. Alternatively he may opt for a combination of two or all of these methods at a given working place. For example, he may use work sampling to determine the allowances to be included in a " standard time " based on stop-watch observations.

Work sampling is probably the easiest and least controversial method of assessing the percentage of time worked and the distribution and causes of idle time. Since it is based on random observations, its reliability depends on sampling and sample size that can give a certain degree of confidence. Hence, if work sampling is to be attempted, a consultant should first determine what sort of confidence level is needed. The answer will depend on the intended use of his data. If he is interested merely in a quick estimation of the percentage of effective working time, the confidence level may be relaxed and sample size can be smaller.

Stop-watch time study is probably the most widely used method of measuring performance. Through sampling and timing, a consultant arrives at a certain " observed time for a given job ". This has to be converted into " normal time " by a process of performance rating in which he rates a certain pace of performance as " standard ". If he has been timing an operation which he rates as 80 per cent of this standard, then he has to adjust his " observed time " accordingly. However, performance rating is based on judgement and as such is a subject of controversy. Various suggestions have been made to cope with this problem, but rating is still based on the judgement of the observer to a great extent. Achieving a certain consistency can be enhanced both by experience and by cross-checking with other observers.

The transformation of a " normal time " into a " standard time " requires the addition of allowances for delays normal to the job, allowances for personal needs and fatigue allowances. The latter two, sometimes grouped together under the title of relaxation allowances, again raise controversy. Some research has been undertaken to determine what should be the fatigue allowance for a given job content and working conditions. It is difficult, however, to imagine an answer that can cater for all possible work situations. It is also uncertain whether research applicable to certain ethnic, climatic and other very specific conditions can be extrapolated to apply to different conditions. In making his assessment of allowances, a consultant should discuss them freely in order to achieve an agreement with both workers and management.

Predetermined time standards (PTS) offer certain advantages. They permit a quantitative means of comparing alternative methods of work without disturbing the existing methods and can be used even before an operation has been established. They also avoid the rating problem and hence help to develop more consistent standards. They do, however, suffer from several weaknesses. They are generally designed for mass production and can become expensive for individual jobs; they also have limitations in machine-controlled operations, and the basic idea on which they are based, i.e. motions can be added and subtracted, has been challenged.

Another issue is that over 200 different systems of PTS exist at present and are known by trade names, such as MTM, WF, DMT,[1] and so on, and a consultant has to decide which one is most appropriate for his purposes. He may, in this case, rely also on assistance not only from the literature but from associations such as the MTM Associations which exist in certain countries.

Before leaving this area, it may be useful to summarise the approach a consultant can follow to determine the standards of performance, and ensure consistency as much as possible. The main steps can be as follows:

(1) identify the jobs or activities for which standards are desirable, considering the cost and practicality of developing and applying such standards;

(2) on that basis determine the degree of coverage needed (standards to be established for all or certain jobs, departments and/or products);

(3) break the jobs into elements and attempt to have as many common elements as possible;

(4) decide whether he wants to use macroscopic systems (e.g. stop-watch time study) or microscopic systems (predetermined time standards) or a combination of both, in which case he decides what parts of the job will be measured by what system (the nature of the job and costs being a determining factor);

(5) if stop-watch time study is used, check for consistency among common elements performed in various areas of the workplace, and

---

[1] MTM = Methods-Time Measurement; WF = Work Factor; DMT = Dimensional Motion Times.

make sure he has enough data to enable an estimation of observed time with a required degree of confidence;

(6) if PTS is used make sure that the elements of the job can be readily deduced from the system of PTS that was chosen; it is also preferable to make spot checks with a stop-watch to verify whether PTS timetables do not need readjustment (this may become necessary when using a PTS table in another culture).

Needless to say, the development of performance standards assumes that the method of work has already been improved or cannot be varied, since any change in the working method would necessitate another standard setting.

Production planning

The choice of the planning method to be used depends on the nature of the operation. In normal process and mass production operations, various methods of planning can be applied ranging from the sophisticated use of mathematical models for queuing or waiting line to normal scheduling and charting. However, when planning is intended for a special project with a long lead-time, such as the building of a ship or the construction of a plant or a building, network planning may be used since it allows for a more rational use of resources and enables a comparison to be made of various cost-time combinations.

In the case of production that is geared to distribution (as distinct from special projects such as the manufacturing of airplanes, large diesel engines, steam turbines or ships) the starting point for a planning process is the forecast of demand which is established with the assistance of the marketing department. A production consultant should check on the reliability of such a forecast before going into production planning itself. A discrepancy between sales forecasting and production planning can result in either lost orders or carrying excess inventory, and is often a subject of contention between the marketing and production managers and their staff. In addition to the forecast which is translated into an aggregate of operations for various products in the product mix, the consultant has to calculate the machine hours required for each product component, determine the total working time and introduce a certain flexibility in his planning system to allow for emergency situations.

The difficulty often lies in the fact that there are *bottleneck operations*, but instead of concentrating on them many consultants gear their planning and scheduling to all operations. An effective analytical and planning exercise should indicate shortages of machine or operators' hours in certain work centres and present proposals in that respect to management.

It is important, once a production plan is established, that a control system for reporting and feedback be also set up to check on the progress and to correct future plans accordingly.

In the case of special project network planning, using techniques such as CPM or PERT [1], the crucial task for the consultant is to consider the use of alternative schemes, each with its cost factor, time limit and specific requirements on organisation and control of operations.

Planning of production, particularly with a large product mix or where hundreds of components are involved, becomes far more manageable if a computer is used. [2] This is also usually true of planning networks containing more than 200 activities.

Inventory control

Most consultants approach the problem of inventory control by analysing values to determine the " A " items (few in number but most costly) as distinct from " B " and " C " items (the latter being the great multitude of relatively cheap items that are carried in stock).

An ordering strategy is then developed for the " A " items which rests on the use of inventory models to determine the economic order-quantity by balancing ordering costs against carrying charges. The required buffer stock is then calculated by balancing opportunity costs (the probability of lost sales if one runs out of stock) against carrying charges. For the " B " items ordering is carried out through regular review of stock or whenever a minimum level is reached, and for " C " items mass orders may be placed at certain points in time.

This is in effect the ideal situation. In actual practice, the skill of the consultant depends on his ability to move from the ideal to the practical. For example, in the case of a wholesaler of various widths and varieties of lumber, a comparatively arbitrary choice must be made of the items to be classified as " A " items. In addition, the economic order-quantity may prove impractical for various reasons. If the lumber wholesaler imports certain varieties from, say, the USSR or Canada, shipping is not always possible during the winter season, hence the need to readjust ordering points. Apart from that, an order-quantity may prove too small to be shipped to a distant area or an attractive discount can be obtained if the quantity is increased.

The question of buffer stock also needs careful consideration. In many cases uncertainty of sources of supply or of transportation, the availability of foreign exchange or the anticipation of inflationary trends necessitate a reassessment of the level of buffer stock to be carried.

---

[1] CPM = Critical Path Method; PERT = Programme Evaluation and Review Technique.

[2] See Chapter 20.

The objective of the above discussion is not to dissuade a consultant from applying scientific methods to inventory control, but to impress on him that once such inventory strategies have been devised, they should be discussed with management and readjusted if need be.

The organisation of stock records is another area for intervention. In some cases the feasibility of introducing computerised inventory systems should be investigated. In other cases it might even be possible to do away with record-keeping and depend on physical control for the sake of simplicity. For example, a retail outlet keeping several " in-out " stock records for an item like ribbons (a " C " item) depending on their width, colour and material, may well be advised to discard such entries in favour of a simple visual method such as the " two-bin " system.[1]

19.3 The human aspects of production

The human element is the determining factor in any operation. It would be naive to propose, let alone implement, any recommendation without the involvement of the people concerned and without examining the impact on people. There are four major areas in production management consultations to be considered in this respect.

Physical working conditions

The consultant should pay attention to the measures at the place of work to protect the worker from adverse conditions with respect to temperature, humidity, light and noise levels, as well as air-contaminants, dust and radiant energy, exposure to which may cause poisoning or occupational diseases. In many cases, safety standards exist, but whether they are applied is a different matter.

Secondly, an enquiry should be made as to whether adequate health care, including emergency and sanitation facilities, exists and if a health education programme, particularly in plants dealing with hazardous products, is operational.

Safety

It is not uncommon to find management concentrating on the so-called technical aspects of accident prevention, i.e. the provision of protective gloves, boots or goggles, and guards for machinery. In most plants, however, well over

---

[1] A system whereby stock is divided and placed in two boxes etc.; when the first box is empty, this is a signal for reordering.

half of the accidents are caused more through human misjudgement and negligence than through the absence of guards or protective equipment.

Many revealing facts can emerge from an analysis from past records of accidents by cause, department, hour of the day and day of the week, or even by person. These can provide invaluable information that can advantageously be used for introducing a scheme of safety which should invariably include training.

Job satisfaction

Most production consultants are productivity conscious and neglect job satisfaction. The issue is extremely broad as many factors contribute to job satisfaction. However, in the context of a production shop, the process design, the method of work, the arrangement of the workplace and the organisation of work groups, affect the worker's satisfaction a great deal. To this extent, a consultant would do well to examine the implications his proposals have in this field and modify them, if need be, to achieve a balance between productivity and job satisfaction.

More specifically, he should consider the possibilities of both job enlargement and job enrichment. Task time cycles can be lengthened particularly in the case of tedious monotonous jobs, work can be made more varied by adding other tasks, such as routine maintenance, to it, or more authority may be delegated to a worker to make his own decisions on certain matters connected with his work.

Jobs may be enriched by designing work around a group rather than individual activity, and by giving these groups a certain degree of autonomy to allow them to interchange tasks and conduct more interesting and varied jobs.

Involvement

A good deal of the success of a production consultant depends on his ability to get people involved in the diagnosis of the problems, in preparing proposals and in implementation. A consultant who approaches his assignment with a feeling of knowing all the answers and wanting to impose his views will invariably fail. There are many technical and human aspects of each job that have to be taken into consideration when designing or modifying an operation, and a consultant cannot be expected to know every detail. He may be surprised to find how readily people will respond to his enquiries and offer helpful suggestions or improvements if they feel he is sincere, appreciates their views and has their needs and interests at heart.

CONSULTING IN INFORMATION SYSTEMS AND DATA PROCESSING 20

This chapter deals with consulting in two closely related areas. The first—information systems—can form part of any general or functional management assignment (without necessarily touching upon the technology used to process information). The second—data processing—will usually require examination, and frequently substantial redesign of both the information system and its processing methods. Before dealing with computer applications and their relationship to the management problems as seen and handled in management consulting, we will first discuss the more general and basic issues of management information systems.

20.1 Information versus decision and control systems

No information system is an end in itself. An experienced consultant is well aware of this, but in practical situations this apparently obvious general truth takes the form of more specific questions and answers. Frequently, the consultant hears managements' complaints about the absence of appropriate information, or about the excessively long delays with which information is submitted to managers—delays owing to which too many opportunities may be missed.

If this is the problem submitted to the consultant, he should examine the relationship between information and the various types of managerial action for which this information may be needed. What to management appeared to be simply an information problem may be revealed as a weakness in the decision system: for example, are delivery lead times being agreed without reference to those responsible for production scheduling or raw materials supply? A whole new area of enquiry into organisational structure and relationships is thus opened up and the consultant must ensure that his client approves a change in the terms of the assignment to permit such an enquiry.

Arguments the consultant can justifiably employ include:

— improving availability of information without making sure that it will be purposefully used achieves very little;

— the extra time and effort required to look at the decision system in greater depth may be more than offset by savings on hardware or systems development costs;

— many a detailed problem analysis intended to lead to developing a computer-based system has solved the problem without recourse to a computer.

Management, however, may employ arguments such as:

— they want a computer even if they don't really need one;

— " Old Bill ", responsible for negotiating suppliers' lead-times, can only be brought into line by the exigencies of computer discipline (" let's blame it on the computer "); which means, in other words, that weaknesses in the decision system will be patched automatically by the superior quality of information (especially if this is processed by a computer), and that organisational relationships will evolve to facilitate new information flows.

The consultant may have to work within these constraints, in which case he must pay special attention, at the implementation stage, to day-to-day arrangements for furnishing and utilising the information provided.

20.2   How much information, when, and how

If client and consultant have agreed that part—at least—of the problem can be solved by improved information, the consultant may now face difficulties in controlling a process which he himself has set in motion. Initially he will have worked hard to broaden management's notions of the types of information that could be made available and the uses to which that information could be put. But having fired a new enthusiasm for information the consultant may have to restrain management's tendency to want to know about everything, all the time, from a multiplicity of analytical directions. The consultant must keep firmly in view the use to which information is put and the difference between vital information and that which it " would be nice to have ", and help his client to maintain the same perspective.

This can be achieved quite painlessly if the client is made aware that information has both a cost and a value. The value of information is notoriously difficult, but by no means impossible, to quantify. For example, " if we have current and accurate information on suppliers' lead-time promises and performance for sub-assemblies and a contingency margin on components to allow us to build in the event of non-delivery, then we can reduce stockholdings by 15%". Cost is less difficult. Certainly the client can have a data base and a data base management system which will immediately answer virtually any query, but at what cost! The consultant has a responsibility to make his client aware of the cost/benefit aspects of information and to justify information system proposals with cost/benefit analysis.

There are also various " when " and " how " questions to be asked. Are stock status reports, debtor analyses, machine loading statements, etc. needed monthly, weekly, daily, hourly, instantly, and to what level of detail? Is it equally important that a production schedule be accessible both by job number and machine number? The consultant should be the objective arbiter between conflicting requirements and priorities. He may require specialist help in assessing the implications of a certain information request on the structure of a data base and on processing complexity; however his objective should be to present his client with costed alternatives (with ensuing benefits), a statement of where the law of diminishing returns begins to apply, and his own recommendations based firmly on the foreseen utility of information.

20.3 Systems improvement and integration

All organisations have a multiplicity of existing information systems both formal or informal, at a number of levels, and of varying degrees of effectiveness and relevance. The consultant needs to determine:

  (i) the extent to which existing systems, if " cleaned up " and adjusted to provide information at the right level and in the right form, could satisfy newly identified needs;

  (ii) the degree of compatibility between systems, and the extent to which they interact;

  (iii) whether to recommend improvement (in accuracy, currency, form, content, etc.) of existing systems, thereby minimising supporting structural changes, or to adopt a " clean sheet " approach which, although less easily assimilated, is unencumbered by " we've always done it this way " attitudes;

  (iv) given that few information systems stand alone, whether to plan for over-all systems improvement (in which all the interactions between sub-systems are clearly perceived) or to concentrate on a crucial functional area or decision level.

It should be remembered that because of the dynamism of information requirements and the complexity of organisational relationships, total integration of an organisation's information system may be practically impossible. It may be wiser, as a start, to aim for vertical integration within a function (for example, operational-level production reports for first-level supervisors, shop production summaries for middle management, departmental output and cost statements for senior management) or horizontal integration between functions (information between sales, inventory, production and finance, etc.). Valuable as master plans and strategies are, the client wants tangible results from his information system.

Any degree of systems integration requires the existence of data files which serve the needs of multiple users. However a frequent obstacle to effective integration has been the failure to rationalise different versions of the same data which exist simultaneously in an organisation. Costing and pricing data held in sales, cost and accounting departments are good examples of data files which by reason of differences in use, frequency of updating, and perhaps the criteria used to establish values (marginal costing versus absorption costing) may be incompatible. The consultant should take care to discover why differences exist and ensure that different user needs are satisfied by the integrated file. The implications for all users of changes in master data should be appreciated and agreement reached on common updating procedures and responsibility for file maintenance.

20.4 Computer data processing

At some point of an assignment dealing with information systems the consultant may be asked the question: " Could we (or should we) use a computer? " Or he may himself raise the same question if, in his assessment, the client organisation is able to respond to innovations which may have far-reaching effects.

System feasibility

The first important question is one of feasibility. The problem with many computer-based information systems is that although they are technically feasible (i.e. they work on the computer) they do not work effectively in the larger environment of the organisation as a whole. Typical of this situation is the sophisticated computer system processing " garbage " (inaccurate data). For example, most computer-based systems presuppose the availability of accurate input data presented in a specific, often exactingly accurate, form according to an equally exacting schedule. Can the client organisation guarantee such inputs?

It may well fall to the management consultant to determine whether, under present conditions, a system will work outside the data processing department, or whether the conditions for success can be created. The starting point is to ensure that the output from the system is what is needed in terms of its basic content, its degree of summarisation, its accuracy, frequency and currency, its presentation, etc., subject to the compromise between perfection and cost and the observance of other criteria for effective systems implementation referred to above.

On the input side the consultant should be on the look out for illogicalities in the designated sources of data. For instance, the fact that the stores controller has always supplied certain data does not mean that he is necessarily the only—or best—source, particularly if data are now required in a modified form, with a greater degree of accuracy, or at a different point in a procedure. Generally speaking data will be provided faster and more accurately if they form part of the normal operations of an organisational unit. The consultant should avoid proposing data origination and collection tasks which are extraneous to normal work content, do not result in any feedback (other than brickbats) for the furnisher, or which demand accuracy, frequency or exactitude of presentation beyond his capabilities. It is not realistic to demand unsoiled machine-readable production batch slips from the oil-stained hands of a machinist; yet many a sophisticated system has been predicated—and has foundered—on just such assumptions. Clerical accuracy demands clerical training, and it is up to the consultant to make this clear if he is in any doubt about the feasibility of his or others' input proposals.

File creation

The consultant may also have a role to play in the frequently under-estimated task of file creation. A system master file for order allocation, stock control, despatch and billing contains data elements from files held in a number of separate departments (order processing, pricing, stock records, warehouse, despatch, invoicing etc.). Collation of this data needs careful planning and a broad perspective which may be beyond the capabilities, or the authority, of the systems designer. Points for the consultant to watch include:

(i) the accuracy and currency of data at the time of transfer to the computer file (can the transfer of stock balances be made immediately after a physical stock check? is it feasible to mount such a check other than in a slack trading period? can the transfer be made progressively, and if so what are the problems of control?);

(ii) availability of files (can the order section release their pricing files for transfer to the computer file? what happens to price changes notified during the transfer period?);

(iii) need for extra staff (since the " old system " must continue to operate during the transfer period, can the additional tasks of file creation and validation be undertaken without the need for extra staff? how can work be organised and responsibilities assigned so as to create maximum contributions and minimum disruption?);

(iv) the feasibility and desirability of parallel running (can the " old " and " new " systems run in parallel? if so, for how long? what happens if the results disagree? is there a real commitment to the new system?).

The consultant—client relationship in computer applications

Earlier chapters stressed the importance of this relationship and made it clear that " ultimate success is a joint accomplishment ".[1] In few other consulting fields is it so essential that this axiom be taken to heart, for a great many of the problems that beset organisations in their attempts to use computers are the direct result of management's reluctance to become involved in the development of computer-based systems. Apparent technical complexity and specialist jargon have created psychological barriers which many managers have found difficult to cross, thus the computer specialist has been left to develop systems which work to his satisfaction but not necessarily to management's. It is clear that a key determinant of success in information systems development is the creation of a partnership between the information systems designer and the users of information. This partnership depends on the *informed* (not blind) commitment of top management to the over-all objectives of an information system and to the investments in time and money which it entails, and the working involvement of those whom the system will service in specifying requirements, ensuring system feasibility, and agreeing and contributing to the systems design at each stage in its development.

The management consultant is better placed than the computer technician to ensure the full participation of management. He has a clear responsibility to educate management to a full understanding of the potential and limitations of computers in the provision of information, and can bridge, at least temporarily, the gap between technician and user. Finally, since his work concerns the organisation and management of an enterprise to attain its objectives, he can make management aware that an information system which truly responds to key decision needs will inevitably reshape the organisation it serves. If this reshaping is a conscious effort, undertaken jointly, so much the better.

---

[1] See Chapters 1 and 3.

Limitations on the management consultant's intervention

It therefore follows that a management consultant, whatever his specialisation, must be properly prepared to handle questions concerning possible computer applications in his field of competence. Initially, most computers in commercial and industrial enterprises were installed to process accounting data; thus many well-established consulting organisations in the management information systems and computer field are offshoots or divisions of financial and accounting consultants. Nevertheless, over the years the use of computers in other management areas has become widespread, and a production, marketing or personnel management consultant may expect to be called upon to offer advice on computerised planning or control systems in many types of assignment. The extent to which the management consultant can offer detailed advice on, say, the design of a computer-based production scheduling system will depend on his training and previous experience. However the consultant should familiarise himself with the main applications in his field to which computers have been successfully applied (including the availability of application packages), the orders of magnitude of expense and the pre-requisite conditions for success, the data requirements of the system and their possible organisational impact, the probable time-scale for implementation, and the main characteristics of specialised hardware, particularly that used for data collection.

If the stage is reached where technical decisions outside the range of his experience are required, and the client lacks the necessary expertise " in-house ", then the management consultant should enlist—or advise his client to enlist—specialist services; however there is usually a long road to tread before that point is reached. The management consultant should use his general problem-solving skills, supplemented by his knowledge of computer *applications*, to resolve many of the " if " and " where " questions pertaining to computer use. Only when a clear case for computer use has been made, based on the criteria of cost-effectiveness and feasibility set out above, should the details of data and file handling and processing, hardware capabilities, operating systems, etc. be determined and further specialist help be sought if required. In this connection, it is important to distinguish between the various types of activity falling under the heading of " computer consulting ". Computing is rapidly becoming as polyvalent as management itself; thus consulting specialities have grown up in

— equipment (hardware) selection, installation and operation;
— operating systems, application packages and data base management (software);
— on-line and real-time systems and data communication;

— data processing standards;

— staff selection, recruitment, career planning, training, and professional development;

— the myriad sub-disciplines within the broad spectrum of computer utilisation.

20.5 Some organisational options offered by computer technology

Having asserted that an information system will reshape an organisation, we must sound a word of caution. The advent of large-scale computer facilities, integrated information systems, data bases and data management systems has produced a trend towards centralisation, a trend supported by economies of scale in the acquisition of equipment. However, falling hardware costs, and in particular the availability of mini-computers, remote job entry stations, intelligent terminals, etc., have highlighted the alternatives to full centralisation. Furthermore, centralisation of data processing does not necessarily imply a fully centralised information system and supporting organisation, nor does the centralisation of certain functions preclude decentralised processing where appropriate.

The management consultant may choose from a number of options, including:

(i) *central computing facility*, perhaps with on-line access from a number of decentralised locations, but employing an integrated data base;

(ii) *central computer with linked "front-end" mini-computers and/or intelligent terminals* which, in addition to controlling data transfer to and from the central computer, also provide local facilities for processing specific operational-level systems and editing data for entry to the central data base;

(iii) *central computer with independent mini-computers* where considerations of cost, loading, access time, data security, communication difficulties, etc., indicate the advantages of carrying out more routine, data-intensive batch-processing tasks on the central computer and fast response, on-line access jobs on a mini-computer;

(iv) *mini-computers alone* where processing volumes, communications problems, the independence of systems from each other, or a high degree of organisational decentralisation render a central processing facility inappropriate.

Many other hardware and software options exist, enabling the consultant to propose technical solutions which are not only the most appropriate from a processing standpoint but, in particular, harmonise with the organisational climate in which they will be applied.

20.6   We have a computer but it doesn't work

The previous sections have assumed that the consultant is advising on whether and how to use a computer as an aid to improving the effectiveness of an organisation. The consultant may also be asked to diagnose the failure of a computer system to do what someone (usually the computer vendor or an over-enthusiastic computer specialist) said it would do.

Typical complaints are:
— the information is late or out of date;
— the information is inaccurate;
— there's too much or too little detail;
— it's not what I wanted, so I don't use it;
— why didn't they ask me first?
— where does the computer get that figure from?

First of all, the management consultant should understand that it is most unlikely that machine failure is the cause of the trouble. What has failed is the system not the computer.

Unless the system is designed for the specific purpose of providing, say, accurate accounting data to meet a monthly deadline, the consultant should not get bogged down at the outset in questions of accuracy, currency, and degree of detail. It is more important to establish

— what the system is supposed to do,
— that the objectives were agreed with the user,
— that the user was involved in specifying his requirements and participated in the systems design;

then to move on to an analysis of what the user really wants from the system—if anything. If it is apparent that the system could be useful if . . ., then the consultant can start to concern himself with accuracy, timeliness and presentation and with feasibility aspects.

If, on the other hand, the system is the brainchild of a computer specialist or the panacea of the salesman, predicated on what they thought the user wanted from a limited range of pre-packaged " solutions ", then the consultant should advise his client to cut his losses and to take a fresh look at the problem area with a view to determining the real need for a decision-oriented information system, specified and designed with the full involvement of management.

Less common, but worth a little of the consultant's time, is the possibility that problems are caused by *ineffective management in the data processing department*. The management consultant may need to enlist specialist help if, for example, the quality of programming is called into question, but a computer department is, after all, a sophisticated production shop, and many of the criteria the consultant would use to form a first impression of a production shop are valid for the computer department. He will observe general housekeeping, layout, work flow; he should enquire into scheduling and control procedures and examine machine downtime and job turnround records (if they exist); he should ask for written or verbal job descriptions and discuss existing mechanisms for liaison with users, for error corrections, and for handling complaints and enquiries. If the outcome of this initial survey is disquieting he should take a closer look (possibly with specialist assistance) since it is highly probable that systems and programming work is also substandard.

CONSULTING IN PERSONNEL MANAGEMENT

21

The personnel management consultant deals with the " people " aspects of the organisation. The traditional content of consultations in this area used to focus mainly on personnel administration, job evaluation and wage schemes, but has expanded in recent years to include major aspects of human resources development and application of a broad range of tools and techniques of behavioural sciences to analyse organisations, develop more effective teams, and harmonise individual, group and organisational goals.

In many respects the personnel management consultant is expected to bring new knowledge into organisations, and act, therefore, as a resource consultant. Nevertheless, process consulting [1] is increasingly being used as the main approach to the solution of problems in personnel management, hence the need for consultants to be versed in the underlying concepts and experienced in the application techniques of process consulting.

21.1 Personnel policies and the consultant's audit

In the early stages of an assignment the personnel management consultant will usually be told that there are organisational policies for dealing with the major elements of the personnel function, e.g. recruiting, training, promotion and transfer, salary increments, labour-management relations etc. The consultant may first attempt to conduct an appraisal of existing personnel policies and procedures by investigating, analysing and comparing policies with actual results obtained over a set period by means of a systematic, in-depth audit.

Before commencing to prepare a research design to uncover the requisite hard data, the consultant is likely to find that the alleged " policies " may often

---

[1] See Chapter 2, p. 18.

only be pious hopes and good intentions. For a personnel policy to be worthy of the name it should fulfil several criteria:

    (i) policy should be written, understandable and present a comprehensive coverage of the function;

   (ii) provision should be made for ensuring dissemination and comprehension of stated policy throughout the organisation;

  (iii) policy should be soundly based, consistent with public policy and comparable organisations;

  (iv) policy should be internally consistent with the organisation's stated general objectives and policies;

   (v) specific personnel policies, e.g. staffing, development and administration, should be mutually supportive;

  (vi) policy should be established as a result of multi-level discussion and consultation throughout the organisation, including consultations with employees' representatives as appropriate.

The purpose of the personnel audit is to provide information on and explanation of personnel practices. To achieve this, information should be sought both vertically through the personnel department, and horizontally across other departments. In other words, the audit is conducted throughout the organisation.

The procedures for conducting the audit may vary considerably. Basically, they consist of obtaining information of a quantitative and qualitative nature from various records and reports supplemented by interviews, questionnaires, surveys, discussions, etc. Information may be obtained by means of a latitudinal study, e.g. a department-by-department assessment of safety records or absenteeism, in which the percentage of lost time and other ratios are calculated on a comparative basis. Alternatively, a longitudinal study may be used where a sample of individuals are examined in depth, with respect to the effects of the organisation's policies on their performance.

A recommended method for setting out a personnel audit is to list the organisation's policies in sequence, to set out the practices regularly employed by the organisation and the results obtained from the study and then draw the appropriate conclusions and recommendations. An example is given in Table 18.

A complete listing of personnel policies for audit purposes would include references to organisation; manpower planning; selection; transfers and promotions; assessment; training and development; communications; remuneration and allowances; job evaluation; fringe benefits; social and welfare benefits; safety and health; industrial relations; discipline; motivation; and administration.

Table 18. The personnel audit (data for the last 12 months)

Stated Policies	Regular Practices	Results of Audit
1. Recruitment To promote, where possible, from within the organisation.	Recruitment from external sources is an on-going and continuous procedure.	95% appointments made from external sources. High staff turnover of 65% per annum.
2. Training No stated policy.	Organisation sends two senior staff members to courses conducted by professional associations at request of individuals concerned.	Staff claim only limited opportunities for promotion and development, feel they have to go elsewhere to " get on ".
3. ...... etc.	......	......

The results of the personnel audit should, if necessary, point out the need for definition, refinement or rewriting of organisational policies. In a similar manner a review of the regular practices may suggest improvements to facilitate conversion of policies to procedures. Inadequacy or total absence of data indicates that urgent attention is required in the field of personnel administration.

Effective personnel administration is the only means whereby management is able to use the personnel audit as a mechanism for telling its story and demanding a fair hearing from its assessors. It is also the machinery which permits the checking, testing and evaluating of managerial performance in the personnel field. Consequently, appropriate, comprehensive and meaningful records and reports describing the results obtained from the personnel policies need to be established and maintained, and the consultant in personnel management will be required to act as a resource and process consultant in this field. It can be recommended that record forms for individuals be prepared which will accommodate all pertinent data concerning the personnel function and will also permit easy assessment of the grouped information (e.g. accidents, overtime, etc.) required for the personnel audit in future periods.

21.2 Methods for improving personnel management

The following notes touch briefly on the subject areas for which a personnel management consultant's specialist services are required.

Staff selection

The selection of one person rather than another for a specific position is usually based on the universal and constant phenomenon known as individual differences. In many instances, procedures and techniques are readily available for identifying and measuring the traits and abilities required in the selection and placement of personnel. The principal selection techniques are testing and interviewing.

Testing involves collecting and examining samples of candidates' behaviour and using them to predict likely future performance. The present trend seems to be to employ achievement tests (i.e. measures of existing skills and knowledge) rather than ability tests (i.e. potential) as the former possess greater validity in predicting occupational performance. Meanwhile consultants have also realised that obtaining the " right " person, with the precise profile called for in the job description, is usually hard to realise and a real need exists to relate testing to manpower planning and staff training programmes to make good the noticeable shortfalls in requisite skills, knowledge and attitudes amongst those finally selected.

Interviewing is a useful diagnostic tool but is recognised to have many imperfections as a predictor of future job performance. Consultants should be well aware of the need for thorough and deliberate training in this technique, and should ensure that clients are aware of the restrictions of this management tool.

Career planning and development

The planning and development of people's work careers [1] is becoming a matter of concern to management in a growing number of organisations. Although personnel management consultants have done little work in this area hitherto, it can be expected that their advice will be increasingly sought. The consultants should prepare themselves to deal with problems such as:

— identifying the principal career paths available to various categories of personnel and defining new paths that management would like to promote;

— analysing organisational, educational, cultural, social and other obstacles which people have to surmount, and in many cases cannot surmount, in their careers;

— installing a system whereby individual workers and other employees will be stimulated to plan their own life careers;

— defining career development policies for the organisation as well as measures (information, training, transfers, etc.) to support and facilitate advancement in careers;

---

[1] See M. S. Kellog: *Career management* (New York, American Management Association, 1972) and ILO: *Career planning and development* (Geneva, International Labour Office, 1976).

— devising career paths for those who are not likely to reach managerial and other senior positions for various reasons.

Staff and organisation development

Recognition is rapidly being accorded to the benefits of a planned approach to development of worker and managerial resources. There is a growing interest in combining staff development with career planning, organisation development and other programmes helping people to improve their working life and gain more satisfaction from it.

A personnel management consultant may advise his client in the following areas:

(i) on the identification of staff development *needs*, in which case the consultant will endeavour to define these needs in relation to the main development trends and long-term objectives of the client organisation; in this framework specific training needs related to particular jobs, or groups of jobs, should be defined;

(ii) on the elaboration of staff development *policies, plans and programmes*, which may be made for several years ahead and include the planning of financial resources for programme implementation;

(iii) on the choice of staff development and training *methods and techniques* appropriate to the various categories of personnel and reflecting the financial and other possibilities of the client organisation;

(iv) on the *use of external training facilities*;

(v) on the *organisation of the training function* and *training of trainers* within the organisation (the consultant would not, of course, offer to design training programmes in special fields outside his own field of competence);

(vi) on a *programme of organisation development*, using methodology corresponding to the culture of the client organisation (viz. its behavioural norms, procedures and climate).[1]

Job evaluation

Because of the widespread ramifications likely to emerge from job evaluation assignments, the consultant is well advised to consult with trade union representatives as well as with management and individual workers. Trade union officials are particularly well placed to advise on special factors likely to

---

[1] See Chapter 4, p. 35.

affect the job rating, such as the need to consider shortages of skilled labour for the jobs being reviewed, existing or planned bargaining agreements or special allowances for seniority of workers.

Many techniques are available for job evaluation but, depending on the job in hand, the order of complexity of the system employed usually moves from (1) job ranking schemes through (2) job classification to (3) points systems and to (4) factor comparison methods.[1]

Motivation

Every organisation whose purpose is to achieve certain economic and social objectives, but which has only limited resources at its disposal, tries to motivate its personnel towards the achievement of a range of goals, which may include societal, organisational, group and individual ones.

A personnel management consultant may be requested to assist in determining what motivational tools and strategies should be used. This may concern, for example:

— the improvement of the over-all organisational climate, the underlying assumption being that this climate, which is determined primarily by the attitudes and behaviour of the leading personalities in managerial positions [2], strongly affects the motivation of people at all levels in the organisation to work and achieve;

— the enrichment of job content, where, by means of changing the structure of the work to be performed, the consultant endeavours to assist in creating intrinsic job interest [3];

— reward systems, where the appropriate behaviour is shaped as a result of certain rewards, in particular financial and material ones; there should, therefore, be a feedback system, so that the incentive used (e.g. pay) is tied as directly as possible to actual performance.

The methods outlined do not operate independently, but affect separate components of the motivational process and call for different levels of intervention on the part of the organisation, and of the consultant. In many assignments, however, the consultant may be requested to assist above all in the examination and reorganisation of the wage and salary system. Logically, the consultant approaches such a problem by conducting a job analysis,

---

[1] For specific techniques see P. Pigors and C. Myers: *Personnel administration* (New York, McGraw-Hill, 1969), G. McBeath and D. Rands: *Salary administration* (London, Business Books, 1976) and ILO: *Job evaluation* (Geneva, International Labour Office, 1960).

[2] See also Chapter 16, p. 178.

[3] Cf. Chapter 19, p. 205.

followed by job evaluation and the building of job structure so as to develop an equitable salary structure and plan which will accommodate periodic reviews, supplementary remuneration and appropriate fringe benefits.[1] As in the case of job evaluation, the consultant cannot see wage and salary problems as purely technical ones and has to be well informed on industrial relations practices related to wages, especially on collective bargaining.

Performance evaluation

Experience has shown that performance ratings generally improve in accuracy as performance levels increase. Unfortunately, experience also shows that performance evaluations as practised in many organisations are usually not objective measures but subjective assessments made by supervisors.

The consultant must realise that evaluations have to be related to actual performance, that raters require training in performance appraisal techniques, and that sensible performance evaluations commence with well-established organisational, departmental, group and individual goals, and are effectively executed by having both required and actual performance levels recorded, measured and compared. Before examining performance evaluation in a client organisation, the consultant should also find out whether its conclusions are used for training, promotion, remuneration, etc. An assignment in performance evaluation is of little use if the management of the client organisation is not able to use its results for any reason.

21.3 Consulting in labour-management relations

Several references have already been made to the need for consultants to take into account industrial relations practices and implications in respect of particular subjects falling within the personnel management function. In this section a brief look will be had at the various points that a consultant in labour-management relations should bear in mind when entering into a consultancy, particularly in an enterprise with which he has little familiarity. Technical advice in this field is in many cases provided by labour-management relations specialists. This does not mean that a personnel management consultant could not develop expertise and provide advice in this area, but he should be well informed and aware of the social, legal, political and financial implications connected with labour-management relations in the given country, sector and particular organisation.

The consultant may be called in because there are problems in labour-management relations under an existing situation, because there are internal or

---

[1] See McBeath and Rands: op. cit.

external forces that are likely to lead to problems in labour-management relations, or where advice is needed in the initial formulation or reformulation of labour-management relations policies. In each case a key question will be the presence or absence of a trade union in or for the enterprise and, where trade union representation does exist, the nature and role of that representation.

The substantive questions of labour-management relations that the consultant may be called upon to face could include one or more of the following:

(1) Advice on dealing with workers' representatives on a day-to-day basis. These may be trade union representatives or representatives directly elected by all the workers with no or only indirect links with a trade union.

(2) The mechanics of handling workers' grievances, including advice on the setting up of grievance procedures.

(3) Collective bargaining and, in particular, management organisation for collective bargaining. The significance of this question will depend to some extent on the level at which bargaining takes place (for the industry as a whole; for the industry in a particular region or locality; for a group of enterprises; or at the enterprise level). But in most cases where there is a trade union presence in the workplace, a certain degree of collective bargaining, be it of an informal character, will take place in the enterprise even if more formal or official bargaining takes place at a higher level.

(4) Machinery and procedures for management-worker consultation and co-operation on issues of common interest such as productivity, welfare facilities, etc. (as opposed to issues of an antagonistic nature such as grievances or bargaining demands).

(5) Dismissal and redundancy principles and procedures (whether within or without the context of collective bargaining).

The above is by no means an exhaustive list of concerns that a labour-management relations consultant may have to meet. But it does suggest some of the factors which a consultant will have to take into account in his advisory activity.

First, one could mention the relevant legal framework of labour-management relations at the enterprise level. This framework, which is highly individual to particular countries, might reflect rules on: trade union recognition; workplace workers' representation; collective bargaining procedures; dispute settlement (including work stoppages); forms of workers' participation in decisions within the enterprise; the formation and content of individual contracts of employment, etc. In charting courses of action to be recommended to clients, consultants of necessity must take account of existing legal rules. It is obvious that substantive rules on conditions of employment must also be taken into consideration. And where necessary, in particularly complex situations for example, recourse might be had to the services of a qualified lawyer specialising in labour law.

But rules resulting from legislation are only one of the significant sets of norms to be considered by the consultant. In virtually all cases of an established enterprise or industry there will be labour-management relations customs, usages and practices which often require the same respect that legal rules may require. At times these customs, usages and practices are common to a region or locality. It is essential that the consultant be fully aware of them.

The consultant must also be fully aware of the relevant provisions of any existing collective agreement that is applicable to the enterprise that he is advising (whether such agreement be for the industry, region or the enterprise itself).

It is also very important that the consultant be familiar, or make himself familiar, with the position and outlook of the workers' representatives who will be involved in any course of action that he might recommend, since possible reactions from the workers' side must be a determinant in such recommendations.

In addition, particularly in so far as the introduction of new labour-management relations policies is concerned, the consultant should recommend that every opportunity for consultations with workers' representatives should be seized. And he himself should, in consultation with the client, consider what contacts with workers' representatives would be appropriate before and during the framing of his recommendations.

The above paragraphs are intended only to give an idea of what some of the more important preoccupations of the labour-management relations consultant should be. It must be recognised that the innumerable and complex factors impinging upon labour-management relations make for a situation where each consultancy is highly particular and individual and where pre-established formulae must yield in most cases to tailor-made specific approaches.

While it is typically management that recruits the consultant, there may be cases where specialists, particularly in respect of very specific aspects of labour-management relations, are engaged jointly by management and the trade union and, sometimes, even by the trade union alone.

CONSULTING IN SMALL ENTERPRISE MANAGEMENT 22

The definition of a small enterprise tends to vary according to the nature of its activities. The criteria for considering a trading concern " small " are usually a limited number of employees or money value of sales. Industrial enterprises are so classified on the basis of the level of capital investment and/or a maximum energy requirement. Other small enterprises use various combinations of these and other factors as an operational definition. Nevertheless, in most discussions and writings on the subject it is conceded that a small enterprise is one in which the general and functional management are in the hands of one or, at most, two or three people who also make all the important decisions in that enterprise.

22.1 Characteristics, opportunities and problems of the sector

The consultant should be aware of factors which usually distinguish the small from the larger enterprise. Firstly, the small enterprise is normally financed from personal or family savings with limited recourse to outside finance during the formative stages. Secondly, the manager has close personal contact with the whole workplace and, thirdly, the enterprise operates in a limited geographical area. These factors greatly influence the consultative process.

In addition to these characteristics there are special opportunities and problems facing the sector which the consultant must know well.

The small enterprise possesses distinct *advantages*, including the ability to fill limited demands in natural markets; a propensity for labour-intensive, high-skill precision work; and flexibility to adapt rapidly to special demands and conditions.

Problems likely to beset a small enterprise are both general and specific in nature. Problems of a general nature involve the legal setting, access to credit and raw materials, lack of appropriate technical and managerial assistance, and so on.

Problems at the enterprise level do not necessarily occur in every instance but the consultant should keep them in mind as they may appear more formidable to the man who is in charge of a small enterprise than problems of a large corporation might appear to its chairman.

A management consultant should be aware, among others, of the following problems:

— whereas large, well-organised enterprises can afford both good line management and specialist staff, the small enterprise manager is a relatively isolated individual dealing with policy and operational problems simultaneously and having to face these problems despite his personal biases and limitations;

— the small enterprise manager often operates with inadequate or, at best, minimum quantitative data; in order to save operating costs he is likely to dispense with information systems, a weakness which becomes glaringly apparent should the enterprise reach a growth stage;

— because the small enterprise can usually only pay minimum wages, has few fringe benefits, offers low job security and few promotional opportunities, it is not unreasonable to expect that there is difficulty in recruiting high calibre employees;

— professional investors are seldom attracted to the new small enterprise and the manager is severely limited in his ability to raise initial capital; this problem is compounded when, as is often the case, the enterprise runs into operating difficulties and the manager attempts to raise additional finance to cope with crisis situations;

— related to this is the problem of limited financial reserves coupled with low capacity to borrow; as a result the small enterprise is vulnerable to economic downturn and recessions;

— although ability to change and adapt rapidly is a natural strength of a small enterprise, this quality may be nullified when the opportunity requiring rapid change suddenly appears, because the manager may be too occupied with on-going operational problems and badly placed to think about the future;

— the hand-to-mouth existence of the enterprise does not encourage opportunities for staff training and development, with the consequent loss of realising the full potential of human resources of the enterprise;

— the manager is not often able to understand and interpret government regulations, actions, concessions etc., to his best advantage.

22.2   The role and profile of the consultant

The consultant dealing with small enterprises handles *the whole spectrum of management* and is required to be more of a generalist than a specialist. It can be taken for granted that he requires professional training and experience in the principles of management and the critical elements of small enterprise development. Of prime importance is the knowledge of the interaction of functions of the enterprise since it is rare that change in one function does not have immediate repercussions in other functions. Furthermore, it is useful for the consultant to be familiar with the various "entrepreneurial" development approaches which have provided the conceptual basis for current small enterprise development practices.

As with any combination of skill and art, mastery of the fundamentals is essential for a successful career in consulting for small enterprises. When assisting the manager of a small enterprise it is important to ensure that all managerial tasks are completed, even if not perfectly, rather than have only 75% of the tasks completed to perfection, with the remaining 25% left neglected. The consultant must always keep in mind the " total " picture of the business in order to assist in seeing that all functions of administration and operation are harmonised in an integrated manner.

Patience and dogged perseverance is required in encouraging the manager to complete managerial chores ranging from accounting to staff training and preventing sole concentration on preferred technical activities, e.g. the actual manufacture of furniture.

That being said, the role becomes further complicated in that the consultant's main duties lie in development of the manager and other people contributing to the management of the enterprise, while he is expected to provide feasible practical solutions to a whole range of specific problems of finance, sales, production, purchasing and so on. In other words, the subject matter is specific, but as a rule exceeds the limits of a particular function or technique. The consulting technique is broad, including assistance with implementation wherever necessary, and informal training in many cases.

It is perhaps needless to add that the consultant's routine reports submitted to larger organisations do not apply in this case. Written reports should be short, simple and limited to an absolute minimum.

The consultant should also appreciate that his clients are not necessarily the best educated and skilled managerial resources required for the job in hand. Moreover, there are often no training facilities readily available to help remedy obvious deficiencies. Thus, rather than a professional air and emphasis on expertise to influence clients, a simpler style of coax, cajole, praise and reprimand is likely to be more effective in obtaining desired results.

The client-manager of the small enterprise is often known to suffer a severe sense of failure when forced to use the services of a consultant. The consultant, therefore, should be alert to the possible need to restore the client's self-esteem in addition to providing the more technically-oriented assistance usually required.

Unquestionably, lack of data is a major handicap in undertaking assignments with a small enterprise. Usually, the sole source of information is the manager who is "too busy" to be interviewed. This calls for ingenuity, persistence and tenacity on the part of the consultant to keep after his man until he extracts the required information.

During the last twenty years many governments, trade associations and chambers of commerce have established special services and facilities for small enterprises in industry and other sectors. These embrace, among others:

— supply of credit (loans and guarantees);

— reduced tax rates (to enable accumulation of capital necessary for survival and growth);

— preferential treatment for goods and services (special government subcontracts);

— industrial estates or parks;

— product design and quality control services;

— advisory services on export possibilities;

— economic, market and feasibility studies;

— advantageous purchases of raw materials, etc.

A manager or owner of a small enterprise may find it difficult to decide when and how to use such services. Although he will probably be able to obtain some advice directly from technicians who are in charge of a particular service, an all-round management consultant has to be able to advise on the whole range of services and make recommendations to the manager on priorities, and on the acceptable cost of a special service.

Good health and endurance are major assets. The small enterprise manager has little respect for conventional working hours, and once he overcomes his preliminary fears he quickly learns how to ask for help whenever and however he sees fit. Clients are often astonished to learn that consultants require time off for meals and might even wish to see their families on weekends or evenings. The consultant is very similar to the family doctor in that he is always on call—and some clients will, fortunately or unfortunately, take this for granted.

Responsibility is also disproportionate. In most conventional consulting assignments for large organisations there is some tolerance for error, reports are checked by supervisors and very important reports are examined by a manager of the consulting unit. However, when dealing with small enterprises, failure on the part of the consultant may mean annihilation of the organisation requesting assistance. As this assistance tends to be direct and immediate, the consultant has limited possibilities to check his ideas and proposals with his seniors. Not irreverently, the Asian Productivity Organisation has set out the role of the small enterprise consultant in the form of a " Consultant's Prayer ": [1]

" God grant me

COURAGE to change what I can,

PATIENCE to accept what can't be changed, and

WISDOM to know the difference ".

Timing may be a critical issue. The consultant is usually under extreme pressure since assistance is often not sought until a critical situation has developed.

22.3   Some practical consulting situations

The review of management problems dealt with by consultants in Chapters 16-21, includes a number of thoughts and experiences relevant to consulting in small enterprises. Nevertheless, there are some quite specific situations in which a small enterprise may use the consultant's help.

Situation 1 : At the very beginning

Biographical evidence suggests that successful small enterprise people, sometimes referred to as entrepreneurs (which definition has, in fact, wider implications than for small enterprises only) commonly possess distinctive qualities. They are often the first-born of a family or have had to assume a more than average amount of responsibility at an early stage in life. In many cases they are the offspring of self-employed persons, but not necessarily in the same occupational grouping, trade or service. Such people have had a sound but not necessarily extended education and, as a rule, more than five years' experience working in real-life conditions.

From a personality point of view they are inclined to be optimistic, moderate risk-takers as opposed to gamblers or no-risk-whatsoever types, and

---

[1] APO: *Productivity through consultancy in small industrial enterprises* (Tokyo, Asian Productivity Organisation, 1974), p. 28.

have a feeling that control over their own destiny rather than just making money is a key motivating factor in their life. Such people are usually married, with minimum distractions caused by family life—at least there is usually an understanding spouse who may not, in fact, care for the sort of life-style which results, but understands and appreciates the demands made on the marriage partner.

A key characteristic is that such successful types are mentally and physically very active. Success may result not so much from the quality, but from the quantity of schemes they prepare and develop. In short, the greater the effort, the greater the chances seem to be of success.

The consultant, when dealing with such a beginner, should take stock of his background and interests to ascertain whether he is dealing with a probable or a possible entrepreneur, and develop the assignment accordingly.

Situation 2: Starting up

Assuming that a client wishes to launch a new enterprise, the consultant should, after reviewing the proposal, prepare for three possibilities and develop appropriate contingency plans, viz.:

(i) what is the best that might happen;

(ii) what is likely to happen;

(iii) what is the worst that can happen.

The consultant should talk freely with his client about the first two possibilities, which are usually " creative " type problems, whereas the third alternative, which is a " corrective " type problem, should be reserved for his own counsel. In the first place the client is unlikely to listen to or agree with the " worst possible " alternative and, secondly, encouragement rather than discouragement should help to attain full potential of the proposal. The consultant must, however, draw up detailed contingency plans for all three alternatives if for no other reason than to make allowances for "Murphy's Law".[1]

A good small enterprise manager is usually capable of generating a great many ideas very rapidly. The consultant should encourage this and assist the client to obtain and record relevant quantitative data for two major reasons: first, to assist in making a logical choice between alternatives and, secondly, to use as supporting evidence should the manager experience uncomfortable afterthoughts about the scheme once he has started.

Mistakes will happen, particularly in the early stages—it is part of the general learning process. The consultant's task is to minimise errors made by

---

[1] " Murphy's Law ", put simply, states that " if anything can possibly go wrong—it will ! "

the manager in the early stages. It is, however, better to have an ineffective scheme fail in the early stages rather than to attempt to salvage an impossible project at a later date. There is a consulting maxim: " Giving birth is a lot easier than resurrection ". If necessary, the proposal may be allowed to lapse and the client encouraged to try afresh when more evidence and support is available. If it is decided to go ahead with the enterprise, full commitment should be encouraged. Effective decision making and action are vital: there is little room for compromise in the new enterprise.

From a functional point of view the consultant should encourage his client to use the services of some specialists from the outset if he can possibly afford them because, hopefully, as the enterprise grows they will be familiar with its history, practice and results, and thus be able to assist in a very meaningful way. The specialists include:

— *a legal firm* (of good repute and the best to be afforded),

— *an accountant* (possessing the same qualities as required of the legal firm),

— *a banker* (a man, not an institution, so that rapport and trust are established at a personal level),

— *an insurance agent* (similar qualities as required in the banker),

— *a marketing representative* (which may take several forms depending on the type of enterprise being developed; where the enterprise is not basically marketing-oriented, it is often sound practice to tie up with experts during the formative stages).

Reference has been made to the fact that a wide range of functional expertise is required in a small enterprise consultant. Perhaps the most important considerations revolve around financial matters, which are difficult both in terms of attracting formation capital and later in controlling expenses and income. A small enterprise management consultant who is not well versed in these activities is a danger to clients and cannot, in the true sense of the word, claim professional competence.

It is often only by means of thorough financial appraisal that the consultant is able to undertake the necessary though unpleasant task of recommending the discontinuation of an enterprise rather than encouraging a holding operation which will eventually lead to insuperable problems for all involved.

This fear of tragedy deserves greater emphasis in the start-up stages of the enterprise than may seem warranted. Often family and friends' savings are used to finance the capital requirements of the new enterprise simply because " no one else will lend the money ". This finding, alone, suggests that the scheme is probably not a particularly good one. If none of the surprisingly large number of financing agencies consider a proposal as worthwhile, (although they take into account a percentage allowance for failures), why should a consultant recommend that family savings be jeopardised for what is obviously a risky undertaking? By all means there should be proprietor equity in a venture, but not simply because no one else is prepared to support the scheme. When preparing the third (worst-of-all) contingency plan, if failure is likely to cause undue hardships the consultant is professionally obliged to dissuade his client from undertaking such a venture.

During the start-up phase the consultant might reflect on the following checkout routine which has been based on a considerable number of studies designed to pin-point potential problem areas in small enterprises. In descending order of importance for diagnosing trouble areas the consultant is likely to find deficiencies classified as the seven " M "s:

— managerial (lack of experience);
— monetary (lack of capital, poor cost control);
— material (poor location, too much stock);
— machines (excessive purchase of fixed assets);
— marketing (inappropriate granting of credit);
— mental (lack of planning for expansion);
— motivation (wrong attitudes to work and responsibility).

Situation 3: Getting bigger

Having weathered situations 1 and 2 the consultant is now rewarded by being presented with a brand new set of events which emerge as the enterprise commences to mature and the consulting approach takes on a progressive look. This is the right time for a thorough examination not only of weaknesses that have to be overcome, but, in particular, of opportunities for further development, and of alternative resource allocations that will help the enterprise to benefit from the most interesting opportunities. When assisting the manager to allocate resources, the consultant may refer to the 4 to 1 principle according to which, as a rule of thumb:

— 20% of the customers account for 80% of the business,
— 20% of stocks result in 80% of movements,
— 20% of staff causes 80% of the problems,
— 20% of salesmen create 80% of the sales, and so on.

The consultant should encourage the manager to " play percentages " and concentrate on appropriate critical areas. During this maturation phase of the enterprise the manager, submerged in day-to-day operational problems, often does not pay enough attention to long-term or medium-term planning essential for continued growth and survival. The consultant can assist by encouraging him to look to the future. For example, he can present organisation charts and attendant job descriptions and then prepare charts as they should look in five or ten years to show how the enterprise should change. New developments usually require a little inspiration, considerable incubation, and a whole heap of perspiration. Therefore the consultant should make sure that the manager plans appropriate resources and the time required for future developments.

One noticeable feature of successful managers is that they are exceptionally well organised. This virtue must be encouraged in management development. This requires introducing systems, encouraging managers to read on management subjects, and insisting on forecasts, budgets and controls. Probably during this maturation phase an accountant (financial controller) post should be established.

The consultant will also have to draw on his knowledge of comparable enterprises to judge the productivity of the client under review. Knowledge of a range of interfirm comparisons, in the form of input/output ratios, becomes an invaluable asset at this time, especially if corrective measures become the order of the day.

Situation 4: The end of the road

Eventually the manager finds that his enterprise may have grown to a stage where it can no longer be considered small, and issues to do with growth, finance, corporate structure, delegation and the like will arise. The small enterprise consultant should then judiciously refer the manager to specialists capable of assisting in the new situation.

Alternatively, the manager may decide he no longer enjoys the routine running of an enterprise and may prefer to start something new, revert to becoming an employee, retire or what have you. In any event, disposal of the enterprise becomes the crisis problem of the moment.

Assessment of the monetary value of an enterprise is usually made in any of three ways:

   (i) liquidation or forced sale value, where the enterprise is virtually put up for auction and sold to the highest bidder (if any);

   (ii) book value, where items are assessed at cost less depreciation and sold piecemeal to selected markets;

   (iii) market value, where the entity is sold as a going concern and items such as goodwill are included in the price.

Varying conditions (e.g. death of the owner) may determine which of these assessment methods will be used. Generally speaking, the market value method provides the best return to the seller.

The consultant is obliged to assist his client in obtaining the best possible deal. Nevertheless, the consultant should keep in mind that the best sales are those involving a willing seller and a willing buyer. To arrive at this happy situation the consultant should encourage the seller to " leave something in it " for the new owner. By doing so the chances of a sale are enhanced, time is often saved and the possible opportunities for recrimination are reduced. Trying to squeeze the last drop of money out of the new buyer can well carry the sale beyond the borders of diminishing return.

Another end-of-the-road situation occurs when the manager is succeeded by a member of his family or someone else. With small enterprises, apart from areas of obvious equality and responsibility, e.g. a partnership of doctors, lawyers, etc., it is seldom that shared management succeeds. For purposes of direction, control and responsibility it is usually better to have one identified manager, rather than to split the authority between, say, two brothers. There is a saying which has some bearing on this subject: " If you want a job well done choose one man, if you want half a job choose two, if you want no job at all choose three or more ".

As a general rule family succession in an enterprise should follow only after the offspring have been exposed, if possible, to working in outside situations, otherwise managerial in-breeding is likely to occur.

LITERATURE TO PART IV

Chapter 16 Consulting in general management

American Management Association: *A basic approach to executive decision making* (New York, AMACOM, 1978); 229 pp.

Ansoff H I.: *Corporate strategy* (Harmondsworth, Middx., Penguin Books, 1968); 200 pp.

Ansoff H. I.: *Strategic management* (London, Macmillan, 1979); 236 pp.

Bennis W.: *Organisation development: its nature, origins and prospects* (Reading, Mass., Addison-Wesley, 1969); 90 pp.

Dalton G. W., Lawrence P. R. (eds.), Lorsch J. W.: *Organizational structure and design* (Homewood, Ill., Irwin and Dorsey, 1970); 310 pp.

Drucker P.: *Management* (New York, Harper and Row, 1973); 840 pp.

Drucker P.: *Managing for results* (New York, Harper and Row, 1964); 240 pp.

Drucker P.: *The effective executive* (London, Pan Books, 1970); 180 pp.

Drucker P.: *The practice of management* (London, Pan Books, 1970); 480 pp.

Eden C., Harris J.: *Management decision and decision analysis* (New York, Halsted Press, 1975); 257 pp.

Galbraith J. R.: *Organization design* (Reading, Mass., Addison-Wesley, 1977); 426 pp.

Koontz H., O'Donnell C.: *Principles of management* (New York, McGraw-Hill, 1972); 760 pp.

Martin C. C.: *Project management: how to make it work* (New York, AMACOM, 1976); 312 pp.

Maynard H. B. (ed.): *Handbook of business administration* (New York, McGraw-Hill, 1967); 2050 pp.

McGregor D.: *The human side of the enterprise* (New York, McGraw-Hill, 1960); 246 pp.

Reddin W. J.: *Managerial effectiveness* (New York, McGraw-Hill, 1970); 350 pp.

Steiner G. A.: *Business and society* (New York, Random House, 1975); 610 pp.

Steiner G. A., Miner J. B.: *Management policy and strategy: text, readings and cases* (New York, Macmillan, 1977); 1014 pp.

Steiner G. A.: *Top management planning* (New York, Macmillan, 1969); 800 pp.

Chapter 17 Consulting in financial management

Accounting standards 1977 (London, The Institute of Chartered Accountants in England and Wales, 1977); 272 pp.

Beranek W.: *Working capital management* (Belmont, Cal., Wadsworth).

Carsberg B. V., Edey H. C.: *Modern financial management: selected reading* (Harmondsworth, Middx., Penguin Books, 1969); 411 pp.

Davidson S., Weil R.: *Handbook of modern accounting* (New York, McGraw-Hill, 1977); 1500 pp.

Frecar J.: *Financing decisions in business* (London, Accountancy Age Books, 1973).

Helfert E. A.: *Techniques of financial analysis* (Homewood, Ill. Irwin, 1972); 270 pp.

Horngren C. T.: *Cost accounting: a managerial emphasis* (4th ed.) (London, Prentice-Hall International, 1977); 934 pp.

Hunt P., Williams Ch. M., Donaldson G.: *Basic business finance* (Homewood, Ill., Irwin, 1966); 1020 pp.

ILO: *How to read a balance sheet.* An ILO programmed book (Geneva, International Labour Office, 11th impr. 1975); 124 pp.

Keller I. W.: *Management accounting for profit control* (New York, McGraw-Hill, 1957); 435 pp.

Kirkman P. R. A.: *Accounting under inflationary conditions* (London, Allen and Unwin, 1974).

Moroney M. J.: *Facts from figures* (Harmondsworth, Middx., Penguin Books, 1969).

Nickerson C. B.: *Accounting handbook for nonaccountants* (Boston, Cahners, 1975); 590 pp.

Newbould G. D.: *Business finance* (London, Harrap, 1970).

Robson A. P.: *Essential accounting for managers* (London, Cassell, 1968); 132 pp.

Samuels J. M., Wilkes F. M.: *Management of company finance* (London, Thomas Nelson & Sons Ltd, 1971); 518 pp.

Weston J. F., Sorge B. W.: *Guide to international financial management* (New York, McGraw-Hill, 1977); 409 pp.

Wilson R. M. S.: *Cost control handbook* (Epping, Essex, Gower Press, 1975); 500 pp.

Chapter 18 Consulting in marketing management

Buell G.: *Handbook of modern marketing* (New York, McGraw-Hill, 1970); 1400 pp.

Elliot K., Christopher M.: *Research methods in marketing* (London, Holt, Rinehart and Winston, 1973); 250 pp.

Fiber A.: *The complete guide to retail management* (Harmondsworth, Middx., Penguin Books, 1972); 320 pp.

Kotler P.: *Marketing management* (Englewood Cliffs, N. J., Prentice-Hall, 1972);
630 pp.

McCarthy E. J.: *Basic marketing, a managerial approach* (Homewood, Ill., Irwin,
1971).

Seibert J. C. *Concepts of marketing management* (New York, Harper and Row,
1973); 570 pp. (includes a useful bibliography).

Staudt T., Taylor D. A.: *A managerial introduction to marketing* (Englewood Cliffs,
N. J., Prentice-Hall, 1970).

Tull D., Hawkins D. I.: *Marketing research: meaning, measurement and method* (New
York, Macmillan, 1976); 736 pp.

Chapter 19 Consulting in production management

Barnes R. M.: *Motion and time study: design and measurement of work* (New York,
Wiley, 1968).

Biegel J. E.: *Production control, a quantitative approach* (Englewood Cliffs, N. J.,
Prentice-Hall, 1971); 295 pp.

Birchdale D.: *Job design: a planning and implementation guide for managers* (Epping,
Essex, Gower Press, 1975); 141 pp.

Bowman E. H., Fetter R. B.: *Analysis for production and operations management*
(Homewood, Ill. Irwin, 1967); 870 pp.

Buffa E. S.: *Operations management: the management of productive systems* (New
York, Wiley, 1976); 686 pp.

Gilchrist R. R.: *Works management in practice* (London, Heinemann, 1970); 216 pp.

Greene J.: *Production and inventory control handbook* (New York, McGraw-Hill,
1970); 800 pp.

ILO: *Introduction to work study* (Geneva, International Labour Office, 3rd edition,
1979); 442 pp.

Juran, J. M., Gryna F. M., Bingham R. S.: *Quality control handbook* (3rd ed.) (New
York, McGraw-Hill, 1974); cca 1600 pp.

Kanawaty, G. (ed.): *Managing and developing new forms of work organisation*
(Management Development Series No. 16) (Geneva, International Labour
Office, 1980); approx. 160 pp.

Larson S.: *Inventory systems and control handbook* (Englewood Cliffs, N. J., Prentice
Hall, 1976); 288 pp.

Lewis B. T.: *Developing maintenance time standards* (New York, Farnsworth, 1967);
428 pp.

Luck D. J.: *Product policy and strategy* (Englewood Cliffs, N. J., Prentice-Hall,
1972); 118 pp.

Maycr R. R.: *Production and operations management* (New York, McGraw-Hill,
1975); 660 pp.

Maynard H.: *Handbook of modern manufacturing management* (New York,
McGraw-Hill, 1970); 1100 pp.

Maynard H.: *Industrial engineering handbook* (New York, McGraw-Hill, 1971);
1980 pp.

Morris A.: *Analysis for materials handling management* (Homewood, Ill., Irwin, 1962)

Morrison A.: *Storage and control of stock for industry and public undertakings* (London, Pitman, 1967); 273 pp.

Muth J. F., Thompson G. L., Winter P. R. (eds.): *Industrial scheduling* (Englewood Cliffs, N. J., Prentice-Hall, 1963); 400 pp.

Muther R.: *Practical plant layout* (New York, McGraw-Hill, 1955); 370 pp.

Reed R.: *Plant location, layout and maintenance* (Homewood, Ill., Irwin, 1967); 193 pp.

Riggs J. L.: *Production systems: planning, analysis and control* (New York, Wiley, 1970); 604 pp.

Ross J. E.: *Managing productivity* (Reston, Virg., Reston Publishing Comp., 1977); 190 pp.

Starr M. K.: *Production management, systems and synthesis* (Englewood Cliffs, N. J., Prentice-Hall, 1972); 525 pp.

Stuart F., Farrell V.: *Purchasing; principles and applications* (Englewood Cliffs, N. J., Prentice-Hall, 1971); 460 pp.

Tersine R. J.: *Materials management and inventory systems* (New York, Elsevier North-Holland, 1976); 425 pp.

Walters R. W. and associates: *Job enrichment for results : strategies for successful implementation* (Reading, Mass., Addison-Wesley, 1975); 307 pp.

Whitmore D. A.: *Work study and related management services* (London, Heinemann, 1976); 338 pp.

Chapter 20 Consulting in information systems and data processing

Davis G. B.: *Computer data processing* (2nd ed.) (New York, McGraw-Hill, 1973); 662 pp.

Hartman W., Matthes H., Proeme A.: *Management information systems handbook* (New York, McGraw-Hill, 1969); cca 500 pp.

Kanter J.: *Management guide to computer system selection and use* (Englewood Cliffs, N. J., Prentice-Hall, 1970); 250 pp.

Li D. H.: *Design and management of information systems* (Chicago, Science Research Associates, 1972); 312 pp.

Murdick R. G., Ross J. E.: *Information systems for modern management* (Englewood Cliffs, N.J., Prentice-Hall, 1971); 560 pp.

Sanders D. H.: *Computers in business : an introduction* (New York, McGraw-Hill, 1975); 657 pp.

Tomeski E. A.: *The computer revolution* (New York, Macmillan, 1970); 270 pp.

Chapter 21 Consulting in personnel management

Armstrong M.: *Handbook of personnel management practice* (London, Kogan Page, 1977); 408 pp.

Craig R. L. (ed.): *Training and development handbook: a guide to human resource development* (2nd ed.) (New York, McGraw-Hill, 1976); 866 pp.

Courtis J.: *Cost effective recruitment* (London, Institute of Personnel Management, 1976); 92 pp.

Famularo J.: *Handbook of modern personnel administration* (New York, McGraw-Hill, 1972); 1200 pp.

Flippo E. B.: *Principles of personnel management* (4th ed.) (New York, McGraw-Hill, 1976); 592 pp.

French W.: *Personnel management process* (Boston, Houghton Mifflin, 1974); 760 pp.

Hamner W. C., Schmidt F. L. (eds.): *Contemporary problems in personnel* (Revised edition) (Chicago, St Clair Press, 1977); 510 pp.

ILO: *An introductory course in teaching and training methods for management development* (Management Development Manual No. 36) (Geneva, International Labour Office, 5th impr. 1977); 350 pp.

ILO: *Career planning and development* (Management Development Series No. 12) (Geneva, International Labour Office, 1976); 140 pp.

ILO: *Job evaluation* (Geneva, International Labour Office, 8th impr. 1976); 150 pp.

Janger A. R.: *The personnel function: changing objectives and organisation* (New York, The Conference Board, 1977); 133 pp.

Kellog, M. S.: *Career management* (New York, American Management Association, 1972); 200 pp.

McBeath C., Rands D.: *Salary administration* (London, Business Books, 1976; 320 pp.

Paterson T.T.: *Job evaluation,* Vols. 1 and 2 (London, Business Books, 1972); 428 pp.

Pigors P., Myers C. A.: *Personnel administration: a point of view and a method* (New York, McGraw-Hill, 1977); 546 pp.

Plumbley P. R.: *Recruitment and selection* (London, Institute of Personnel Management, 1974); 214 pp.

Schein E. H.: *Career dynamics: matching individual and organizational needs* (Reading, Mass., Addison-Wesley, 1978); 276 pp.

Stewart V., Stewart A.: *Practical performance appraisal* (Farnborough, Hampshire, Gower Press, 1978); 192 pp.

Taylor B., Lippitt G. L. (eds.): *Management development and training handbook* (London, McGraw-Hill, 1975) 650 pp.

Thakur M., Gill D. *Job evaluation in practice* (London, Institute of Personnel Management, 1976); 97 pp.

Thomason G.: *A textbook of personnel management* (London, Institute of Personnel Management, 1976); 540 pp.

Torrington D.: *Encyclopaedia of personnel management* (London, Gower Press, 1974); 474 pp.

Yoder D.: *Personnel management and industrial relations* (Englewood Cliffs, N. J., Prentice Hall, 1970); 780 pp.

Chapter 22 Consulting in small enterprise management

Allen L. L., *Starting and succeeding in your own small business* (New York, Grosset and Dunlop, 1968); 160 pp.

APO: *Productivity through consultancy in small industrial enterprises* (Tokyo, Asian Productivity Organisation, 1974); 500 pp.

Baumback C. M., Lawyer K., Kelley P. C.: *How to organize and operate a small business* (Englewood Cliffs, N.J., Prentice-Hall, 1973); 612 pp.

Baumback C. M., Mancuso J. R.: *Entrepreneurship and venture management* (Englewood Cliffs, N.J., Prentice-Hall, 1975); 335 pp.

BIM: *Know your business! Vol. I: Business analysis; Vol. II: Managing the smaller company* (developed from the Swedish original) (London, British Institute of Management, 1973)

Clarke P.: *Small businesses: how they survive and succeed* (London, David and Charles, 1972); 400 pp.

Harper M.: *Consultancy for small businesses (the concept; training the consultants)* (London, Intermediate Technology Publications, 1976); 254 pp.

ILO: *Small enterprise development: policies and programmes* (Management Development Series No. 14) (Geneva, International Labour Office, 1977); 250 pp.

Kilby P.: *Entrepreneurship and economic development* (New York, The Free Press, 1971); 384 pp.

McClelland D. C., Winter D. G.: *Motivating economic achievement* (New York, The Free Press, 1969); 410 pp.

Meredith G. G.: *Small business management in Australia* (Sydney, McGraw-Hill, 1977); 350 pp.

Putt W. D.: *How to start your own business* (Cambridge, Mass., The MIT Press, 1974); 260 pp.

S.I.E.T.: *10 years of SIET (Small Industry Extension Training Institute, Hyderabad)* (Madras, B.N.K. Press, 1972); 160 pp.

Staley E., Morse R.: *Modern small industry for developing countries* (New York, McGraw-Hill, 1965); 430 pp.

Stanworth M. J. K., Curran J.: *Management motivation in the smaller business* (London, Gower Press, 1973); 195 pp.

Steinhoff D.: *Small business management fundamentals* (New York, McGraw-Hill, 1978); 512 pp.

Walker E. W.: *The dynamic small firm: selected readings* (Austin, Texas, Austin Press, 1974); 484 pp.

Walsh J. E.: *Guidelines for management consultants in Asia* (Tokyo, Asian Productivity Organisation, 1973); 210 pp.

White R. M.: *Entrepreneur's manual; business start-ups, spin-offs, and innovation management* (Radnor, PA., Chilton Book Co., 1977); 419 pp.

Wood E. G.: *Bigger profits for the smaller firm* (London, Business Books, 1972); 191 pp.

Wortman L. A.: *Successful small business management* (New York, MACOM, 1976); 262 pp.

PART V

ORGANISATION OF CONSULTING

MAIN TYPES OF CONSULTING ORGANISATIONS 23

23.1 Specialisation in management consulting

To meet the criteria of professional competence and effectiveness, management consulting organisations have had to develop and apply specialisation of services commensurate with the specialisation and sophistication of clients' needs.

Specialisation by *management functions* is an old feature of consulting. Most established consulting firms started up on a functional basis (in production management, financial management and accounting, personnel administration, etc.). This traditional specialisation has continued until the present time and in some instances increased, as in the case of consulting services offering special methods and techniques such as job evaluation, operations research, productivity measurement, or market research.

When general management became an area in which more and more organisations requested advice, it also developed as a special function of consulting concerned particularly with the co-ordination and integration of services provided in other areas. Hence the emergence of the leading role of general management consultants in conducting diagnostic surveys and in managing complex assignments embracing several functional areas of management.

Specialisation of services by *sectors* has also gained importance in recent years. Consulting in sectoral management tends to concentrate on areas of management where sectoral differences are predominant and where the links of management with technology are most apparent: it is confined mainly to production and operations management. In such areas as personnel, general administration or management accounting, emphasis on sectoral differences is not as important.

Examples of sectoral services are management consulting in construction, distribution and related activities, specific aspects of transport, banking and, last but not least, in small enterprise management.

Specialisation of services requires a correspondingly specialised expertise in the professional consulting staff, but consulting organisations of different sizes do not have to follow the same pattern. To guarantee a required level of expertise, single consultants (sole practitioners) have to specialise in a narrow field either on a functional or sectoral basis, or both. But larger consulting organisations can afford to offer a wide range of specialised services without sacrificing that specialisation in their professional staff which is so desirable.

Concerning the *geographical coverage* of management consulting services, the recent trend has been towards consulting across national boundaries, which reflects the general tendency in business and management patterns. Multinational corporations, for example, in many cases can only use consultants who are able to examine their problems in the socio-economic and institutional context of the countries in which they are operating. New areas of consulting have also emerged, such as international financial management and transnational industrial relations.

A growing number of consulting organisations (including the smaller ones) are prepared to accept assignments outside their home countries, and a number of them have themselves become multinationals, setting up regional or branch offices, or creating subsidiaries in a number of countries.

23.2 Organisational and legal forms of consulting units

External consulting services

In external consulting[1] the most prevalent type of organisational unit is the *consulting firm*. Sizes range from sole practitioners and small partnerships to large firms employing more than 1,000 consultants, operating both nationwide and internationally. Alternatively, management consulting may be only one of a range of services offered by a firm of professional accountants, engineering consultants, EDP consultants or by similar organisations.

Most consulting units start on a limited scale, with a relatively very small investment in fixed assets. Operating costs are predominantly labour costs and can normally be considered as fixed costs. But consulting is in a high-risk financial category, with very modest financial reserves (made in " better times ") and little security against a slump in the consulting market. The real asset is brain power which, unfortunately, has no financial value as collateral.

---

[1] See Chapter 1, p. 12.

These constraints usually mean that most units have small beginnings, with expansion generally coming from self-generated funds.

From a legal viewpoint, most consulting firms are established as a sole ownership, partnership, private limited company or public limited company.[1]

Sole ownership. This form may involve either the sole practitioner, or the owner, plus a small and variable number of associates employed perhaps only for the duration of specific assignments.

Partnership. A true partnership, where all partners are joint owners and share joint liabilities, is usually confined to a comparatively small number of people. If a unit expands beyond this number, it may still retain something of the spirit and the title of partnership, but for legal purposes would be converted into a private limited liability company.

Private limited company. There are probably more independent units in this form than any other, in their own right or as management consulting departments of companies offering other types of consulting services (e.g. in accounting or engineering). The conditions of employment of the staff may vary from those of ordinary salaried staff to those embracing the principles of partnerships and co-operatives. Some firms return part of the operating profit as a bonus or commission; some offer shares so that the staff may become part-owners.

Public limited company. It is unusual for a consulting firm to start with a public subscription, but there have been instances of subsequent conversion.

Independence is usually mentioned as an essential feature of consulting firms.[2] The real degree of independence is, however, not unrelated to the ownership pattern. In this respect there may be some difference between firms owned by the consultants themselves and firms financially controlled from outside by another company. For example, in 1970-71 a certain number of consulting firms in Europe were taken over by banks, computer firms and other business companies.[3] In such cases, the controlling company (e.g. a vendor of computer equipment) may take a number of policy decisions which the consulting firm has to observe.

The second major type of external management consulting is a unit established in or attached to various organisations, institutions or associations. As a rule it is non-profit-making, although it may charge for its services. We

---

[1] In some countries the terminology used may be different.

[2] See Chapter 1, p. 7.

[3] See *Management of the consulting firm* (FEACO professional conference, Lucerne 7-8.10.71), conference papers (Paris, FEACO, 1971; mimeographed), p. 67. Further references to FEACO findings made in Part V are also from this source.

shall call it *an institutional unit*. In some countries this may be the main or only form in which consulting is available.

The range of organisational and legal forms of institutional units is very wide. They may be in a position of relative independence (including financial autonomy) similar to that of an independent firm. For example, in some country a government ministry may establish a consulting unit for small and medium enterprises in a productivity centre and provide it with a substantial financial subsidy so that management consulting services can be made available to local businesses at a reasonable price. At the same time, however, the statutes drawn up for the unit may stipulate that the services must be confidential, that the choice of the clients will not be made by the ministry, etc.

The most common organisational arrangements of institutional units are as follows:

(i) consulting departments are created within management or productivity centres, business schools, management and trade associations, chambers of commerce, industrial development centres, small business development and advisory centres, etc.;

(ii) no special consulting departments are established, but the professional staff members (teachers, trainers, research workers, designers and the like) of the institutions undertake consulting work as one of their duties (for example, a management trainer's time may be split between training and consulting assignments);

(iii) consulting units are organised as separate institutions (centres, bureaux, services, offices, etc.) with some legal, administrative and financial linkage to the government ministry or independent association which has created them.

The final type of external consulting in management is a service which is provided on a personal, frequently rather informal, basis by individuals who are professors of management, research workers and the like, but whose practical expertise is recognised, and counsel sought, by management circles.

Internal consulting services

Internal consulting services in both the public and private sectors are also organised in different ways. There are organisation and methods departments, management services departments, rationalisation departments, industrial engineering departments and so on.

With regard to the degree of their independence, extreme situations are possible. The first one is that of strong dependence. The unit's services are available on request by managers, but top management to which the unit reports may direct it to undertake surveys and submit proposals for, say, reorganisation or productivity improvement in any unit in the organisation. The consulting unit may also be expected to monitor various aspects of productivity and efficiency to indicate where its services might be needed. Though not requested, it may propose an assignment and supply higher-level management with full information on the under-utilised resources discovered in a particular plant or department. The opposite arrangement provides an internal consulting unit with a degree of independence similar to that prevailing in an external consulting organisation.

Between these extremes there may be varying degrees of independence according to objectives and conditions of operation. There is, however, a general tendency towards greater independence of internal consulting units, to make their work more effective and to facilitate the role of clients in assessing the quality of consulting provided.

TECHNICAL SERVICES OF CONSULTING ORGANISATIONS

24

In addition to their main function of providing consulting services, consulting organisations usually possess other technical services which furnish internal technical support to the consulting activity and supplement consulting assignments by special client services. A short review of both types of service will be made in this chapter.

Every consulting unit has to decide what range and volume of technical services it needs and can afford. A small unit may have no special technical services and some of the activities discussed below have to be carried out by the unit's manager. In medium-sized consulting organisations some elements of organised technical services will usually be found, while large-scale consulting organisations can usually be expected to have a developed network of special services.

24.1 Technical support services

Promotional activities

The promotion of consulting services is an essential activity in every consulting organisation. The purpose is to identify new clients and maintain contacts with former ones, in order to obtain new requests for consulting work.

The main responsibility for promotion tends to rest with the senior people in the consulting unit. In independent consulting companies these people spend 40 – 70% of their time in promotional activities. This notwithstanding, every professional member of the unit should be involved in promotion. Large units have specialised officers or a department responsible for promotion and public relations. As a general rule, priority is given to promotion which builds a public image of the consulting organisation (its technical competence, independence, reliability, integrity) in a way that appeals to management circles, over various techniques of direct selling of services.

The most frequently used promotional media [1] include:

(i) technical articles, books, speeches and conference papers written and presented by the staff of the consulting organisation;

(ii) teaching assignments at training centres and business schools;

(iii) information pamphlets;

(iv) recommendations made by past or present clients, the clients' banks, trade associations, etc.;

(v) social meetings (in societies, clubs or other places);

(vi) visits to potential clients.

Advertising is a controversial means of promotion. As already mentioned [2], most associations of management consultants have banned the consulting profession from using standard advertisements in the daily and business press. This practice is, however, not recognised by all consulting firms some of which may advertise in the daily press or send sales letters in a way similar to any other commercial firm.

Information services

A dynamic and reliable information and documentation service is needed for two principal reasons:

— information on new developments in management relevant to the work of the consulting organisation has to be collected and channelled to the consultants (who often work far from their headquarters, where new books, professional reviews, or other information sources are not easily available and the consultant is too busy to search for new information);

— information on work methods used and results obtained in previous assignments must be available for any new assignment.

The information service has responsibility for collecting, extracting, storing and retrieving managerial and technical information contained in important *publications*, for use by the appropriate consultants. Suggestions are also made to consultants concerning new materials they should study. The consulting unit should have at least a reference library of the standard management handbooks, a selection of the best textbooks on general and functional management, and references on special techniques.

---

[1] Cf. ACME: *Professional practices in management consulting* (New York, Association of Consulting Management Engineers, 1966), pp. 22-27.

[2] See Chapter 5, p. 50.

The consulting unit should subscribe to a number of leading management and business *periodicals* and also to an *abstracting service*. While some periodicals may be for general circulation, an information service may also select and photocopy articles and abstracts that are of direct interest to particular consultants. The unit may also subscribe to those newspapers that regularly issue business or industrial supplements, or use an agency specialising in screening and copying published matter for its subscribers.

Whoever runs a periodicals or clippings service may also collect companies' annual reports, brochures, advertising and descriptive matter, government economic plans and reports, and so on. These may provide useful information for initial meetings with potential clients in the private and public sectors, and for both surveys and operating assignments.

These are costly services, but consultants must keep up to date. Some excellent operating procedures can often be traced to an idea picked up from an article or book, not necessarily directly related to the particular subject.

The organisation and use of the information service requires inputs from both ends of the information flow. The information section should take the initiative in looking for new sources and suggesting what might interest whom, while the consultants should present specific demands clearly indicating the nature and scope of the information required for their priority tasks.

The second essential part of an information service is the *reports library*. Survey reports, survey notes, and operating and follow-up reports have to be classified, indexed and filed. They grow into an invaluable reference library for the further guidance of consultants in their work. Although complete solutions cannot usually be transferred unchanged from one situation to another, the methods used and results achieved may provide examples and give inspiration. Reports are also needed for the training of new consultants and for the development of internal operational guides and manuals.

The reports library must have an efficient means of information retrieval and for this an indexing system has to be established and maintained. Reports may be indexed by client, sector, country, operating function, subject within a function, or technique applied.

Thus, an enquiry as to what work has previously been done in, say, production planning in food canning with the use of EDP, could result in either the extraction of a report, or the reply that no assignment of this nature has been undertaken, or that there has been one assignment, but without any EDP application.

A long-term view is needed when deciding on an indexing system. It is easier to start with something that will be suitable in twenty years time than to change twenty years' reports from one system to another.

Clients' reports are confidential papers and the library must be run on lines of strict security. Copies lent to consultants must not be taken into other clients' premises, nor left open in public places.

Research and development

Consulting organisations do not normally have sizeable research and development departments. They prefer to follow relevant research projects undertaken by management faculties, business schools or research institutions and acquire the results when these become available. The development of new methods and techniques is often a feature of consulting practice, especially when new types of assignments are tackled.

In some cases, however, the larger consulting organisations may set up a separate research and development programme and attach some consultants full- or part-time to it. They may, for example, be developing a new technique or establishing a new specialisation. This could be later removed from the research and development function and set up as a new line of consulting activity or a headquarter's service for clients.

Staff recruitment, selection and training

These activities or their elements will exist in any consulting organisation, especially in a growing one. However, larger organisations can be expected to have special units with full-time specialist staff for this purpose.[1]

24.2   Special client services

In recent years there has been a tendency in many consulting organisations to widen the scope of services to clients by adding other management services to consulting. There is logic behind such a move when, for example, management training, which is closely allied to consulting in nature, may be needed to solve a particular problem. Another supporting reason occurs when the same professional staff alternate between consulting assignments and central client services. Finally, consulting assignments frequently create demand for other management services and vice versa. Some large consulting organisations prefer to satisfy these new demands themselves rather than direct clients to other service organisations.

Consulting units that include a broad range of capabilities and resources required not only for counselling clients but also for providing assistance in implementing action programmes, are sometimes called " full service management consulting companies ".[2]

---

[1] These questions will be discussed in greater detail in Part VI entitled " Developing management consultants ".

[2] P. W. Shay: *How to get the best results from management consultants* (New York, Association of Consulting Management Engineers, 1974), p. 1.

A detailed description and analysis of special client services is not included in this book, as these services are beyond the scope of management consulting in spite of existing links. Brief comments on the most common services are offered as follows:

Follow-up services

A brief reference to follow-up services was made in connection with the operating assignments and assignment reports.[1] It is a policy of some consulting organisations to try to establish a follow-up service at the end of any operating assignment in order to maintain a continuing relationship with a client. The advantages to the consulting organisation are obvious. The follow-up service is an invaluable source of information on the real impact of operating assignments and on new problems that may have arisen in the client organisation. New assignments may develop from these visits, which may not cost the consulting organisation anything if follow-up is provided on a paying basis.

Many client organisations may also find that follow-up services are a useful form of assistance through which new problems can be discovered and resolved before they become a headache. However, no client should be forced to accept follow-up arrangements if they are not felt to be required.

Follow-up visits are usually made, according to an agreed schedule, by operating consultants who have worked with the client.

Training centre

Many consulting organisations run their own centres for management and specialist training. In addition to scheduled programmes the centre may offer bespoke programmes for particular clients or their groups. The teaching staff is frequently drawn from experienced consultants, some of whom return to consulting after a period spent with the centre. Experiences from consulting assignments are often utilised in the preparation of training materials. Many assignment reports constitute excellent case-study material and can be used in training if information likely to reveal the particular client is disguised.

Economic and feasibility studies

As most of these studies require special skills (industrial economics, market research, business forecasting, etc.), and often may be carried out as off-shoots of main assignments, some large consulting organisations have

---

[1] See Chapter 15, pp. 165 and 166. Follow-up is called "servicing" by some consultants.

concentrated them in specialised service units. There are also consulting organisations that are fully specialised in this particular type of service.[1]

Systems development and computing services

This activity has become very important in the last decade. The services range from feasibility studies for computer applications, through systems analysis and design and training of specialist staff, to computing services or facilities management provided on a temporary or continuing basis.[2] Some consulting organisations have their own computing centres, or have established special companies for this purpose.

Executive search (management recruitment) service

Executive search (management recruitment) is another service offered by some larger management consulting units, or by consultants who are fully specialised in this function.[3] It is increasingly used by business and other organisations to fill important managerial positions, the advantage of an executive search specialist being that he can develop information on potential sources of recruitment and undertake a systematic search and objective selection in a way that usually is beyond the normal possibilities of a line or even personnel manager.

The executive search function involves the building of extensive files with names of potential candidates and recruitment sources, assistance to clients in analysing the job to be filled and defining the ideal candidate, active and methodical search for candidates (by direct approach, search through various business contacts, in some cases advertising, etc.), contacts with candidates for the purpose of interviewing them and getting them interested in the job, evaluation and preliminary selection of candidates, arranging the client's interviews with preselected candidates, and follow-up contact with the selected candidate and the client.

Executive search consultants form their own professional associations (e.g. in the USA) or are members in national associations of management consultants. Codes of ethics for executive search have been adopted in several countries. For example, such codes forbid charging fees to the candidates and accepting any payment from them: the cost of the search operation is charged to the client according to an agreed scheme. In no case is the fee for a search made contingent on the placement of an executive.

---

[1] See Chapter 2, p. 19 and Chapter 23, p. 245.

[2] See also Chapter 20.

[3] See e.g. J. H. Kennedy (ed.): *The handbook of executive search* (Fitzwilliam, N.H., Consultants News, 1974).

STRUCTURING AND CONTROLLING A CONSULTING ORGANISATION 25

If managers are expected to take the consultant's advice seriously, they must be able to recognise that the consulting unit itself provides an example of sound organisation, competent management and efficient administration. If this is not the case, the operating consultant's advice may be considerably devalued.

25.1 Organisational structure

Chapters 23 and 24 have set out several alternatives in specialisation, size, legal form and range of services provided by consulting organisations. Many variables have to be considered, including the personality of the men at the top. There is, therefore, no one rigid structure for a consulting organisation. Only certain examples and common principles can be provided.

Let us consider the organisation of a *basic operating consulting unit* which may be part of a larger consulting organisation consisting of several units, specialised, for example, for operating in different geographical areas. However, such a unit may make up a whole consulting company, or a consulting department in a management development or productivity centre.

The unit is structured as shown on Figure 9, and contains a total of approximately 30 consultants, which is roughly the number that one director or manager can control.

A unit of this size requires one senior consultant to fill the survey (diagnostic) role and four seniors as supervisors. Each supervisor is responsible for about five operating consultants, and in addition he may have new consultants in training. Such a unit may also have one senior consultant for special surveys, and for conducting difficult general management assignments. The figure of 30 is by no means universal. It simply indicates that there is a limit to the number of clients and assignments that a director or manager can

Figure 9.   Structure of a basic consulting unit

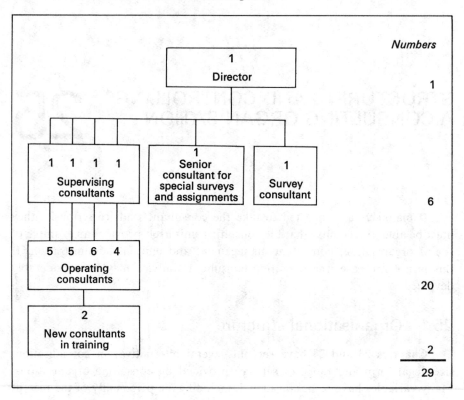

effectively know and follow at any one time. Assuming, in our case, that 16 operating consultants are working singly, and 4 in a team, the director has to know and keep in touch with 17 clients.

There are several other factors to be considered in setting the size of the operating unit. Each supervisor is responsible, as the senior member of the operating team, for the smooth running of several assignments. He should personally visit each of these assignments every 1-2 weeks—that is why each supervisor should (as stated above) have about five operating consultants under him. More experienced operating consultants may require less supervision, and the supervisor's time thus saved can be used for maintaining contact with past clients, making contact with new clients, attending training courses, examining reports and undertaking other administrative work associated with the unit. In addition, more experienced seniors are preparing themselves for promotion to the next level—supervisors to become survey consultants, and survey consultants to become directors.

The operating consultants will, as a rule, be specialists in various management functions. Hence three supervisors in the unit may also be specialised in supervising individual assignments for specific management functions, while the fourth may be a general management consultant supervising assignments embracing several functional areas.

The small consulting firm may never expand beyond the size of 27-30, as the owner or manager may wish to keep personal control of all the operations and clients. In this case, the top man may have a small office and staff to support the operation.

If *expansion* takes place, and a unit employs more than 30 consultants, it may split into two sub-units. The survey consultant may become the head of the second unit, which he builds up to full size. During this expansion more seniors will be required, and in time central support services may be set up. The additional seniors are needed to co-ordinate and administer these separate units, or to set up specialist units and support services.

The key factors determining expansion are market demand and the availability of operating consultants with sufficient experience and knowledge to be appointed as supervisors. At least four years of experience encompassing both a range of assignments with companies and a variety of techniques is required. To replace the operating consultants as they rise to higher levels or leave, new consultants must be ready trained. For this reason a stable organisation always includes two or three trainee-consultants in every group of 27-30, as shown in Figure 9.

Another factor governing expansion is the ratio of specialist to generalist consultants. Where an assignment calls for several disciplines, the supervising consultant may accept over-all responsibility but call on a specialist to oversee special techniques as required. Usually, operating consultants have wide general experience and knowledge, and keep occupied by undertaking a variety of assignments. To meet the full range of client demands, however, the consulting organisation may employ some specialist consultants, e.g. in corporate planning or electronic data processing. It is more difficult to find a constant demand for these types of services within a smaller unit.

If several types of specialists are working in a region or area they may operate under a *matrix structure*, where each consultant has two directors. One director is responsible for the special technique of the consultant and the second director for the general administration of consultants to meet client requirements. The specialist director may have consultants located in several units reporting to him in their specialities.

In some cases it may be convenient to staff the operating units with generalist consultants, retaining the specialists in centrally controlled units. This has the advantage of providing a wider opportunity for work in their own field because they can operate over a wide geographical territory. The disadvantages lie in the difficulties of travel and family separation, and in providing supervision.

Management consulting

Figure 10 gives a general pattern of organisation followed by many *larger consulting companies* in Great Britain and some other countries.[1]

Figure 10. Typical organisation of consulting companies

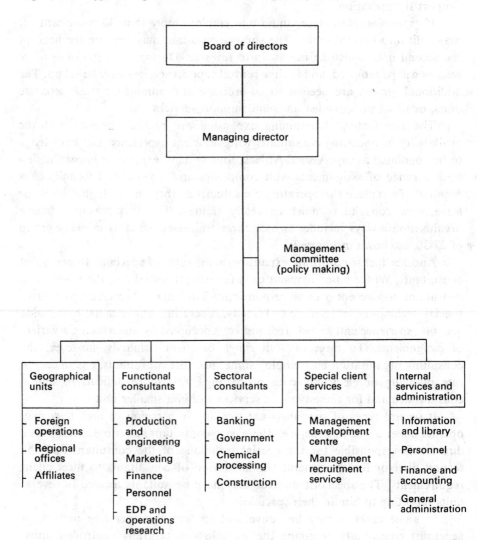

---

[1] Adapted from an organisational chart developed by a FEACO research project.

25.2 Top management

The pattern of the consulting organisation's top management depends very much on its legal statute.

In consulting firms constituted as limited companies there will be a *board of directors*. In a smallish unit the directors would generally be the general manager (managing director) and some of the senior consultants. In a large unit there may also be external board members who, being non-executives, may play a useful role in the sense that they may preserve the same detachment in guiding the unit as the consultants have in guiding their clients. They also tend to be chosen because of their range of business interests and contacts.

In the institutional consulting units, there may be a *governing body* comprising a cross-section of managers from private and public enterprises, representatives of chambers of commerce and employers' federations, senior government officials and possibly other members.

The key position in the management hierarchy is that of the *chief executive officer*, who may be called (in various countries) principal, general manager, president, managing director, director general or simply director.

This top man will possibly have been a career consultant with considerable experience and managerial talent. But on reaching the top, he may experience problems similar to those faced by research managers—he must stop being a technician and concentrate on managing.

In large and complex consulting organisations the top functions involve considerably more than guidance and control of consulting work. Promotion has been mentioned, and the establishment of strategies and policies for the unit's further development is no less important. There is, moreover, the difficult function of co-ordinating a wide range of diversified services. In some consulting organisations top managers have, therefore, been recruited from individuals who have had considerable management experience, but not necessarily in professional management consulting. It may, for example, be quite advantageous to recruit a manager who, in addition to personal qualities, has had reasonable experience with the *use* of consultants in his organisation.

In large organisations there may be an executive committee, management committee or policy formation committee, composed of the general manager and several other senior partners, divisional or regional managers and consultants.

25.3 Professional guidance and control of quality

It is recognised that a consulting unit should not simply recruit a number of consultants, even if they are competent and experienced people, and send them on assignments. Clients with problems address themselves to a consulting organisation and not merely to an individual in this organisation. High-level *professional guidance* of all senior and operating consultants, and *quality control* of consulting assignments are, therefore, principal management functions within consulting units. They concern both the content of consulting work—the particular subject areas in management—and the methodology used.

To exercise such functions is probably more difficult in consulting than in other industrial or professional service organisations. The reasons for this are the great variety of subject areas and specific problems the consultants have to deal with; the often great distances between headquarters and the client's premises; the fact that only 1-2 consultants are attached to most assignments and possibilities of teamwork remain limited; and the consultants' personality traits that tend to develop after a few years of consulting, so that many of them become strong individualists proud of their own work methods and not easy to guide.

Professional guidance does not mean that consultants (with the exception of trainees and beginners) would be told what to do in particular cases. The problem is how to ensure *before* the consultant starts his work that results will be satisfying, and how to identify and correct cases where the consultant's advice to his client risks being below the necessary professional level.

The top management of the unit has primary responsibility in this area, but methods of professional guidance and control will vary from case to case.

Guidance may be provided in the following ways [1]:

(i) dissemination to consultants of information on developments in management theory and practice, and model reports from previous assignments in their technical fields;

(ii) personal guidance provided by the unit's manager to the senior consultants who, in turn, guide operating consultants on assignment, etc.;

(iii) internal technical meetings and conferences of the unit on matters of policy (these cannot usually be very frequent; for example, the whole organisation may meet only once a year, and a regional or special functional division once every three months);

(iv) training and retraining of the consultants (off-the-job);

(v) use of operating manuals, guides, checklists, report outlines and other material that standardise consulting approaches and work methods on the basis of the unit's best practical experience.[2]

---

[1] As some of these ways are discussed in other parts of the book in greater detail, they are referred to only briefly here.

[2] Some well-established consulting organisations have dozens of internal operating manuals, which are regularly revised and up-dated.

A systematic control of quality of consulting work is also necessary, in order to ensure the real impact of the professional guidance and orient it towards areas where the unit's work has gaps or deficiencies.[1]

In a small unit the control of quality is exercised by the manager and the senior consultants more or less informally. The larger the unit the greater the tendency to install formal procedures and internal bodies for this purpose.

Quality control involves in particular:

    (i) control of the competence and development of the staff (with special regard to individuals stagnating for various reasons);

    (ii) review of new assignments (i.e. analysis of conclusions presented in preliminary surveys, assignment strategies and plans);

    (iii) control by supervisors of the operating consultants' behaviour, work methods used and proposals developed in the course of operating assignments;

    (iv) examination of key reports by senior members of the unit before their submission to clients;

    (v) evaluation (including rating) of staff performance at the end of each operating assignment;

    (vi) assessment of end results achieved by clients, thanks to the implementation of the consultant's proposals (if a regular follow-up service [2] has not been foreseen, the management of the consulting unit should nevertheless inform itself about results by visiting former clients and checking client satisfaction indirectly with their banks, business associates or other reliable sources close to the client).

25.4 Financial and operational control

In this section the main financial and operational control techniques used in consulting units will be discussed; a simple example of the hypothetical small unit described in Section 25.1 above [3] will be used for this purpose.

Operating budget

A hypothetical consulting unit employing 29 professional staff members (including one director and two trainees) might establish its annual operating budget as shown in Table 19 below.[4]

---

[1] See ACME: *How to control the quality of a management consulting assignment* (New York, Association of Consulting Management Engineers, 1972).

[2] See Chapter 24, p. 255.

[3] See pp. 257-259.

[4] The structure of the unit was shown in Figure 9 (p. 258). The salary rates and other figures are also hypothetical.

Table 19. Operating budget of a consulting unit

		$
EXPENSES	Professional salaries:	
	Director, per annum	20,000
	Senior consultants, 6 × $16,000 p.a.	96,000
	Operating consultants, 20 × $13,000 p.a.	260,000
	Trainees, 2 × $10,000 p.a.	20,000
	Administration:	
	Salaries	45,000
	Social security, etc.	40,000
	Headquarters expenses	68,000
	Travel and other expenses	81,000
		630,000
INCOME	To meet expenses	630,000
	For profit and reserves	140,000
	For profit tax	50,000
		820,000

Profit planning

In profit planning, consulting companies frequently use a ratio:

$$\frac{Profit}{Income}$$

A ratio between 0.1 and 0.2 is considered normal, but depends on various factors. The actual volume of profit before tax that the unit needs to achieve depends on the level of taxation and the need to establish security reserves, increase working capital and finance capital expenses. If a consulting company is in a period of growth, which it has to finance from its own profits, a higher profit may be needed.

In budgeting and planning the unit's work, the following main ways of achieving higher profits are available (see Table 20).

Management has to consider which method to adopt depending on the market, the opportunity to recruit new consultants, and the unit's ability to enhance promotional efforts, improve internal organisation and planning of its activities, and so on.

Income-generating activities

The reader is now well aware that not all the services provided to clients generate income for the consulting unit. For example, in our hypothetical unit only the 20 operating consultants and one senior consultant (the consultant for

Table 20. Methods of achieving higher profits

Method	Achieved by
Sell more	Providing new types of services Recruiting more consulting staff Utilising staff better Enhancing promotional efforts
Charge more	Increasing fees Charging for services provided free hitherto
Spend less	Reducing operating expenses Reducing overhead (general) expenses

special surveys) may do chargeable work, while the remaining five senior consultants are engaged in preliminary surveys and supervisory functions. Earnings from the 21 consultants have to support the unit, everyone in it and all general expenses.

A frequently used ratio is:

$$\frac{Number\ of\ senior\ (non\text{-}fee\text{-}earning)\ consultants}{Number\ of\ operating\ (fee\text{-}earning)\ consultants}$$

In our case one of the senior consultants is fee-earning; the ratio would, therefore, be $5 : 21 = 0.24$. This is an acceptable figure. Should it be higher, the unit would probably have too many consultants in non-fee-earning jobs.

Fee-earning days

As services to clients are charged on the basis of the number of consultant-days provided, it is essential to plan and attain the required number. It may be determined as indicated in Table 21 (assuming a five-day working week).

The 180 chargeable days represent the normal expectation of the consulting unit for the planned period. This is a 69% utilisation of the total time, as determined by the ratio:

$$\frac{Chargeable\ time}{Total\ time} = \frac{180}{260} = 0.69$$

The number of lost days (25) is not a standard figure; every consulting unit has to establish its own figure based on experience and future strategy. It appears, however, that a utilisation rate of 65-70% is considered a normal basis for achieving satisfactory incomes. Some consulting units achieve rates of 75-85%, but utilisation below 60% is not exceptional.

Table 21. Chargeable time

Item	Weeks	Days
Total time	52	260
—annual leave	4	20
—public holidays [1] etc.		10
—reserved against sickness		10
—reserved for training, annual meetings, etc.		15
Days available		205
—lost time		25
Chargeable time		180

Fee per day [2]

Calculation of the daily fee rate can then be made as follows:

$$\frac{Total\ income}{Fee\ earning\ days} = \frac{\$820{,}000}{21 \times 180} = \$127$$

This is an average figure. The rate for each assignment is individually weighed against circumstances; the senior consultant doing special surveys may earn a considerably higher rate; etc.

Most consulting organisations charge their clients fees that relate to the number of days worked by the consultants on operating assignments.

Fee/salary ratio

Another control ratio used by consulting organisations compares the fee-earning consultants' salaries (plus social charges) to the fees as follows:

$$\frac{Total\ fees\ earned\ (total\ income)}{Salaries\ and\ social\ charges} = Factor$$

Several European consulting firms, members of FEACO, indicate that their ratio (i.e. the factor) is between 2.0 and 3.0.

In our hypothetical case the factor would be (assuming that social security charges are about 27,000):

$$\frac{820{,}000}{276{,}000 + 27{,}000} = \frac{820}{303} = 2.7$$

---

[1] In some assignments, public holidays may be charged for.

[2] See also J. Marre: " Le vrai prix d'un conseil " (The real price of a consultant) in *Travail et méthodes*, No. 338-339/1977, p. 48.

Planning the forward workload

The very nature of their services requires that consulting organisations maintain a backlog of orders for several weeks ahead. For any unit there is an optimum figure that provides a reasonable safety margin and still allows new jobs to start without undue delay. To maintain this margin, the volume of new assignments (in fee-earning days) negotiated every week should be equal to the average volume of consulting work performed by the unit in a week.

In our case it will be:

$$\frac{180}{52} \times 21 = 72.6 \text{ days}$$

This, of course, is a theoretical figure, but it provides guidance to the unit's work planners. If the unit is selling at a rate below this figure, its forward load is decreasing and there may be danger ahead. If selling is at a greater rate, the order book is lengthening and clients will have to wait longer for assignments to commence unless the number of operating consultants can be increased.

In practice, promotion and the planning of work have to be less global: ideally the structure of the forward load should correspond as closely as possible to the relative numbers of operating consultants of different professional profiles.

Preliminary surveys and operating assignments

Operating assignments depend on successful preliminary surveys. In time, a unit is able to derive an average for a ratio of *surveys made to assignments sold*. If this were 1.5, it means that in the long run three surveys yield two assignments. That 100 surveys yielded 65 assignments may, however, be cold comfort if the last ten surveys made no sales. What is certain is that there must always be a number of surveys in the pipeline: waiting to be made, in progress, or pending decision. Further, there must always be a number of initial meetings booked with prospective clients or there will be no surveys.

Impact of length of assignments

The intensity of promotional activity should be heavily influenced by the duration of the current assignments and the length of the assignments waiting to start. If the average length were three months, each operating consultant would start four assignments a year and a unit having 20 members would need to find clients for about 80 assignments a year.[1] Could it, however, make

---

[1] Assuming that all consultants work individually.

120 surveys in a year? A few pointers begin to emerge from this simple arithmetic: either the average assignment should be longer, or more survey consultants should be employed, or fewer operating consultants engaged.

Coincidence of assignment completions

From the foregoing considerations, it can now be seen that the ultimate nightmare would be for all operating consultants to finish their current assignments in the same week. Statistically, this may seem unlikely, but it is not impossible. If records are properly kept and the progress of all assignments is controlled by the unit's manager, such a contingency will be foreseen in advance and extraordinary efforts made to avert it (without, however, keeping consultants on assignments purely for convenience of the unit).

Key controls

In summary, the management of a consulting unit will be interested in following, usually on a monthly basis, certain key controls, which may include:

- forward workload,
- actual vs. budgeted fee rate,
- actual vs. budgeted utilisation of total time,
- number of surveys made to number of assignments negotiated,
- cumulative actual fee-earning days against planned fee-earning days,
- cumulative fees earned against fees budgeted,
- cumulative fees earned against cumulative expenses,
- monthly billings,
- number of weeks (months) of outstanding fees,
- outstanding fees as a percentage of total income.

Any deviation from the unit's standards, or the discovery of an undesirable trend, requires deeper analysis and prompt action by management.

25.5 Internal administration

Only selected elements of administration, specific to consulting units, will be described below.

Operating records

Records serve to ensure that operating data are collected for the purposes of management control, clients properly charged and consultants paid their salaries and expenses.

Notification of assignment

At the beginning of every assignment the supervisor (or the survey consultant) prepares a form of notification, which is intended to inform many sections within the consulting unit. It initiates or supplements a client file for the commercial aspects of the unit's work with him. The form caters for information as indicated in Figure 11 on the next page.

When, during the course of an assignment, additional operating consultants, specialists or trainees become involved, a supplementary notification is made.

Consultants' time records

These records are the source of data for invoicing clients and for much of the control information needed by the unit's management.

One standard form suffices for operating and senior consultants. It is returned to the office either weekly or monthly depending on the requirements for invoicing and control.

The form should cater for the following:

— consultant's name
— dates of period covered
— client names (for up to, say, five assignments, surveys or visits)
— fee rates for paid work
— number of fee-earning days per client
— number of non-fee-earning days per consultant divided into:
    — leave
    — sickness
    — unassigned
    — unpaid operating
    — receiving training
    — giving training
    — supervision
    — preliminary survey
    — promotional activity
    — attending public and professional events.

Operating consultants normally enter one name—their current client, the fee-earning days to be charged and the non-chargeable days.

Survey and supervising consultants enter the names of all clients dealt with personally during the period, the days spent on non-chargeable work, the days of chargeable work, fee rates, and the use made of all non-fee-earning time.

Figure 11.   Notification of assignment

NOTIFICATION OF ASSIGNMENT	Assignment No.
Client	Industry
Address	Phone
Assigner (main contact)	
Invoices to	

Type of assignment
Preliminary survey ☐   Operating ☐   Follow up ☐
Paid survey ☐   Training ☐   Other (specify below) ☐

Fee rate	Special invoicing instructions
Expenses rechargeable to client	
Operating function	
Operating consultant(s)	
Survey consultant or supervisor	
Others (trainees, etc.)	

Starting date	Planned duration	Finishing date

Briefing and special conditions	Other comments

Date	Issued by	Signature

Consultants' expenses

The unit may have a standard scale of expense allowances, and rules for their application which cover an assumed normal set of conditions. This is surprisingly difficult to draw up and administer: the "every situation is different" character of operating assignments often extends to the consultants' actual expenses. As a rule, consulting organisations are prepared to consider any case of higher than standard expenses at the consultant's request.

The main sources of expenses are:

— accommodation while away from home,
— travelling,
— communication (cables, telephone calls, etc.),
— entertainment of client and contacts.

Whether other out-of-pocket expenses are reimbursed may depend on the consultants' terms of employment. The expenses claim form caters for any items that are to be recharged to the client.

Assignment reference report [1]

This report, prepared at the end of operating assignments, was described in Chapter 15.[2]

Invoicing

The consultants' time record described earlier is a simple device which acts as a trigger for the invoice.

Most consulting organisations bill their clients monthly, especially if assignments are long and billing in shorter periods might cause some annoyance. However, some consultants prefer to invoice clients weekly.

Office staff

Because the majority of the professional staff—the operating consultants—are able to use their clients' administrative services, the unit needs only a small office staff at its headquarters. But the smaller the staff, the more its members have to be able to help in any part of the daily work. The work is straightforward but must be done with the efficiency that befits a professional body. The office staff, therefore, needs to be rather above average in ability, versatility and discretion. In a small unit the following staff may be employed:

---

[1] This report is called "assignment summary" by some consultants.
[2] See p. 167.

Secretary to the director (May also act as administrative assistant and office manager, and type confidential reports for both operational and internal matters.)

Accounts clerk/cashier (Would keep time records, invoice clients, pay salaries and expenses, and purchase office supplies.)

Receptionist/telephonist/copy typist (Would type routine documents such as invoices and purchase orders.)

Stenotypists (Would type routine communications, and reports that should not be typed by the clients' personnel; they can also assist in various secretarial duties.)

25.6 Headquarters accommodation

The question of where and how to house the headquarters of a consulting unit raises a surprising number of issues. Our approach here is to start with the first essentials and go on to consider what may be needed through growth and the addition of professional services.

General considerations

In all circumstances headquarters accommodation should be designed round the fact that consulting is predominantly a field operation and not a head-office activity. The premises should be modest and the location carefully chosen. There is a balance to be struck between the prestigious image of a professional service and the economy of its operation.

A " good address " is liable to be expensive. The right address is usually close to the sources of business. This tends to locate it in or near the commercial quarter of the capital city or the major industrial centre, which in many countries is the same place.

The accommodation needed for the internal administrative and commercial services is self-evident. The more difficult points arise from the kind and number of the professional services to be housed, and how much space should be allocated for the consultants themselves.

Accommodating professional services

The basic essentials are:

(1) *Library space*. The reports library may start in a small way with a few lockable filing cabinets but in time may need a room of its own. This

it might share at the beginning with the reference library of books and other documentation files, but with the growth of the unit more space will be needed for this purpose.

(2) *Room for interviewing and contact meetings.*

(3) *Training area.* This has modest requirements so long as the unit is small, and the training is intermittent and restricted to a few at a time. Working space is supplemented by a room for training aids, equipment, and files on course literature. If training assumes larger proportions, and particularly if it becomes a special client service, the headquarters, in its commercial environment, may cease to be the right place for it. The large units usually set up a separate establishment in either a suburban or accessible country area.

Consultant accommodation

Since supervisors and other senior consultants have no other base, they need office space at headquarters. Although the regular meetings with the unit's manager will probably take place in his office, consultants nevertheless need at least a desk each though perhaps not individual offices.

The operating consultants' places of work are normally with their clients. Some operating work may legitimately be done off the clients' premises and a small amount of space at headquarters may be desirable. A good deal depends on how widely the consultants are dispersed.

In some situations, particularly for institutional units in developing countries, the matter of consultants' accommodation takes on certain other aspects. There are places where almost all the operating assignments are in a compact area about the headquarters. Client companies tend to be small and assignments short, and it also happens that the consultant cannot proceed with his work as scheduled because the client is absent, documentation has not been prepared, or for other reasons. There is a tendency for operating consultants to spend more time at headquarters.

The number of consultants sitting at their desks instead of working with clients is generally considered to be an indicator or danger signal which requires careful examination.

LITERATURE TO PART V

ACME: *How to control the quality of a management consulting assignment* (New York, Association of Consulting Management Engineers, 1972); 30 pp.

ACME: *Key operating ratios in management consulting firms* (New York, Association of Consulting Management Engineers, 1977).

ACME: *Professional practices in management consulting* (New York, Association of Consulting Management Engineers, 1966); 100 pp.

ACME: *Survey on compensation for professional staff in management consulting firms* (New York, Association of Consulting Management Engineers, 1977).

ACME: *Survey on professional consulting fee arrangements* (New York, Association of Consulting Management Engineers, 1975).

Batten W. E. (ed.): *Handbook of special librarianship and information work* (London, ASLIB, 1975); 430 pp.

ILO: *Management and productivity: an international directory of institutions and information sources* (Management Development Series No. 13) (Geneva, International Labour Office, 1980); approx. 250 pp.

Kennedy J. H. (ed.): *The handbook of executive search* (Fitzwilliam, New Hampshire, Consultants News, 1974); approx. 150 pp.

Mahon J. J.: *The marketing of professional accounting services* (New York, Wiley, 1978); 189 pp.

Management of the consulting firm (FEACO professional conference, Lucerne, 1971), conference papers (Paris, FEACO, 1971; mimeographed); 121 pp.

Martin C. C.: *Project management: how to make it work* (New York, AMACOM, 1976); 312 pp.

Morrell J. C.: *Preparing an organization manual* (London, British Institute of Management Foundation, 1977); 120 pp.

Shay P. W.: *How to get the best results from management consultants* (New York, Association of Consulting Management Engineers, 1974); 60 pp.

The management of consulting engineering firms (FIDIC Forum 1976) (The Hague, International Federation of Consulting Engineers, 1976); 85 pp.

Vernon K. D. C. (ed.): *Use of management and business literature* (London, Butterworths, 1975); 330 pp.

PART VI

DEVELOPING MANAGEMENT CONSULTANTS

CONSULTING AS A CAREER 26

In the previous five parts of this guide, management consulting has been shown to be a special profession, which has its own objectives, methods, rules and conditions of work. To individuals who become members of this profession, consulting is a *career*, in which they may spend the main part of their working life.

26.1 Personal characteristics of consultants

To become a career management consultant is a major life decision. Both individual candidates and consulting organisations should, therefore, consider the characteristics of a suitable candidate.

Management consultants have discussed these characteristics at many meetings and conferences. The conclusion has been the same as in any other profession which has attempted to define an ideal candidate profile—there is no ideal against which every entrant could be compared, but there are certain common characteristics affecting the success of consulting work and the consultant's job satisfaction. These common characteristics differentiate the consulting profession from other occupations that also require a high level of technical knowledge and skill, but have other objectives and use different methods of action (e.g. research, technical design work, or management jobs with direct decision-making authority and responsibility). In management consulting, particular importance is attached to skills in the behavioural area, and in communicating and helping other people to understand the need for change and the way to implement change.

On the basis of the experience of a number of American consulting firms, P. W. Shay summarises the key characteristics as follows [1]:

---

[1] P. W. Shay: *The common body of knowledge for management consultants* (New York, Association of Consulting Management Engineers, 1974), pp. 41-42.

(1) Good physical and mental health.
(2) Professional etiquette and courtesy.
(3) Stability of behaviour and action.
(4) Self-confidence.
(5) Personal effectiveness (drive).
(6) Integrity (the quality that engenders trust).
(7) Independence. (The successful consultant must be self-reliant, not subordinate to the opinions of others. He must be able to form his own judgements in the areas of his competence and experience. At the same time, he must recognise the limitations of his competence, experience, and judgement.)
(8) Intellectual competence.
(9) Good judgement (the faculty of sound appraisal with complete objectivity).
(10) Strong analytical or problem-solving ability (the ability to analyse, assemble, sort, balance, and evaluate the basic factors of problem situations of different degrees of complexity).
(11) Creative imagination (the ability to see with a fresh pair of eyes).
(12) Skill in interpersonal relationships.
    a. Orientation toward the people-aspect of problems.
    b. Receptivity to new information or points of view expressed by others.
    c. Ability to gain the trust and respect of client personnel.
    d. Ability to enlist client participation in the solution of problems.
    e. Ability to effect a transfer of knowledge to client personnel.
    f. Ability to apply the principles and techniques of planned change.
(13) Ability to communicate and persuade (with above-average facility).
    a. Oral.
    b. Written.
    c. Graphic.
(14) Psychological maturity. (The successful consultant is always ready to experience people, things, and events as they really are with their unique individual characteristics; to view them in perspective and to take action needed in a calm and objective manner without being diverted from a sound, logical, and ethical course by outside pressure.)

How should such a list of personal characteristics be interpreted? Some characteristics may be considered as necessary conditions and a candidate who does not possess them should be discouraged from becoming a consultant. For example, a candidate who is shy, lacks self-confidence and has difficulties in presenting ideas orally in a clear and organised manner at the age of 32, after 7 years of job experience, is probably not a potentially good management consultant, although he may know his technical subject well. It is, however, important to consider what characteristics can and will be further developed during the initial training of a consultant and in the first years of work with clients.

26.2 Recruitment and selection

The key decisions on careers in consulting are made at the moment of recruitment: only candidates who meet certain criteria will have good chances of advancing up the career ladder to their own and the consulting unit's full satisfaction. Hence the extraordinary importance of a thorough appraisal of candidates.

General requirements

Although consulting organisations apply different requirements in recruiting new consultants, the comparison of their practices allows for some general conclusions concerning personal characteristics, education, job experience and age.[1]

Personal characteristics were discussed in the previous section and there is no need to return to them.

Education has to be carefully examined in every case. University level or higher education (a doctorate or corresponding degree) is required at the present time for nearly all management consulting positions. The relevance of the field of study to the particular field of consulting is considered and in some cases candidates should have a specific educational background—for example, a doctorate in psychology for work in the behavioural science area. The consulting organisation is equally interested in the *performance* of the candidates during their university studies.

Experience in a practical management situation is required by all consultant organisations. A minimum of 5 years is a general preference, but there are exceptions. For example, shorter experience may be accepted for work in operations research or systems design if the candidate has the right educational background. Longer experience tends to be required in marketing[2] and in special cases, for example if senior people have to be recruited from outside to start new lines of consulting and head new divisions.

The age at which candidates are recruited reflects the required education and experience as discussed above. The lower age limit is, therefore, between 26 and 30 years. But in many cases there is also an upper age limit. It may be difficult for a senior manager or specialist, who has reached an interesting position in his employment, to switch over to consulting, unless he is directly offered a senior position with a consulting organisation. This, however, would happen only in special cases as mentioned above. Consulting emphasises certain work methods and behavioural patterns and some people would find it difficult to learn them after a certain age. The upper limit for recruitment tends to be, therefore, between 36 and 40 years.

---

[1] Cf. for example ACME: *Interviewing and testing techniques used in selecting management consulting personnel* (New York, Association of Consulting Management Engineers, 1971).

[2] See ACME: op. cit., p. 3.

Sources of recruitment

Logically, by far the most important source of recruitment is industrial and other enterprises. But any other source is acceptable provided it gave the candidate the required sort of experience in management.

Many consulting organisations advertise job opportunities in business journals and management periodicals and thus open their doors to any candidates who meet the criteria.

A good source might be found in the client organisations, but in most cases a consultant must not use this source for reasons already explained.[1] But of course there are exceptions to this. For example, a client may willingly authorise a consultant to offer a job to an employee whose personal qualities would be better utilised in consulting than in his present job. In a similar vein, a national management centre in a developing country may need to attract talented trainers and consultants from certain enterprises with which it co-operates, in order to establish a service needed by the entire local management community.

Interviewing and testing

Candidates for consultants' posts are asked to fill in the usual application forms (personnel questionnaires), supply detailed curricula vitae and provide other evidence of professional work (articles, papers, a doctoral thesis, etc.). References given by the candidate and other references identified by the consulting organisation are checked for every candidate who looks interesting (by correspondence, personal visits and telephone calls).

Applicants are subject to multiple interviews: by the personnel officer, a manager of the consulting organisation, a supervising consultant to whom the candidate might be attached after recruitment and one or two other consultants. Both structured and unstructured interviews are used; in both cases emphasis is on obtaining as complete a picture as possible of the technical knowledge and experience of the candidate and of personal characteristics which are essential to consulting.[2]

In some consulting organisations (more frequently in the USA than in Europe) tests are used as aids in selecting new consultants. These include both cognitive tests (designed to measure mainly knowledge) and psychological tests (related to personality, attitudes, interests and motivation). If personality and

---

[1] See Chapter 5.

[2] On interviewing see, for example, E. Sidney, M. Brown and M. Argyle: *Skills with people: a guide for managers* (London, Hutchinson, 1973) or H. and Z. Roodman: *Management by communication* (Toronto, Methuen Publications, 1973).

attitude tests are used, the evaluation of results should be made by a professional psychologist.[1]

Tests can convey useful information on the candidate, but their importance in the choice of consultants should not be overrated. They sometimes provide distorted information because of the ambiance in which the test is administered, or because some tests that are widely used become well known and hence less effective. In general, mature candidates do not like these tests.

Medical examination

A medical examination will be required, as is usual in the case of long-term employment. This will take account of the way of life of consultants, which in most cases is more demanding on the individual's physical and mental fitness, resistance and endurance than many other jobs with a comparable professional content.

Selection

As any new entrant to the profession is to be seen as a potential career consultant who may stay with the organisation for many years, the selection of those who will be offered employment requires very careful evaluation of the applicants, based (as mentioned above) on all information provided by the applicant himself, reference checking, multiple interviews and, possibly, tests. Managers of consulting organisations should avoid making authoritative decisions on selection without consulting a number of colleagues: every case of recruitment warrants a final collective assessment by a competent team of senior consultants.

26.3 Career development

A typical career structure

In an ideal case, the consultant's professional career will have a progressive structure, as shown in Table 22.

The consultant will be recruited at a junior level and for some time (say 6 to 12 months) will be considered as a *trainee* or junior consultant, whose main task is to master the essential consulting skills as quickly as possible, so as to be able to start on operating assignments.[2]

The actual first level in the career is that of *operating or resident consultant*.[3] He is the front-line man of the organisation who does most of the consulting

---

[1] See, for example, ACME: op. cit., pp. 15-20.
[2] Problems of initial training will be discussed in detail in Chapter 27.
[3] See also Chapter 9, p. 100.

Table 22. Career structure in a consulting unit

Level	Title	Main function	Age and other requirements
Junior	Trainee, Junior consultant	Learn the consulting skills	26-30 years Good education 5 years of experience
Operating	Operating (resident) consultant	Execute consulting assignments in his field of speciality	26-30 years Induction training completed
Senior	Supervising consultant, Team leader	Supervise operating consultants Act as team leader for complex assignments	32-38 years Minimum 4-7 years of operating experience Supervisory skills
Senior	Survey (diagnostic) consultant	Diagnose organisations Prepare and negotiate new assignments	Operating experience Knowledge of the broad spectrum of management problems Diagnostic skills
Managerial	Director, Manager, Partner, etc.	Manage a consulting organisation or its division Negotiate new assignments	Considerable consulting experience Managerial competence

work directly at client organisations. Every operating consultant has a special field of competence, as a rule in one management function, such as production management, or in special techniques, such as operations research. Normally the consultant would undertake a number of operating assignments in varying situations for a period of 4 to 7 years before being considered for promotion to the next level.

At the senior level, the first position is that of *supervising consultant*. He must have considerable experience to be able to guide and control the work of operating consultants in a specific field (for example, a marketing supervisor may be in charge of 4 to 6 different assignments in marketing) or have sufficiently broadened his knowledge and experience to be able to control complex assignments requiring expertise in general management, and including work in several functional areas.

Survey (diagnostic) consultants represent the next senior level in the career ladder.[1] The additional expertise which is required is the ability to examine organisations, identify their problems, and prepare and negotiate assignments.

---

[1] In some countries, for example in the United States, there are many consulting organisations where the difference between a supervising and a survey consultant is marginal or where both functions may be entrusted to the same consultant.

Finally, there is the *managerial level*, which in larger organisations includes divisional and regional managers, or directors, in addition to the top manager.[1]

Factors affecting careers

Not all consultants will pass through every level of the career ladder and become managers or directors of the unit. An obvious reason is that if there are, for example, 20 posts of operating consultant in a unit, there is only one management post. But there are some other reasons.

At the operating level, there are individuals who join a consulting organisation for a few years only and then prefer to return to business, continue as management teachers or trainers and so on. This is a normal and perfectly correct thing to do, although the unit's manager may regret to see some able individuals leave.

There are also consultants who prefer to stay in operating for their whole career—for example, because they prefer to do technical work themselves instead of guiding and controlling other consultants. In many organisations they would be recognised, and appreciated, as senior consultants after some time, without being given supervisory responsibilities.

The number of supervising and survey consultants in a consulting unit is not high and their actual career patterns may take a variety of forms.

As a rule, only a few of them have a tendency to seek other careers outside consulting—they like the professional challenge and independence of consulting and do not look for job satisfaction elsewhere. Another point is that a man who has been an effective senior consultant is unlikely to be happy in anything less than a top executive position, which means that he would have to immediately take responsibilities which were those of his clients—and it is difficult to exchange these two very different roles overnight.

In larger organisations there may be further opportunities for promotion within the senior consultant category, for example to survey consultant as indicated in Table 22, to senior posts in training and to other client services. There are also general management posts available in regional, sectoral or functional divisions and positions as directors. Some senior consultants become members of various management committees.

It should not be forgotten, either, that some senior consultants may establish new consulting organisations—it may be their own consulting firm, or a new institutional unit set up at the request of the government, a chamber of commerce or similar body.

---

[1] See also Chapter 25, p. 261.

Finally, it may be useful to emphasise that the principal factors in a successful career in consulting are, as for many other professional occupations, individual effort, drive and flexibility. Consulting organisations have to keep abreast of changes in the economy and in management and only consultants who are prepared to learn and to adjust their work methods to new opportunities can expect to achieve a career fully satisfying both to themselves and their organisation.

Career planning

The management of the unit should discuss career opportunities and problems with every consultant at regular intervals, say, every two years. The consultant should be encouraged to define his own goals and criteria, while the manager will consider what opportunities he can provide, and whether the individual's plan is realistic from the organisation's point of view. A career plan should be established by common agreement.[1]

---

[1] See ILO: *Career planning and development* (Management Development Series No. 12), (Geneva, International Labour Office, 1976).

TRAINING OF NEW CONSULTANTS 27

Most new recruits to the profession of management consulting have considerable knowledge and experience of one field of management, e.g. production, marketing or finance. Few have any knowledge or experience of management consultancy. They need training to make good this lack before they can assist clients to improve their management performance. If they start operating without initial training the quality of work will be poor, clients will be dissatisfied and the consultant organisation may have a short life.

27.1 Objectives of training

The over-all objective of an initial training programme for consultants is:

> To ensure that the consultant has the ability and confidence to carry out assignments in his field of management.

As consulting is not an easy activity, initial training must explain and demonstrate this, but at the same time provide enough guidance to the new entrant for him to start his first assignment confident in his ability and enthusiastic in his determination.

The over-all objective shown above can be broken down into four sub-objectives as follows:

> 1. To ensure that the consultant can investigate an existing situation and design improvements.

This requires the ability to gather information and analyse it critically, to identify all aspects of the problem, and then to design practical improvements using imagination and creative ability.

2. To ensure that he can gain acceptance of his proposed changes, both face-to-face and in writing, and can implement them satisfactorily.

Easily made contacts with people, a sound knowledge of the techniques of communication and persuasion, and good interaction with people during implementation, are vital aspects of a consultant's armoury. They are stressed and practised during initial training.

3. To ensure proficiency in his field or discipline.

This includes knowledge of all the technical aspects of his field, some of which he may not have encountered in his previous career, and the ability to apply them to a client's problems. At the same time, a consultant must be able to see the problems of his particular functional field in the broader context of an over-all management strategy, and relate them to problems of other functional areas and to the environment in which an enterprise operates.

4. To satisfy his seniors that he is capable of working independently and under pressure to the required standard.

It would be unrealistic to require new consultants to be able to tackle any difficult assignment immediately after training. Nevertheless, by the end of his initial training period the consultant must have demonstrated to the satisfaction of his seniors his ability to embark on a first field assignment. At the same time, a systematic evaluation of the trainee's performance should give the consulting unit enough information on the strengths and weaknesses of the new colleague, so that his supervisor can help him by proper guidance and coaching during the first operating assignments.

27.2 Patterns of initial training

The design of an initial training programme depends on many variables, including the specific needs of individual trainees and the resources and possibilities of the consulting organisation. The practices of consulting organisations vary. There is a broad range of initial training programmes, from precisely planned and organised programmes lasting 1 to 4 years to totally informal programmes of undetermined duration. It is not the purpose of this chapter to prescribe one particular pattern for all conditions. There are, however, certain principles which should be reflected in any programme for new consultants and also certain patterns which have given good results in varying situations.

Individualisation

New entrants have different backgrounds in terms of knowledge and experience and different personal characteristics.[1] There should be no uniform initial training programme, although some elements of initial training will be given to every new consultant for obvious reasons. We will show below how the training programme can be individualised without becoming too difficult and expensive for the consulting unit to organise.

Practicality

Some aspects and methods of consulting can be explained and practised in a course, but most of the training has to take the form of practice in carrying out the various steps of a consulting assignment, and interacting with clients, under the guidance of a senior consultant. The programme must include both the observation of experienced consultants in action and the execution of *practical tasks or projects* involving change.

Stretching the trainee

The programme should demonstrate that consulting is demanding in time, effort and brainpower, so that the trainee is under no illusions about the responsibilities he has accepted in his newly chosen profession.

Length of programme

Although it could be argued that a new consultant will need several years of experience to become fully competent and be able to operate with little guidance and supervision, it would be unpractical, and psychologically unsound, to maintain new consultants in the category of trainees for too long. Assuming normal conditions of recruitment[2], the period of initial training would not exceed 6 to 12 months.

Basic components of the training programme

The programme of initial training has three basic components:

- training course for new consultants;
- practical field training at client organisations;
- individual study.

---

[1] See Chapter 26, pp. 277-278.
[2] As discussed in Chapter 25.

A training course for new consultants will cover those aspects of consulting which have to be given to all trainees, and can be dealt with in a classroom situation, using a variety of teaching methods as discussed below in Section 27.5. As a rule, this will be a full-time residential course and its total duration may be between 6 and 12 weeks. Large consulting organisations can afford longer courses, and hold them at their own headquarters or training centres. Small consulting organisations may have to rely on sending their new members to an external course for management consultants, complementing such a course by a short seminar dealing with their specific problems and work concepts.

Field training is intended to develop a range of practical skills, demonstrate consulting in action and mould the trainee's attitudes towards his new profession on the basis of his own first-hand experience. In planning this part of the training the consulting organisation enjoys great flexibility, provided however it has enough clients willing to receive trainees, and experienced consultants who have the time and the ability to train new colleagues.

Whether the trainee's time spent at a client organisation should be charged to the client is a delicate matter, which should be frankly discussed with clients, without imposing arrangements that clients would accept reluctantly. While it is justifiable to ask clients to pay some fee if a trainee's work led to measurable improvements, it is not reasonable to expect clients to bear directly the cost of training new consultants, as this should be a general overhead cost of the unit. A compromise solution may be found in a reduced fee, or a fee paid only for a certain part of the trainee's time.

The same applies to the trainer's time—if the trainer is an operating consultant, time spent on guiding and advising trainees should not be charged to the client.

Individual study is another component which provides for flexibility of training. A new consultant can be asked to fill some gaps in his knowledge by reading professional literature, final assignment reports, operating manuals and so on.

Combining the three components

In an ideal situation, the initial training may be scheduled as follows:

(1) first (introductory) part of the course for new consultants (say 4 to 10 weeks);

(2) field training (length as necessary and feasible);

(3) second part of the course (say 2 to 3 weeks), including seminars on operating methods, familiarisation with technical services, people and documentation at the consulting unit's headquarters;

(4) field training continues as appropriate;

(5) no specific period is reserved for individual study—this will be done in parallel with the course and with field training (the consultant may have to foresee many overtime hours for this).

A consulting organisation may, however, find it impossible to follow this schedule for various practical reasons; for example the number of trainees may not warrant an in-house course, even though no external course is available in the country. The training task may thus become more difficult for everybody concerned: for example, a new entrant will have to pick up much more through individual reading and from discussions with the operating consultant—his field trainer.

27.3 The trainer's role

During recruitment and selection, the new consultant meets senior people in the organisation for a short time. He cannot get to know them well, nor can he obtain more than a superficial view of the work a consultant really does. The trainer is the first member of the organisation the new consultant gets to know well. He sets an example of how a consultant behaves, and how he achieves results largely without the authority to impose his ideas. The trainer, therefore, plays an important part in developing the characteristics that differentiate the consultant from the manager, executive, accountant or planner. Apart from instilling knowledge, he sets the tone for the new consultant in his work with clients.

Head office trainer

The head office trainer is a senior person with wide experience of consulting and training. He has over-all responsibility for the new consultant's training, including the programming of field training. He is in charge of the central training course for new consultants and will give a number of sessions in the course himself. He may visit new consultants during field training to ensure that all is well.

In a central training course for consultant induction, each trainee is viewed as an individual who will spend much of his time as the sole operating consultant on assignments. However, his behaviour within the group and ability to join in the common cause is also noted. So are his reactions to the problems and ideas discussed during the course.

The trainee may find it difficult to get adjusted to the course. His move may involve more than the change of job: incidental domestic problems could be a source of distraction. The trainer does not take a teacher-and-pupil attitude and the atmosphere in the course room is not that of a schoolroom. This point may seem obvious but a trainer also has to learn to do the job for the first time and may start by being a bit of a pedant. A trainee should find the trainer a good friend and counsellor on whom he can rely at any time for guidance and help.

Field trainer

The field trainer is an operating consultant with a client. He is already practising in the field in which the new consultant will operate, and arranges for him to gradually take over a part of the assignment. He too must have training capabilities, be sympathetic to the needs of the new consultant, and be able to impart enthusiasm to him for working with a client. In particular, he has the responsibility of ensuring that the new consultant can operate successfully on completion of the training.

The field trainer develops a very special relationship with the new consultant. As he will be spending some evenings with him, a strong bond of friendship is usually born, and this may persist for many years after training is completed.

The senior consultant supervising the operating consultant has a minor role to play in field training. Apart from ensuring completion of the programme on time, and approving any training reports, he makes sure that the new consultant is happy in his work and has no worries.

Both the headquarters' and the field trainer have important responsibilities concerning the evaluation of the new consultant, as discussed in Section 27.6 below.

27.4 Subjects to be covered by initial training

Although we have emphasised the individual character of initial training for new consultants, some general guidance on programme content can be given. It will concern the main areas to be covered in most cases, assuming that the planners of these training programmes make the appropriate adjustments for the individual needs of the trainees. In doing so, they will also decide on the use of the basic components of training (central course, field training and individual study) to deal with specific subject areas of the total programme.

While there may be considerable differences in the professional profiles of new consultants when they join the consulting organisation, attempts have been made to summarise attributes which should be common to competent management consultants working with different consulting organisations. This has led to the development by some professional associations of a " body of knowledge " for management consultants.[1] To the planners of training programmes, such documents provide useful checklists of subjects.

By and large, the initial training of management consultants is geared to the enhancement of knowledge and skills in four subject areas:

(1) orientation to consulting;
(2) investigational and problem-solving techniques;
(3) communication and change;
(4) theory and practice of management.

Orientation to consulting [2]:

— the nature, purpose and history of consulting;
— specialisation, functions, organisation, and management of consulting units;
— public relations; contacts; preliminary surveys; types of operating assignments; consulting terms of reference;
— the consultant's basic roles and personal characteristics;
— relationships between various consulting functions (operating, supervising, diagnosing, etc.);
— consultant-client relationships;
— professional behaviour and the code of conduct;
— administration and financial control in a consulting unit.

Investigational and problem-solving techniques:

— systematic approach to problem solving;
— defining the problem; diagnosing organisations;
— assignment planning and scheduling;
— obtaining the facts; methods and techniques; work study; interviewing and other techniques;
— examination of facts; methods and techniques of fact analysis;
— developing proposals; evaluation and choice of alternatives; demonstration of benefits;
— presenting proposals;
— specifying solutions; design of working systems and procedures; form design;

---

[1] See Chapter 5, p. 46.
[2] This includes orientation both to the consulting profession and to policies and work methods of a given unit.

- implementation; preparations, tactics and control; training the client's staff; evaluation of final benefits;
- maintenance and control; measures to prevent backsliding; preservation of standards; controls; follow-up service.

Communication[1] and change:

- introduction to behavioural sciences and their findings about communication and change in organisations;
- oral communication; effective speaking and listening; investigational and other interviewing;
- group leading and control; meetings; presentations;
- persuasion;
- written communication; the message and its medium; report writing;
- the process of change in organisations and in people;
- strategies and tactics for implementing change;
- the role of the change agent.

Theory and practice of management:

- economic, social, and other environments (national and international) and their impact on management;
- principal management functions and basic concepts of managing organisations;
- general management;
- financial management and accounting;
- marketing management;
- production and supply management;
- research and development management;
- personnel management;
- operations research and other quantitative techniques applied to management;
- office and records management;
- management information systems and computer applications in management.

---

[1] See Appendix 6 " Person-to-person communication in consulting " and Appendix 7 " Consultant report writing ".

Table 23.   Structure of the central training course

Subject area	Share of time in %
Orientation to consulting	15
Investigation and problem solving	40
Communication and change	20
Theory and practice of management	25
Total course	100

As mentioned, the proportions between these areas may differ from case to case. A rough guide for structuring the central training course is given in Table 23.

The list of subject areas given above also includes some aspects that were listed under the personal characteristics [1], or qualities, of a good consultant. Both the central course and the field component of training should provide opportunities and time for improving characteristics such as good judgement, analytical and problem-solving ability, skill in inter-personal relationships and ability to communicate and persuade. The training programmes will also aim at improving other qualities such as self-confidence, integrity and independence. These, however, cannot be the subject of a particular session or exercise, but an overriding objective of the trainers' and trainees' common efforts. It should be noted too that the demands on the initial training programme must not be unrealistic: most young consultants will need several years of experience to acquire fully the qualities that characterise a competent member of the profession.

27.5 Training methods

Training course methods

The training course uses a variety of training methods [2], with emphasis on participative methods, and those where the trainee himself can adjust the pace of learning to his capabilities.

Subjects which involve mainly the imparting of knowledge require some lecturing, which, however, should be supplemented by discussions, training

---

[1] See Chapter 26, pp. 277-278.

[2] See ILO: " *An introductory course in teaching and training methods for management development* " (Geneva, International Labour Office, 1972) and further references at the end of Part VI.

films [1], and other audio-visual aids. In many cases lecturing can be replaced by reading texts (e.g. on the origin and history of consulting, on types of specialisation of consulting organisations) or using audio-visual learning packages (e.g. videotapes).

Subjects involving skill-improvement require techniques that allow for practising skills. This can be done to some extent in a training course by using properly chosen and prepared *case studies* and *simulation exercises*. Case studies should introduce the trainee to various consulting situations; the consulting unit should be in a position to prepare a number of such case studies from previous assignments. Exercises should lead the trainee through various common consulting practices, such as:

— effective speaking and persuasion;

— investigational interviewing;

— analysing company accounts and preparing ratios;

— discussion leading and control;

— written communication;

— methods charting;

— designing systems and procedures;

— work measurement.

Role-playing provides an excellent way of introducing consulting practice into learning situations. It takes place in a controlled situation, i.e. in a classroom, where mistakes are used to teach and have no disastrous consequences. As a large part of a consultant's work on assignment consists of presenting proposals to clients and their staff, it is useful to organise role-playing exercises in:

— persuading members of the client's staff to accept a new method of operation;
— interviewing staff to obtain facts about an assignment problem;
— dealing with awkward situations or complaints from staff about proposed changes;
— explaining to the client conclusions drawn from his financial reports;
— presenting an assignment report to the client;
— dealing with embarrassing questions from the client or members of his staff.

Role-playing exercises need to be realistic, and test the participants in as near true conditions as possible. Some feedback after the exercise is also essential. This suggests four requirements:

— a trainee himself playing a consultant;
— other trainees playing client or other roles;
— at least two trainees acting as observers, with a brief to watch for certain features of the players' behaviour;
— thorough briefs have to be prepared for all participants.

---

[1] A list of selected training films applicable in the training of consultants is given in Appendix 8. Other management development films can be chosen from ILO: *Films* (Management development manual No. 15, Rev. 1.), (Geneva, International Labour Office, 1975).

Time is allowed for briefing the role-players and observers, and for the absorption of the material including the preparation of any figures. After the role-playing, observers comment and a general discussion leads to the identification of lessons. Aids such as tape recorders or closed circuit television may be used in this connection.

Field training methods

In field training, the principal training technique is *practical problem-solving and project work*. As this is done in a real consulting situation, which may be very sensitive to errors and faux pas, the trainee will be guided and controlled by the trainer in more detail than might be necessary in another situation. It may not, however, be easy to find situations in which the new consultant could practise not only a few, but a wide range of investigational and other techniques that should eventually make up his consulting kit.

Role-playing can be used to rehearse activities before the " live " show later. In this role-playing, the new consultant and trainer rehearse in the office or at home in the evening, and are able to anticipate and correct snags.

27.6 Evaluation of training

The new consultant's progress in training is carefully watched by those in contact with him, and a series of confidential reports is issued. The purpose is to ascertain whether the training is achieving its objectives, propose corrective measures (extension of the training programme, inclusion of new subjects for individual study and the like) and gather information on the strengths and weaknesses of the new member of the unit (this is invaluable to those who will supervise his first assignments). Needless to say, evaluation also helps to improve the training policies and programmes of the consulting unit.

Evaluating the trainee

Many consulting organisations use a system of confidential reports in which the trainers (both at head office and in the field) give their personal appraisal of the trainee. At least three reports are required:

— one at the end of the initial head office training course;

— one at the end of field training;

— one at the end of the final head office training.

Additional reports may be required, for example if the initial training is broken down into several periods, or if the length of field training warrants interim progress reports.

The reports (see an example of a report form in Figure 12) evaluate the new consultant under a number of headings. The assessments are usually on a

Figure 12. Training report form

TRAINING REPORT (confidential)		Report number	Date
Trainee		Trainer	
Supervisor		Client	

Type of report	Interim report ☐ Final report ☐	Head office training ☐ Field training ☐

Reporting period	starting date	finishing date	duration in weeks

Description of work performed

Evaluation (mark x in the appropriate column; comments are required if marked other than satisfactory)	A - satisfactory			
		B - satisfactory with reservations		
			C - unsatisfactory	
				Comments
I. Personal attributes Intellectual capacity				
Professional conduct				
Physical appearance and bearing				
Initiative and energy				
Person-to-person communication				
Social behaviour				
II. Technical qualities (general) Diagnostic skills				
Preparing suggestions				
Techniques of introducing change				
Verbal reporting				
Written reports				
III. Specific functional or sectoral skills				

Figure 12.   (continued)

Evaluation	A	B	C	Comments
IV. General observations Attendance and punctuality				
Course contribution (as individual)				
Course contribution (to group work)				
Contribution to field work				
Meeting set deadlines				
Speed and accuracy				

Over-all assessment by the trainer

Supervisor's comments

Recommendations concerning first assignments and further training

Other comments or decisions

numerical scale with supporting comments and examples. The scale can have a range of numbers or letters on it, a common system being a five- or three-point scale as follows:

1. Excellent   or   A. Satisfactory
2. Very good   B. Satisfactory with reservations
3. Standard   C. Unsatisfactory
4. Poor
5. Unsatisfactory

The standard against which the new consultant is measured is the standard expected of an operating consultant on his first assignment. The question to be answered is: " On present showing, will he be ready to operate at the end of training? " Consistency of interpretation of the standard by the central trainer, field trainers and supervisors comes from their common experience and their knowledge of current operating requirements.

The trainers review with the trainee how he is progressing, informally during work and training sessions, and in formal discussions which are held when an evaluation report is prepared. The new consultant must be told of his strengths, weaknesses, and any other aspects of his work.

In addition to these discussions, senior members of the consulting organisation interview the new consultant during training. Apart from giving an opportunity to talk about the work and progress, these interviews ensure that the new consultant becomes a fully integrated member of the organisation. They show that management is interested in him, aware of progress, and planning for his first assignment after completion of training.

The importance of open criticism and frankness need hardly be stressed. Both the future effectiveness and life of the consulting organisation, and the long-term career prospects of new consultants, depend on the excellent professional work of the individual. Any doubts about a new consultant's ability are not hidden, but are discussed with him and with the seniors in the unit. If the doubts cannot be resolved by the end of the training course, a decision is required on whether the new consultant stays or terminates his employment. On balance, termination of employment at this early moment may be the better choice, both for the new consultant and for the organisation. This, however, should be rather an exception, if the initial selection of candidates is carried out in a competent manner.

At the end of the total initial training programme it is useful to draw conclusions on the further training needs of the new consultant, and on the best ways of meeting them (by giving preference to certain types of assignments at the beginning, by further individual study, etc.).

Evaluating the training programme

Several ways of evaluating are open to trainers, and particularly the head office trainer who has responsibility for the whole course. Trainees may be asked to comment on the course in the usual way.[1] This can be a general comment, or specific ones on the content and manner of the individual speakers, or their exercises. Care is necessary to preserve confidence—trainees may be reluctant to comment if they feel that adverse criticism may be turned against them later. However, the feedback to individual speakers can be a spur to them to improve their presentations.

Comment and criticism may be obtained from senior consultants responsible for the early assignments. They may find the new consultants lacking in specific skills; this may be due to gaps, or poorly covered subjects, either in the initial head office training course or in the field training. The new consultant should also be asked, during and after field training, whether he found the practical preparation for the first assignments adequate.

27.7 Training new consultants in developing countries

The general approach to initial training of new management consultants discussed in this chapter is not confined to any particular country or type of economic environment. The basic objectives and guidelines apply to the training of consultants in both the public and private sectors of industrialised as well as developing countries. There are, however, certain factors in many developing countries which call for adjustments of the general approach discussed above.

There are three typical shortages which make the training of new consultants considerably more difficult.

Shortage of recruitment sources: It is difficult to find people who in addition to a good educational background have the required 5-7 years of practical experience and the personal characteristics of a management consultant. Those who meet most or all the criteria may have important and interesting jobs in business or government and would seldom consider abandoning them.

Shortage of internal training capabilities: The existing young consulting units have not been in the profession for long enough to have their own trainers, curricula and materials needed for a complete training programme for new consultants.

---

[1] See for example, A. C. Hamblin: *Evaluation and control of training* (London, McGraw-Hill, 1974), pp. 74-84.

Shortage of suitable training situations: There may not be a sufficient number of diverse assignments in which the new entrant to the profession could practise the various consulting methods and techniques on the job, in the presence of a more experienced colleague who maintains primary responsibility for the assignment.

Against these shortages stands the requirement to which many governments and local business communities have subscribed: to develop the local management consulting and training capabilities *in a shorter time* than was needed in countries industrialised today.

This calls for the imaginative application of certain *strategies*, which could be summarised as follows:

(1) to make sure that at least a few members of a new consulting unit will meet all criteria concerning education, previous experience and personal profile;

(2) to accept shorter practical experience in the case of other new recruits, but so design their initial field training that it would replace a part of missing previous experience;

(3) to use international or other experts for local training of management consultants (the expert works as an operating consultant-trainer, his main task being to guide and control 2-3 trainees);

(4) to make sure that every assignment entrusted to foreign management consultants is used as a training opportunity for local consultants; to include a corresponding provision in every contract;

(5) to reduce gradually the use of foreign consultants for simple assignments; to use their services instead only for particularly difficult and important projects;

(6) to arrange projects whereby foreign management consultants:

— would organise the practical training in consulting of nationals from developing countries in industrialised countries;

— would accept responsibility for the establishment of a local consulting unit, including its organisation, operating procedures and training of staff;

(7) to establish and develop internal consulting units [1] in important government and business organisations; such units can also assume responsibility for internal training and for a range of productivity and management improvement measures; in this way some of the advantages of disseminating effective management practices through consulting work could be maintained

---

[1] See also Chapter 1, p. 12, and Chapter 23, p. 248.

without, however, withdrawing competent people from organisations which employ them;

(8) to link external consulting services [1] very closely with local management education and training institutions, and with internal consulting units in important organisations, so that they would support each other in their common effort to develop their country's managerial capability.[2]

---

[1] See Chapter 1, p. 12 and Chapter 23, p. 246.

[2] Cf. ILO: *Effective managers for development (the Management Development Programme of the ILO)*, (Geneva, International Labour Office, 1975) and M. Kubr: " Trends in co-ordination and planning of management education ", in *Management International Review*, Vol. 14, 1974, No. 1.

FURTHER TRAINING AND DEVELOPMENT OF CONSULTANTS 28

In management consulting the idea of permanent, life-long education is not new. A number of consulting organisations have gained excellent professional reputation thanks to their efforts invested in the development of staff. An individual who becomes a consultant should realise that he is joining a profession which has to change continuously, because its object—the practice of management in the contemporary economic and social environment—also changes rapidly. The consequences to the individual are obvious—he must be prepared to continue learning, to develop receptivity to new ideas, to abandon obsolete concepts without regrets, and to develop a strong will to learn under working conditions that are not always ideal.

28.1 Principal directions of consultants' development

Upgrading functional proficiency

Keeping abreast of developments, and improving performance in his own field, is the basis of an operating consultant's further development. Most training and development activities in a consulting organisation are geared to this objective.

Mastering new fields

A consultant may learn subjects complementary to his main field in order to broaden his ability to undertake assignments touching on several management functions. A typical case is the broadening of the consultant's competence with a view to becoming a general management consultant, able to lead teams of mixed functional specialists, to act as advisor on general management problems and to undertake diagnostic surveys.

Another reason for learning new subjects may be the consulting organisation's intention to start activities in new technical fields. As a rule, consulting organisations prefer to transfer their more dynamic consultants, familiar with the organisation's philosophy and practices, to these new activities rather than staffing them with new recruits.

Preparing for career development

As explained in Chapter 26, career advancement in consulting involves the acceptance of new roles, such as supervising or diagnostic ones; the general requirement being that the consultant is able to define the clients' needs and the strategies required for new assignments, and to guide and control other consultants. Thus career advancement carries with it the need to adopt a broader approach and develop technical competence in several fields.

28.2 Organisation and methods of further development

There are certain features in consulting practice which make further training and development difficult to organise. For example, most consultants in the same discipline are geographically dispersed on individual assignments. To arrange a technical discussion may, therefore, require a special organisational effort. Furthermore, the highly individualised character of consulting work encourages consultants to become individualists, and this creates a constant problem in transferring effective work experiences from one consultant to another.

Nevertheless, the profession has many features which greatly facilitate the consultant's development. As distinct from a manager involved in the same technical field, a consultant's energy and time are much less absorbed by routine matters and established procedures. He can approach each new assignment as a practical exercise where innovation may be possible and desirable. He can thus refine his method virtually continuously and is never short of opportunities for the practical application of ideas and suggestions found in the literature or other sources. Furthermore, it would be totally wrong to assume that in the consultant-client relationship only the consultant is teaching and the client learning. A consultant learns a great deal from any client organisation, but to reinforce his learning he must compare, generalise, conceptualise and try to apply a new, more effective approach to successive assignments. He has to avoid the pitfall of mechanically applying routine solutions to every situation.

The following staff development methods are used in many consulting organisations.

Consultant self-development

Because of the very nature of consulting work, with its attendant opportunities and organisational difficulties, self-development is the main method of staff development. Consultants have to acquire the habit of reading the main professional periodicals and important new publications relevant to their field. But the kernel of self-development is the above-mentioned continuous search for new types of more effective solutions to the management problems of clients.

Professional guidance by senior consultants

As already emphasised [1], supervising consultants are responsible, among others, for the development of operating consultants who report to them. They provide guidance when examining work progress and discussing solutions proposed by the operating consultant. Such discussions can easily be broadened to inform the operating consultant of experience from other assignments or techniques used by colleagues. A major feature of guidance by senior consultants is that it should help operating consultants develop their personal characteristics and communication skills.[2]

Dissemination of information

While dissemination of information by itself does not guarantee training and development (e.g. information may be ignored or misunderstood), it is a basic input for learning in the consulting organisation.[3] A properly organised system of information and documentation should supply operating consultants with facts and ideas which they should know and, if appropriate, apply in their assignments. Additional information may be forthcoming as a result of a consultant's membership of a professional association.

Seminars and conferences

Short seminars and conferences for professional staff are organised in many consulting organisations. For example, there may be an annual conference, which in addition to policy and administrative matters deals with technical topics useful to all consultants. Seminars may be organised in functional divisions, on a regional basis, etc.

---

[1] See Chapter 10, p. 114.

[2] See Chapter 26, p. 277, and Appendices 6 and 7.

[3] Cf. Chapter 24, p. 252. See also chapter " Collection and dissemination of information within a consulting firm " in the report *Management of the consulting firm* from the FEACO conference on 7-8.10.1971.

Acting as trainers

One of the best methods of self-development is training other people. Consultants have many opportunities to do this, either for the client's personnel during assignments or at the consulting organisation's training centre.[1]

Special training courses

If new techniques or subject areas need to be learned (e.g. computer applications in production planning and control, or accounting concepts and techniques for non-accountants), consultants can participate in normal management and specialist courses, or the unit can arrange internal courses for its staff.

Research and development assignments

Assignments such as developing a new line of consulting or preparing an operating manual based on the unit's past experiences are excellent learning opportunities for senior staff members.

Training for supervisory functions

Promotion to the role of supervisor usually follows several years in an operating role. Some experience of the role is gained by seeing the senior in action, and by guiding new consultant trainees.

Training on promotion is usually quite short and is provided by experienced seniors who happen to be good trainers. Training is given partly in formal sessions at head office and partly with experienced seniors in action. Head office training requires about three weeks, while the training with an experienced senior may extend over some months. During this time the promoted consultant works largely on his own, with only occasional guidance and advice from his more experienced colleague.

28.3 Planning and budgeting for training and development

From the viewpoint of an individual member of the consulting organisation it is useful to establish specific training objectives against which the consultant can measure his progress. In particular, such objectives should be defined for the first years of operating on the basis of the evaluations made at the end of the initial training programme.[2]

---

[1] See Chapter 24, p. 255.
[2] See Chapter 27, p. 295.

There should be some individual training standards, i.e. every consultant should know what is expected from him, and what time and resources will be allocated to him for training and self-development. For example, the average allocation may be 10 working days of formal training per year, plus current reading of professional literature, for which no special time allocation is made.

For the consulting organisation, training other than on the job is non-fee-earning time [1]; but the annual planning and budgeting should include a provision for training as an item of the unit's fixed expenses. For reasons already explained consulting units must not seek savings by compressing allocations for training below reasonable limits.

---

[1] See Chapter 25, pp. 265-266.

LITERATURE TO PART VI

ACME: *Interviewing and testing techniques used in selecting management consulting personnel* (New York, Association of Consulting Management Engineers, 1971); 22 pp.

ACME: *Personal qualifications of management consultants* (New York, Association of Consulting Management Engineers, 1971); 36 pp.

ACME: *Professional practices in management consulting* (New York, Association of Consulting Management Engineers, 1966); 100 pp.

ACME: *Study guide to professional practices in management consulting* (New York, Association of Consulting Management Engineers, 1960); 53 pp.

Craig R. L. (ed): *Training and development handbook; a guide to human resource development* (2nd ed.) (New York, McGraw-Hill, 1976); 866 pp.

Davies I. K. (ed.): *The organisation of training* (London, McGraw-Hill, 1973); 113 pp.

Farnsworth T.: *Developing executive talent* (London, McGraw-Hill); 162 pp.

Hague H.: *Executive self-development* (London, Macmillan, 1974); 240 pp.

Hamblin A. C.: *Evaluation and control of training* (London, McGraw-Hill, 1974); 200 pp.

Harper M.: *Consultancy for small businesses (the concept; training the consultants)* (London, Intermediate Technology Publications, 1976); 254 pp.

Humble J. (ed.): *Improving the performance of the experienced manager* (London, McGraw-Hill, 1973); 350 pp.

ILO: *An introductory course in teaching and training methods for management development* (Management Development Manual No. 36), (Geneva, International Labour Office, 5th impr. 1977); 350 pp.

ILO: *Career planning and development* (Management Development Series No. 12), (Geneva, International Labour Office, 1976); 140 pp.

ILO: *Films* (Management Development Manual No. 15, Rev. 1), (Geneva, International Labour Office, 1975); 118 pp.

ILO: *Management and productivity: an international directory of institutions and information sources* (Management Development Series No. 13) (Geneva, International Labour Office, 1980); approx. 250 pp.

Kellog M. S.: *Career management* (New York, American Management Association, 1972); 200 pp.

Lopez F. M.: *Personnel interviewing; theory and practice* (New York, McGraw-Hill, 1975); 356 pp.

Mailick S. (ed.): *The making of the manager, a world view* (New York, Anchor Press-Doubleday, 1974); 480 pp.

Markwell D. S., Roberts T. J.: *Organisation of management development programmes* (London, Gower Press, 1969); 182 pp.

Pedler M., Burgoyne J., Boydell T.: *A manager's guide to self-development* (London, McGraw-Hill, 1978); 231 pp.

Plumbey P. R.: *Recruitment and selection* (London, Institute of Personnel Management, 1974); 214 pp.

Revans R. W.: *Developing effective managers* (London, Longman, 1971); 220 pp.

Shay P. W.: *The common body of knowledge for management consultants* (New York, Association of Consulting Management Engineers, 1974); 43 pp.

Sidney E., Brown M., Argyle M.: *Skills with people: a guide for managers* (London, Hutchinson, 1973); 230 pp.

Stewart V., Stewart A.: *Managing the manager's growth* (Westmead, Farnborough, Hants, Gower Press, 1978); 257 pp.

Taylor B., Lippitt G. L. (eds.): *Management development and training handbook* (London, McGraw-Hill, 1975); 650 pp.

Warr P., Bird M., Rackham N.: *Evaluation of management training* (London, Gower Press, 1970); 110 pp.

APPENDICES

ASSOCIATIONS OF MANAGEMENT CONSULTANTS IN SELECTED COUNTRIES

AUSTRALIA	Institute of Management Consultants in Australia Inc. (IMCA) 32, Buckingham Street, Surry Hills 2010 Sydney
AUSTRIA	Vereinigung Osterreichischer Betriebs und Organisationsberater (VOB) Strauchgasse 3, 1010 Wien
BELGIUM	Association belge des Conseils en organisation et gestion (ASCOBEL) c/o CICB, Rue Ravenstein 3, 1000 Bruxelles
CANADA	Canadian Association of Management Consultants (CAMC) Box 289, Toronto-Dominion Centre, Toronto III, Ontario
DENMARK	Den Danske Sammenslutning AF Konsulenter I Virksomhedsledelse (DSKV) Nørrevoldgade 34, 1358 Copenhagen K.
FINLAND	Liikkeenjohdon Konsultit (LJK) Korkeavuorenkatu 29 A 11, Helsinki 13
FRANCE	Chambre syndicale des sociétés d'études et de conseils (SYNTEC) 3, rue Léon Bonnat, 75016 Paris
GERMANY (FEDERAL REPUBLIC)	Bundesverband Deutscher Unternehmensberater (BDU) E.V. Konrad Adenauer Platz 11, 5300 Bonn/Beuel

INDIA

Management Consultants Association of India (MCAI)
c/o Modern Management Counsel,
3E-1 Court Chambers, New Marine Lines, Bombay 20

ITALY

Associazione Fra Società e Studi di Consulenza
Organizzativa (ASSCO)
Piazza IV Novembre, 6, I 20124 Milan

JAPAN

All Japan Federation of Management Organizations
(Zennoren)
Kyoritsu Building, 3-1-22, Shibakoen, Minato-ku,
Tokyo 105

Association of Management Consultants in Japan
Kyoritsu Building, 3-1-22, Shibakoen, Minato-ku,
Tokyo 105

Chusho Kigyo Shindan Kyokai
(Smaller Enterprise Consultants Association)
Ginza Section of MITI, 6-15-1, Ginza, Chuo-ku,
Tokyo 104

Meikokukai, Japan Productivity Center
3-1-1, Shibuya, Shibuya-ku, Tokyo 150

NETHERLANDS

Raad van Organisatie-Adviesbureau
Van Eeghenstraat 86, Amsterdam 1007

NIGERIA

Nigerian Association of Management Consultants
c/o Centre for Management Development
P.O. Box 7648, Ikorodu Road, Lagos

NORWAY

Norsk Forening AV Radgivere i Bedriftsledelse
c/o Industrikonsulent A/S, Aslakveien 14,
Oslo 7

SPAIN

Asociacion Española de Empresas de
Ingenieria y Consultoras (ASEINCO)
Claudio Coello, 86, Madrid-6

SWEDEN

Svenska Organisationskonsulters Förening (SOK)
Bragevägen 9-11, 11426 Stockholm

SWITZERLAND

Association suisse des conseils en organisation
et gestion (ASCO)
Bellariastrasse 51, 8038 Zürich

TURKEY

Turkish Management Consultant Firms Association
Gümüssuyu Cad. 44-4 Taksim, Istanbul

UNITED
KINGDOM

Institute of Management Consultants (IMC)
23-24 Cromwell Place, London SW7 2LG

Management Consultants Association (MCA)
23-24 Cromwell Place, London SW7 2LG

UNITED STATES
OF AMERICA

Council of Management Consulting Organizations
(COMCO)

c/o ACME, 230 Park Avenue, New York,
N.Y. 10017

Association of Consulting Management Engineers
(ACME)
230 Park Avenue, New York, N.Y. 10017

Association of Internal Management Consultants
(AIMC)
Box 472, Glastonbury, Connecticut 06033

Association of Management Consultants (AMC)
331 Madison Avenue, New York, N.Y. 10017

Institute of Management Consultants (IMC)
19 W 44th Street, New York, N.Y. 10036

Society of Professional Management Consultants
(SPMC)
205 W 89th Street, New York, N.Y. 10024

YUGOSLAVIA

Yugoslav Center for Organization and Development
35 Milana Rakica, Beograd

EUROPE

Fédération européenne des associations de conseils
en organisation (FEACO)
c/o SYNTEC 3, rue Léon Bonnat, 75016 Paris

*International associations of consulting engineers whose members are also
involved in management consulting:*

EUROPE   European Committee of Consulting Engineering Firms (CEBI)
83 Bd. Jacquemin, 1000 Bruxelles

LATIN AMERICA   Federación Latinoamericana de Asociaciones de Consultores (FELAC)
Av. R. Rivera Navarrete 451—Piso 3—Of. 3-B
Lima 27

INTERNATIONAL International Federation of Consulting Engineers (FIDIC)
Carel van Bylandtlaan 9
2596 HP The Hague

International Consultants Foundation
5605 Lamar Road
Washington, D.C. 20016

PROFESSIONAL CODES
(Examples)

A. Code of conduct of the FEACO (European Federation of Associations of Management Consultants)

All member Associations must subscribe to FEACO's code of conduct and practice under which it is regarded as unprofessional conduct:

- To advertise in a blatant or commercial manner.
- To accept any trade commissions, discounts or considerations of any kind in connection with the supply of services or goods to a client.
- To have interest in firms supplying goods or services to their clients, or to be under their control, or to fail to make known any kind of interest likely to affect their service.
- To calculate remuneration on any basis other than the agreed professional scale of fees.
- To disclose confidential information regarding their clients' activities.
- To pay or accept payment for the introduction of clients, except in accordance with recognised and generally accepted professional practice in the country concerned.
- To do anything which does not accord with the statutes of the profession.

B. Standards of professional conduct and practice of the ACME (Association of Consulting Management Engineers), USA

Preamble

Purposes of Standards of Professional Conduct

These Standards of Professional Conduct and Practice signify voluntary assumption by members of the obligation of self-discipline above and beyond the requirements of the law. Their purpose is to let the public know that members intend to maintain a high level of ethics and public service, and to declare that—in return for the faith that the public places in them—the members accept the obligation to conduct their practice in a way that will be beneficial to the public. They give clients a basis for confidence that members will serve them in accordance with professional standards of competence, objectivity, and integrity.

They express in general terms the standards of professional conduct expected of management consulting firms in their relationships with prospective clients, clients, colleagues, members of allied professions, and the public. The Code of Professional Responsibility, unlike the Professional Practices, is mandatory in character. It serves as a basis for disciplinary action when the conduct of a member firm falls below the required standards as stated in the Code of Professional Responsibility. The Professional Practices are largely aspirational in character and represent objectives and standards of good practice to which members of the Association subscribe.

The Association enforces the Code of Professional Responsibility by receiving and investigating all complaints of violations and by taking disciplinary action against any member who is found to be guilty of code violation.

The professional attitude

The reliance of managers of private and public institutions on the advice of management consultants imposes on the profession an obligation to maintain high standards of integrity and competence. To this end, members of the Association have basic responsibilities to place the interests of clients and prospective clients ahead of their own, maintain independence of thought and action, hold the affairs of their clients in strict confidence, strive continually to improve their professional skills, observe and advance professional standards of management consulting, uphold the honor and dignity of the profession, and maintain high standards of personal conduct. These Standards have evolved out of the experience of members since the Association was incorporated in 1933. In recognition of the public interest and their obligation to the profession, members and the consultants on their staffs have agreed to comply with the following articles of professional responsibility.

I — Code of professional responsibility

1. Basic client responsibilities

1.1 We will at all times place the interests of clients ahead of our own and serve them with integrity, competence, and independence.

We will assume an independent position with the client, making certain that our advice to clients is based on impartial consideration of all pertinent facts and responsible opinions.

1.2 We will guard as confidential all information concerning the affairs of clients that we gather during the course of professional engagements; and we will not take personal, financial, or other advantage of material or inside information coming to our attention as a result of our professional relationship with clients; nor will we provide the basis on which others might take such advantage. Observance of the ethical obligation of the management consulting firm to hold inviolate the confidence of its clients not only facilitates the full development of facts essential to effective solution of the problem but also encourages clients to seek needed help on sensitive problems.

1.3 We will serve two or more competing clients on sensitive problems only with their knowledge.

1.4 We will inform clients of any relationships, circumstances, or interests that might influence our judgment or the objectivity of our services.

2. Client arrangements

2.1 We will present our qualifications for serving a client solely in terms of our competence, experience, and standing and we will not guarantee any specific result, such as amount of cost reduction or profit increase.

2.2 We will accept only those engagements we are qualified to undertake and which we believe will provide real benefits to clients. We will assign personnel qualified by knowledge, experience, and character to give effective service in analysing and solving the particular problem or problems involved. We will carry out each engagement under the direction of a principal of the firm who is responsible for its successful completion.

2.3 We will not accept an engagement of such limited scope that we cannot serve the client effectively.

2.4 We will, before accepting an engagement, confer with the client or prospective client in sufficient detail and gather sufficient facts to gain an adequate understanding of the problem, the scope of study needed to solve it, and the possible benefits that may accrue to the client. The preliminary exploration will be conducted confidentially on terms and conditions agreed upon by the member and the prospective client. Extended preliminary or problem-defining surveys for prospective clients will be made only on a fully compensated fee basis.

2.5 We will, except for those cases where special client relationships make it unnecessary, make certain that the client receives a written proposal that outlines the objectives, scope, and, where possible, the estimated fee or fee basis for the proposed service or engagement. We will discuss with the client any important changes in the nature, scope, timing, or other aspects of the engagement and obtain the client's agreement to such changes before taking action on them—and unless the circumstances make it unnecessary, we will confirm these changes in writing.

2.6 We will perform each engagement on an individualized basis and develop recommendations designed specifically to meet the particular requirements of the client situation. Our objective in each client engagement is to develop solutions that are realistic and practical and that can be implemented promptly and economically. Our professional staffs are prepared to assist, to whatever extent desired, with the implementation of approved recommendations.

2.7 We will not serve a client under terms or conditions that might impair our objectivity, independence, or integrity; and we will reserve the right to withdraw if conditions beyond our control develop to interfere with the successful conduct of the engagement.

2.8 We will acquaint client personnel with the principles, methods, and techniques applied, so that the improvements suggested or installed may be properly managed and continued after completion of the engagement.

2.9 We will maintain continuity of understanding and knowledge of clients' problems and the work that has been done to solve them by maintaining appropriate files of reports submitted to clients. These are protected against unauthorized access and supported by files of working papers, consultants' logbooks, and similar recorded data.

2.10 We will not accept an engagement for a client while another management consulting firm is serving that client unless we are assured, and can satisfy ourselves, that there will be not conflict between the two engagements. We will not endeavor to displace another management consulting firm or individual consultant once we have knowledge that the client has made a commitment to the other consultant.

2.11 We will review the work of another management consulting firm or individual consultant for the same client, only with the knowledge of such consultant, unless such consultant's work which is subject to review has been finished or terminated. However, even though the other consultant's work has been finished or terminated, it is a matter of common courtesy to let the consulting firm or individual know that his work is being reviewed.

3. Client fees

3.1 We will charge reasonable fees which are commensurate with the nature of services performed and the responsibility assumed. An excessive charge abuses the professional relationship and discourages the public from utilising the services of management consultants. On the other hand, adequate compensation is necessary in order to enable the management consulting firm to serve clients effectively and to preserve the integrity and independence of the profession. Determination of the reasonableness of a fee requires consideration of many factors, including the nature of the services performed; the time required; the consulting firm's experience, ability, and reputation; the degree of responsibility assumed; and the benefits that accrue to the client. Wherever feasible, we will agree with the client in advance on the fee or fee basis.

3.2 We will not render or offer professional services for which the fees are contingent on reduction in costs, increases in profits, or any other specific result.

3.3 We will neither accept nor pay fees or commissions to others for client referrals, or enter into any arrangement for franchising our practice to others. Nor will we accept fees, commissions, or other valuable considerations from individuals or organisations whose equipment, supplies, or services we might recommend in the course of our service to clients.

II — Professional practices

In order to promote highest quality of performance in the practice of management consulting, ACME has developed the following standards of good practice for the guidance of the profession. Member firms subscribe to these practices because they make for equitable and satisfactory client relationships and contribute to success in management consulting.

1. We will strive continually to advance and protect the standards of the management consulting profession. We will strive continually to improve our knowledge, skills, and techniques, and will make available to our clients the benefits of our professional attainments.

2. We recognize our responsibilities to the public interest and to our profession to contribute to the development and understanding of better ways to manage the various formal institutions in our society. By reason of education, experience, and broad contact with management problems in a variety of institutions, management consultants are especially qualified to recognise opportunities for improving managerial and operating processes;

and they have an obligation to share their knowledge with managers and their colleagues in the profession.

3. We recognise our responsibility to the profession to share with our colleagues the methods and techniques we utilise in serving clients. But we will not knowingly, without their permission, use proprietary data, procedures, materials, or techniques that other management consultants have developed but not released for public use.

4. We will not make offers of employment to consultants on the staffs of other consulting firms without first informing them. We will not engage in wholesale or mass recruiting of consultants from other consulting firms. If we are approached by consultants of other consulting firms regarding employment in our firm or in that of a client, we will handle each situation in a way that will be fair to the consultant and his firm.

5. We will not make offers of employment to employees of clients. If we are approached by employees of clients regarding employment in our firm or in that of another client, we will make certain that we have our clients' consent before entering into any negotiations with employees.

6. We will continually evaluate the quality of the work done by our staff to insure, insofar as is possible, that all of our engagements are conducted in a competent manner.

7. We will endeavor to provide opportunity for the professional development of those men who enter the profession, by assisting them to acquire a full understanding of the functions, duties, and responsibilities of management consultants, and to keep up with significant advances in their areas of practice.

8. We will administer the internal and external affairs of our firm in the best interests of the profession at all times.

9. We will not advertise our services in self-laudatory language or in any other manner derogatory to the dignity of the profession.

10. We will respect the professional reputation and practice of other management consultants. This does not remove the moral obligation to expose unethical conduct of fellow members of the profession to the proper authorities.

11. We will strive to broaden public understanding and enhance public regard and confidence in the management consulting profession, so that management consultants can perform their proper function in society effectively. We will conduct ourselves so as to reflect credit on the profession and to

inspire the confidence, respect, and trust of clients and the public. In the course of our practice, we will strive to maintain a wholly professional attitude toward those we serve, toward those who assist us in our practice, toward our fellow consultants, toward the members of other professions, and the practitioners of allied arts and sciences.

Adopted February 1, 1972

Questions about interpretations or Code violations should be sent to:
   Executive Director
   Association of Consulting Management Engineers, Inc.
   347 Madison Avenue
   New York, New York 10017
   212/686-7338

TERMS OF BUSINESS

The terms of business are usually sufficiently standardised to be drawn up as a permanent document for attaching to preliminary survey reports. This avoids having to type them afresh on each occasion. The main non-standard item may be the fee rate. This is left blank, to be filled in when the report is submitted.

The example below gives a typical list of terms. The document may or may not have a blank space at the end for entering any special conditions.

" (i) Our charges for this assignment are $ . . . . per day per consultant employed, inclusive of supervision, but excluding travelling and subsistence when the consultant is engaged on the client's business away from the office or plant to which he is assigned.[1]

(ii) The fee covers all time spent on the client's work whether carried out on his premises or elsewhere. No charge is incurred during absence due to illness or leave, but no deduction is made for public or statutory holidays. Any computer bureau charges will be invoiced at cost. Charges are invoiced and payable monthly.[2]

(iii) We reserve the right to review our fees in the light of operating costs and to adjust them accordingly, but in the event of any change being required at least three months' notice will be given to current clients.

(iv) On concluding an assignment, it is our practice to maintain contact with the client, and to carry out periodic servicing visits to ensure that the benefits secured through our work are maintained.[3] Such visits are charged at

---

[1] Some consulting units indicate a weekly rate. The cost of travel to and from the place of the assignment may be charged separately if the distance is great.

[2] In some circumstances charges may be invoiced weekly.

[3] The reference to servicing (follow-up) visits does not imply that the client has to agree to them in any case. If he so wishes, this clause will be deleted.

$..... per day, including travelling, subsistence and time spent after the visit in preparing a servicing report. A charge of $...... per day is also made for any one-day visits prior to the start of the assignment.

(v) Our work may be terminated on either side by one week's notice in writing.[1]

(vi) All forecasts, and recommendations in this and any subsequent report or letter are made in good faith and on the basis of the information before us at the time. Their achievement must depend among other things on the effective co-operation of the client's staff. In consequence, no statement in a report or letter is to be deemed to be in any circumstances a representation, undertaking, warranty or contractual condition.

(vii) All our consultants are under special contract which protects our clients against the divulging of confidential information. Our consultants are also under agreement not to seek or accept employment with our clients, and it is a condition of the engagement of our company that you will not employ on your staff any member of our company involved in this assignment.[2] "

---

[1] The period of notice for premature termination of an assignment may depend on the reason for it. Some consulting units make this clause 24 hours' notice on either side.

[2] The reason for this clause is obvious. It could be argued, however, that it is an interference with individual liberty and could in time curtail a man's employment opportunities. Some consulting units add " ... within X years of its termination ".

CASE HISTORY OF CONSULTING
IN PRODUCTION MANAGEMENT
(Apollo Garment Manufacturers)

The purpose of this case history is to illustrate in compact form the association between a client and his consultants, from initial source of contact to the point of recommendation and demonstration of benefits and costs. It is a case where the production management consultant acts essentially as a resource consultant.

I. Background

Client:	Apollo Garment Manufacturers
Nature of business:	Manufacture of ready-to-wear clothes for men.
Origin of assignment:	The managing director of the consulting organisation Pinnay, Nesbith and Partners was introduced by a business friend to the two brothers who own the factory. The consultant was invited to carry out a preliminary survey, which confirmed that there were numerous opportunities to raise production and productivity by improving methods of work. As a result of the survey a contract for a consulting assignment was concluded.
Objective of assignment:	The contract set the objective as being to improve plant layout and production methods so that production would increase by at least 20% and costs fall by at least 10% without incurring capital expenditure exceeding $20,000.[1]
Consulting team:	One operating consultant, specialised in production management, under part-time guidance of a supervising consultant.

---

[1] The sign $ is used in this case history to indicate any financial unit.

Duration:	Eight weeks.
Role of consultant:	The client's business was a medium-sized firm owned by two brothers neither of whom had any experience of consultants. They were practical men who had set up the factory and worked out the production methods on what seemed to them sensible lines. They had limited knowledge of production management and looked to the consultant to devise means of improving production methods. In these circumstances the consultant had to act as problem solver, developing most of the improvements in production methods himself and helping the client and his staff to implement them.

II. Orientation facts

During early meetings with the two brothers and the supervisors of the factory the consultant learned the following facts:

1. History

The client had worked as a cutter for a tailor making men's suits to measure. His brother had been an accountant in a large business importing textiles. Ten years ago the two brothers decided that there was an opening in the local market for ready-to-wear men's garments. They took their savings and started the factory. They erected and equipped a two-storey building and started production with 250 workers. After a slow start the business grew. At the time of the consultation two floors had been added to the building and 430 workers were employed.

2. Products

— Shirts, slacks, jackets, raincoats, swimming trunks, bath robes, pyjamas and uniforms for men.

— Skirts, blouses and scarves for women.

— Suits for children.

3. Markets

— Region around factory extending for a radius of about 100 kilometres.

— Sales direct to retailers (about 40).

— Percentage of total regional market unknown.

— Total sales for last financial year $1,250,000.

— Recently obtained some small export orders from local exporter.

4. Summary of latest balance sheet

Table 24. Summary of the balance sheet

		$
ASSETS	Land and Buildings	247,000
	Vehicles	10,000
	Machinery and Equipment	82,000
		339,000
	Inventory of Materials, Work-in-Progress and Finished Goods	170,000
	Accounts Receivable	206,000
	Cash at Bank and on Hand	25,000
		401,000
	Total Assets	740,000
LIABILITITES	Owners' Capital and Accumulated Profits	430,000
	Long-term Loans	50,000
	Accounts Payable	260,000
		740,000
	Profit before tax	110,000
	after tax	68,000

5. Material

Textiles such as poplin, terylene, linen, tweed.

6. Processes

The manufacturing operations are simple and consist of
cutting,
sewing,
pressing,
packing.

7. Organisation

The following informal organisation structure has evolved:

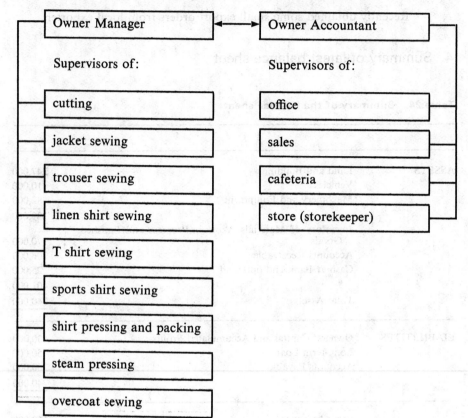

```
  ┌───────────────────────┐        ┌───────────────────────┐
  │ Owner Manager         │◄─────► │ Owner Accountant      │
  └───────────────────────┘        └───────────────────────┘

     Supervisors of:                   Supervisors of:

  ┌───────────────────────┐        ┌───────────────────────┐
  │ cutting               │        │ office                │
  └───────────────────────┘        └───────────────────────┘

  ┌───────────────────────┐        ┌───────────────────────┐
  │ jacket sewing         │        │ sales                 │
  └───────────────────────┘        └───────────────────────┘

  ┌───────────────────────┐        ┌───────────────────────┐
  │ trouser sewing        │        │ cafeteria             │
  └───────────────────────┘        └───────────────────────┘

  ┌───────────────────────┐        ┌───────────────────────┐
  │ linen shirt sewing    │        │ store (storekeeper)   │
  └───────────────────────┘        └───────────────────────┘

  ┌───────────────────────┐
  │ T shirt sewing        │
  └───────────────────────┘

  ┌───────────────────────┐
  │ sports shirt sewing   │
  └───────────────────────┘

  ┌───────────────────────┐
  │ shirt pressing and packing │
  └───────────────────────┘

  ┌───────────────────────┐
  │ steam pressing        │
  └───────────────────────┘

  ┌───────────────────────┐
  │ overcoat sewing       │
  └───────────────────────┘
```

8. Records and reports

Records of sales,

        production,
financial transactions,
inventory movements.

Report to owners — numbers of each garment produced each month,
(managers)   — value of total sales each month,
              — bank balance each day,
              — balance sheet, manufacturing, trading and profit and loss account once a year, about three or four months after the end of the financial year.

III. Assignment facts

1. Objective of business

The owners agreed that the objective of the business was simply to make and sell clothes at a profit. They decided that profit after payment of taxes should amount to 15% of the capital and accumulated profits they invested in the business.

As information on the size of the local market was difficult to obtain they did not set their sales target in terms of a share of this market but preferred to aim at an increase in sales of 20% each year. They wished to push up export sales to the level of 25% of total turnover.

These simple targets provided a basis for planning volume of production, plant capacity and financial resources.

2. Products

A full list of styles and sizes for all garments was compiled.

3. Sales

Sales records provided number and value of sales during each of the previous 12 months for each of the following groups of products:

trousers	suede jackets
shirts	swimming trunks
jackets	children's suits
overcoats	pyjamas and bath robes
uniforms	sundries.

It was found that trousers, shirts, jackets and overcoats accounted for 89% of the total value of sales and 93% of total number of items sold. Uniforms consisted of jackets and trousers. By adding sales of uniforms to those of the four main products it was possible to account for 96% of value of sales and 94% of number of items sold. Obviously the assignment could concentrate on trousers, shirts, jackets and overcoats and largely ignore all other products.

The client drew up a list of selling prices of each style and size of garment in the four main product groups.

4. Costs

The client calculated the cost of each style in each of the four main product groups, e.g. for shirts, cost of

poplin shirt
linen shirt
sports shirt
T shirt.

Cost of each product was broken down into
  materials
  direct wages
  expenses.

By deducting cost from selling price the profit on each garment was obtained. This was verified by multiplying profit per garment by total number of garments sold and comparing this with the total profit shown in the profit-and-loss account.

5. Machines

The client listed the machines in each section of the factory and the space they occupied.

6. Processes

The consultant discussed the manufacture of each product with factory supervisors and observed the manufacturing operations. For each product he compiled a process chart.

He then drafted floor-plan layout and movement charts for each floor of the factory.

He also timed each manufacturing operation.

7. Materials

The client drew up a list of all materials and their prices.

8. Storage

The client estimated the storage space required for each type of material and each group of finished products. The stores records showed the stock of each material and product on hand at the end of each of the previous twelve months. The consultant used this information to verify the client's estimates.

IV. Examination of facts, decisions and recommendations

After devising a number of recommendations for improving plant layout and production methods, the consultant, the two brother owners and the supervisors evaluated the benefits of each and compared their advantages and disadvantages. As a result, they selected the following recommendations for implementation.

1. Plant layout

To improve flow of materials and reduce material movement, transfer some departments to different floors of the building and allocate more space to them; also rearrange machines within departments. The layout was chosen from detailed floor plans and movement charts.

Estimated cost of implementation . . . . $ 4,000

Estimated reduction in manufacturing costs per year . . $ 8,000

Estimated increase in output at least 15%
(depending on output of each department)

2. Production methods

(i) Locate all shirt-making operations in the same department.

Estimated cost of implementation . . . . . already covered under
plant layout

Estimated reduction in manufacturing costs per year . . $10,000

Estimated increase in shirt production 20%

(ii) Instead of laying out patterns over material each time a batch of garments is cut for production, prepare a standard layout for each garment, reproduce by copying machine and use for cutting each production batch.

Estimated cost of implementation . . . . $ 500

Estimated reduction in material and manufacturing costs
per year $60,000

Estimated increase in output of cutting department . . . 66%

(iii) Buy and use a machine to lay out material for cutting.

Estimated cost of implementation . . . . $ 5,000

Estimated reduction in manufacturing costs per year . . $15,000

Estimated increase in output of cutting department . . . included
in (ii) above

(iv) Buy and use a hydraulic press to cut material.

Estimated cost of implementation . . . . $ 1,200

Estimated reduction in costs of material and manufacturing per year $30,000

Estimated increase in output of cutting department . . . 15%
in addition to (ii) above

(v) Simplify pressing and packing operations as indicated by detailed work study.

Estimated cost of implementation . . . . nil

Estimated reduction in manufacturing costs per year . . $16,000

Estimated increase in output of pressing and packing
department 100%
(provided previous operations increase their output to this
extent)

3. Materials handling

(i) Redesign storage shelves and racks and install more of them to
facilitate handling, provide more orderly stacking of material in
process and cater for increased output.

(ii) Replace dead containers by chutes, a small overhead conveyor and
specially-designed trolleys.

(iii) Install chutes between floors.

Estimated cost of implementation . . . . $ 3,000

Estimated reduction in manufacturing costs per year . . $10,000

Estimated increase in output . . . . capable of
handling output increases resulting
from other improvements

4. Management information

Install systems, as planned in detail, to improve recording of customers'
orders, sales, production and inventories, and report prompt up-to-date
information to enable the managing owners and supervisors to plan operations
and control them by exception.

Estimated cost of implementation . . . . $ 2,500

Advantages — possibility of improving planning of sales and production
and reducing the managerial effort required to keep actual
performance in line with plans. As a result of improved
planning and control of production, output should
increase.

5. Summary

The summary of estimated costs and benefits is given in Table 25 below.

In addition unquantified benefits can be expected from improved production planning, better flow of materials and work-in-progress and prompter,
more pertinent and more extensive management information.

These estimated costs and benefits meet the targets laid down in the
objective of the assignment, which were:

increase production by at least 20%

reduce costs by at least 10% . . . . $114,000 per year

costs of implementation not to exceed. . . . . $ 20,000

Table 25.   Estimated costs and benefits

Proposed improvement		Estimated cost of implementation $	Estimated reduction in material and manufacturing costs per year $
1. Plant layout		4,000	8,000
2. Production methods	(i)	0	10,000
	(ii)	500	60,000
	(iii)	5,000	15,000
	(iv)	1,200	30,000
	(v)	0	16,000
3. Materials handling		3,000	10,000
4. Management information		2,500	
Total		16,200	149,000
Estimated over-all increase in output		27%	

CASE HISTORY OF PROCESS CONSULTING
(Apex Manufacturing Company)

In his book " Process Consultation " E. H. Schein [1] provides a case history of the Apex Manufacturing Company to explain the progressive steps and procedures of an assignment using the process-consulting approach.

1. Initial contact with the client and defining relationships

The contact client from the Apex Manufacturing Company was a divisional manager one level below the president. The company is a large manufacturing concern, organized into several divisions. The contact client indicated that there were communication problems in the top management group resulting from a recent reorganization. Because the company expected to grow rapidly in the next several years, they felt they should work on these kinds of problems now.

He spoke openly about his concerns that the president needed help in handling certain key people, shared his worries that the president and his key subordinates were not in good communication, and indicated that recent company history suggested the need for some stabilizing force in the organization. I asked him whether the president knew he had come to me and what the president's feelings were about bringing in a consultant. The contact client indicated that the president as well as other key executives were all in favor of bringing someone in to work with them. All saw the need for some outside help.

Eventually, after many months of working with the president and his six key subordinates, I arrived at a point where all of them saw me as a potentially useful communication link. They asked me quite sincerely to report to each

---

[1] E. H. Schein: *Process consultation* (Reading, Mass., Addison-Wesley, 1969). Reprinted with the kind permission of the author and the publisher.

one the feelings or reactions of others whenever I learned anything I felt should be passed on. At the same time they were quite open with me about each other, knowing that I might well pass on any opinions or reactions they voiced to me. They did not want me to treat everything as confidential because they trusted me and each other enough.

This case was of great interest because of my own feeling that my having to serve as carrier of this type of information was not an ideal role for me, and reflected an insufficient ability on their part to tell each other things directly. Hence I took two courses of action. First, I tried as much as possible to train each man to tell others in the group directly what he thought about an issue. At the same time, I intervened directly in their process by passing on information and opinions if I felt this would aid the working situation.

A simple yet critical event will illustrate what I mean. Two members, Pete and Joe, did not always communicate freely with each other, partly because they felt some rivalry. Pete had completed a study and written a report which was to be discussed by the whole group. Three days before the report was due, I visited the company and stopped in at Pete's office to discuss the report with him and ask how things were going. He said they were fine, but frankly he was puzzled about why Joe hadn't come to him to look at some of the back-up data pertaining to Joe's function. Pete felt this was just another bit of evidence that Joe did not really respect Pete very much.

An hour or so later I was working with Joe, and raised the issue of the report. Joe and his staff were very busy preparing for the meeting but nothing was said about looking at the back-up data. When I asked why they had not done anything about the data, Joe said that he was sure it was private and would not be released by Pete. Joe wanted badly to see it, but felt sure that Pete had deliberately not offered it. I decided there was no harm in intervening at this point by reporting to Joe how Pete was feeling. Joe expressed considerable surprise; and later in the day, he went to Pete, who gave him a warm welcome and turned over to him three volumes of the data which Joe had been wanting to see and which Pete had wanted very much to share with him. I had to judge carefully whether I would hurt *either* Pete or Joe by revealing Pete's feelings. In this case I decided the potential gains outweighed the risks.

Getting back to setting the proper expectations on the part of the company, I have to make it very plain that I will not function as an expert resource on human-relations problems, but that I will try to help the group solve those problems by providing alternatives and by helping them to think through the consequences of various alternatives. I also need to stress my expectation that I will gather data primarily by observing people in action, not by interviewing and other survey methods (though these methods would be used whenever appropriate). Finally, I have to point out that I will not be very active, but will comment on what is happening or give feedback on observations only as I feel it will be helpful to the group.

The fact that I will be relatively inactive is often a problem for the group because of their expectation that once they have hired a consultant they are entitled to sit back and just listen to him tell them things. To have the consultant then spend hours sitting in the group and saying very little not only violates this expectation but also creates some anxiety about what he is observing. The more I can reassure the group early in the game that I am not gathering personal data of a potentially damaging nature, the smoother the subsequent observations will go.

In summary, part of the early exploration with the contact client and any associates whom he involves is intended to establish the formal and psychological contract which will govern the consultation. I feel there should be no formal contract beyond an agreement on a *per diem* fee and a potential number of days to be devoted to working with the client system. Each party should be free to terminate or change the level of involvement at any time. At the psychological contract level, it is important to get out into the open as many misconceptions as possible, and to try to be as clear as possible about my own style of work, aims, methods, and so on.

2. Method of work

The method of work chosen should be as congruent as possible with the values underlying process consultation. Thus observation, informal interviewing, and group discussions would be congruent with:

1. the idea that the consultant does not already have pat answers or standard " expert " solutions, and
2. the idea that the consultant should be maximally available for questioning and two-way communication.

If the consultant uses methods like questionnaires or surveys, he himself remains an unknown quantity to the respondent. As long as he remains unknown, the respondent cannot really trust him, and hence cannot really answer questions completely honestly. The method of work chosen, therefore, should make the consultant maximally visible and maximally available for interaction.

Often I choose to start a consultation project with some interviewing, but the purpose of the interview is not so much to gather data as to establish a relationship with each of the people who will later be observed. The interview is designed to *reveal myself* as much as it is designed to *learn something about the other person.* I will consider the use of questionnaires only after I am well enough known by the organization to be reasonably sure that people would trust me enough to give direct and frank answers to questions.

In the Apex Company, the exploratory meeting led to the decision to attend one of the regular meetings of the executive committee. At this time I was to meet the president and the other key executives to discuss further what could and should be done. At this meeting, I found a lively interest in the idea of having an outsider help the group and the organization to become more effective. I also found that the group was willing to enter an open-ended relationship. I explained as much as I could my philosophy of process consultation and suggested that a good way of getting further acquainted would be to set up a series of individual interviews with each member of the group. At the same time, I suggested that I sit in on the weekly half-day meetings of the executive committee. The interviews then would occur after several of these meetings.

At the initial meeting of the group, I was able to observe a number of key events. For example, the president, Alex, was very informal but very powerful. I got the impression initially (and confirmed it subsequently) that the relationship of all the group members to the president would be the key issue, with relationships to each other being relatively less important. I also got the impression that Alex was a very confident individual who would tolerate my presence only as long as he saw some value in it; he would have little difficulty in confronting me and terminating the relationship if my presence ceased to have value.

It was also impressive, and turned out to be indicative of a managerial style, that Alex did not feel the need to see me alone. He was satisfied from the outset to deal with me inside the group. Near the end of the initial meeting, I requested a private talk with him to satisfy myself that we understood the psychological contract we were entering into. He was surprisingly uncomfortable in this one-to-one relationship, had little that he wished to impart to me, and did not show much interest in my view of the relationship. I wanted the private conversation in order to test his reaction to taking some personal feedback on his own behavior as the consultation progressed. He said he would welcome this and indicated little or no concern over it. As I was to learn later, this reflected a very strong sense of his own power and identity. He felt he knew himself very well and was not a bit threatened by feedback.

Part of the initial mandate was to help the group to *relate to the president.* In the interviews which I conducted with group members, I concentrated quite heavily on what kinds of things went well in the relationship; what kinds of things went poorly; how relationship problems with the president were related to job performance; in what way the group members would like to see the relationship change, and so on. I did not have a formal interview schedule, but rather, held an informal discussion with each member around issues of the sort I have just mentioned.

Intervention by the consultant

In the Apex Company, I found that the treasurer consistently made the operating managers uncomfortable by presenting financial information in an unintentionally threatening way. He wanted to be helpful, and he felt everyone needed the information he had to offer, but it often had the appearance of an indictment of one of the other managers: his costs were too high, his inventory control had slipped, he was too high over budget, etc. Furthermore, this information was often revealed for the first time in the meeting, so that the operating manager concerned had no forewarning and no opportunity to find out why things had gone out of line. The result was often a fruitless argument about the validity of the figures, a great deal of defensiveness on the part of the operating manager, and irritation on the part of the president because the managers could not deal more effectively with the treasurer.

As I observed this process occurring repeatedly over several weeks, I decided that merely drawing attention to the pattern would not really solve the problem because everyone appeared to be operating with constructive intent. What the group needed was an alternative way to think about the use of financial control information. I therefore wrote a memo on control systems (see Section 5) and circulated it to the group.

When this came up for discussion at a later meeting I was in a better position to make my observations about the group, since a clear alternative had been presented. My feeling was that I could not have successfully presented this theory orally because of the amount of heat the issue always generated, and because the group members were highly active individuals who would have wanted to discuss each point separately, making it difficult to get the whole message across.

In working with the Apex group I found the written " theory memo " a convenient and effective means of communication. With other groups I have found different patterns to be workable. For example, if the group gets away for a half-day of work on group process, I may insert a half-hour in the middle (or at the end) of the session to present whatever theory elements I consider to be relevant. The topics are usually not selected until I observe the particular " hang-ups " which exist in the group. I therefore have to be prepared to give, on short notice, an input on any of a variety of issues.

A final method of theory input is to make reprints of relevant articles available to the group at selected times. Often I know of some good piece of theory which pertains to what the group is working on. If I suggest that such an article be circulated, I also try to persuade the group to commit some of its agenda time to a discussion of the article.

The key criterion for the choice of theory input is that the theory must be relevant to what the group already senses is a problem. There is little to be gained by giving " important " theory if the group has no data of its own to link to the theory. On the other hand, once the group has confronted an issue in its own process, I am always amazed at how ready the members are to look at and learn from general theory.

Agenda-setting interventions may strike the reader as a rather low-key, low-potency kind of intervention. Yet it is surprising to me how often working groups arrive at an impasse on simple agenda-setting issues. In a way, their inability to select the right agenda for their meetings, and their inability to discuss the agenda in a constructive way, is symbolic of other difficulties which are harder to pinpoint. If the group can begin to work on its agenda, the door is often opened to other process discussions. Let me provide some case examples.

In the Apex Company I sat in for several months on the weekly executive-committee meeting, which included the president and his key subordinates. I quickly became aware that the group was very loose in its manner of operation: people spoke when they felt like it, issues were explored fully, conflict was fairly openly confronted, and members felt free to contribute. This kind of climate seemed constructive, but it created a major difficulty for the group. No matter how few items were put on the agenda, the group was never able to finish its work. The list of backlog items grew longer and the frustration of group members intensified in proportion to this backlog. The group responded by trying to work harder. They scheduled more meetings and attempted to get more done at each meeting, but with little success. Remarks about the ineffectiveness of groups, too many meetings, and so on, became more and more frequent.

My diagnosis was that the group was overloaded. Their agenda was too large, they tried to process too many items at any given meeting, and the agenda was a mixture of operational and policy issues without recognition by the group that such items required different allocations of time. I suggested to the group that they seemed overloaded and should discuss how to develop their agenda for their meetings. The suggestion was adopted after a half-hour or so of sharing feelings. It was then decided, with my help, to sort the agenda items into several categories, and to devote some meetings entirely to operational issues while others would be exclusively policy meetings. The operations meetings would be run more tightly in order to process these items efficiently. The policy questions would be dealt with in depth.

Once the group had made this separation and realized that it could function differently at different meetings, it then decided to meet once a month for an entire day. During this day they would take up one or two large questions and explore them in depth. The group accepted my suggestion to hold such discussions away from the office in a pleasant, less hectic environment.

By rearranging the agenda, the group succeeded in rearranging its whole pattern of operations. This rearrangement also resulted in a redefinition of my role. The president decided that I should phase out my attendance at the operational meetings, but should plan to take a more active role in the monthly one-day meetings. He would set time aside for presentation of any theory I might wish to make, and for process analysis of the meetings. He had previously been reluctant to take time for process work in the earlier meeting pattern, but now welcomed it.

The full-day meetings changed the climate of the group dramatically. For one thing, it was easier to establish close informal relationships with other members during breaks and meals. Because there was enough time, people felt they could really work through their conflicts instead of having to leave them hanging. It was my impression that as acquaintance level rose, so did the level of trust in the group. Members began to feel free to share more personal reactions with each other. This sense of freedom made everyone more relaxed and readier to let down personal barriers and report accurate information. There was less need for defensive distortion or withholding.

After about one year the group decided quite spontaneously to try some direct confrontive feedback. We were at one of the typical monthly all-day meetings. The president announced that he thought each group member should tell the others what he felt to be the strengths and weaknesses of the several individuals. He asked me to help in designing a format for this discussion. I first asked the group members whether they did in fact want to attempt this type of confrontation. The response was sincerely positive, so we decided to go ahead.

The format I suggested was based upon my prior observation of group members. I had noticed that whenever anyone commented on anyone else, there was a strong tendency to answer back and to lock in on the first comment made. Hence, further feedback tended to be cut off. To deal with this problem I suggested that the group discuss one person at a time, and that a ground rule be established that the person being described was not to comment or respond until all the members had had a chance to give all of their feedback. This way he would be forced to continue to listen. The ground rule was accepted, and I was given the role of monitoring the group to ensure that the process operated as the group intended it to.

For the next several hours the group then went into a very detailed and searching analysis of each member's managerial and interpersonal style, including that of the president. I encouraged members to discuss both the positives and the negatives they saw in the person. I also played a key role in forcing people to make their comments specific and concrete. I demanded examples, insisted on clarification, and generally asked the kind of question which I thought might be on the listener's mind as he tried to understand the feedback. I also added my own feedback on points I had observed in that member's behavior. At first it was not easy for the group either to give or receive feedback, but as the day wore on, the group learned to be more effective.

The total exercise of confrontation was considered highly successful, both at the time and some months later. It deepened relationships, exposed some chronic problems which now could be worked on, and gave each member much food for thought in terms of his own self-development. It should be noted that the group chose to do this spontaneously after many months of meetings organized around work topics. I am not sure they could have handled the feedback task effectively had they been urged to try sooner, even though I could see the need for this type of meeting some time before the initiative came from the group.

In this case, my intervention tended to help the group move from chaotic meetings toward a differentiated, organized pattern. In the end, the group spent more time in meetings than before, but they minded it less because the meetings were more productive. The group has also learned how to manage its own agenda and how to guide its own processes.

Feedback systems to groups and individuals

After getting to know the top-management group through several group meetings, I suggested that it might be useful to interview and give feedback to the next level below the vice-president. There was some concern on the part of the senior group that there might be a morale problem at this level. Initially I was asked merely to do an interview survey and report back to the top group. I declined this approach for reasons already mentioned: gathering data to report to a higher group would violate P-C assumptions because it would not involve the sources of the data in analyzing their own process. I suggested instead that I conduct the interview with the ground rule that all my conclusions would first be reported back to the interviewee group, and that I would tell top management only those items which the group felt should be reported.[1] The group

---

[1] This procedure was brought to E. H. Schein's attention by R. Beckhard. See also R. Beckhard: *Organisation development: strategies and models* (Reading, Mass., Addison-Wesley, 1969).

would first have to sort the items and decide which things they could handle by themselves and which should be reported up the line of authority because they were under higher management control. The real value of the feedback should accrue to the group which initially provided the data; they should become involved in examining the issues they had brought up, and consider what they themselves might do about them.

The above-mentioned procedure was agreed upon by the top management. One vice-president sent a memorandum to all members who would be involved in the interview program, informing them of the procedure, his commitment to it, and his hope that they would participate. I then followed up with individual appointments with each person concerned. At this initial appointment I recounted the origin of the idea, assured the interviewee that his *individual* responses would be entirely confidential, told him that I would summarize the data by department, and told him that he would see the group report and discuss it before any feedback went to his boss or higher management.

In the interview I asked each person to describe his job, tell what he found to be the major pluses and minuses in the job, describe what relationships he had to other groups, and how he felt about a series of specific job factors such as challenge, autonomy, supervision, facilities, salary and benefits, and so on. I later summarized the interviews in a report in which I tried to highlight what I saw to be common problem areas.

All the respondents were then invited to a group meeting at which I passed out the summaries, and explained that the purpose of the meeting was to examine the data, deleting or elaborating where necessary, and to determine which problem areas might be worked on by the group itself. We then went over the summary item by item, permitting as much discussion as any given item warranted.

The group meeting had its greatest utility in exposing the interviewees, in a systematic way, to interpersonal and group issues. For many of them, what they had thought to be private gripes turned out to be organizational problems which they could do something about. The attitude " Let top management solve all our problems " tended to be replaced with a viewpoint which differentiated between intragroup problems, intergroup problems, and those which were higher management's responsibility. The interviewees not only gained more insight into organizational psychology, but also responded positively to being involved in the process of data-gathering itself. It symbolized to them top management's interest in them and concern for solving organizational problems. Reactions such as these are typical of other groups with whom I have tried the same approach.

Following the group meeting, the revised summary was then given to top management, in some cases individually; in others, in a group. My own preference is to give it first individually, to provide for maximum opportunity to explain all the points, and then to follow up with a group discussion of the implications of the data revealed in the interviews. Where the direct supervisor of the group is involved, I have often supplemented the group report with an individual report, which extracts all the comments made by interviewees concerning the strengths and weaknesses of the supervisor's style of management. These focused feedback items have usually proved of great value to the manager, but they should be provided only if the manager initially *asked for* this type of feedback.

In giving either individual or group feedback from the interview summary, my role is to ensure understanding of the data and to stimulate acceptance of it, so that remedial action of some sort can be effectively undertaken. Once the expectation has been built that top management will do something, there is great risk of lowering morale if the report is merely read, without being acted upon in some manner. Incidentally, it is the process consultant's job to ensure that top management *makes this commitment initially* and that high-level officials understand that when the interviews are completed there will be some demands for action. If management merely wants information (without willingness to do something about the information), the process consultant should not do the interviews in the first place. The danger is too great that management will not like what it hears and will suppress the whole effort; such a course will only lead to a deterioration of morale.

The results of interviews (or questionnaires) do not necessarily have to go beyond the group which is interested in them. One of the simplest and most helpful things a group can do to enhance its own functioning is to have the consultant interview the members individually and report back to the *group as a whole* a summary of its own members' feelings. It is a way of hauling crucial data out into the open without the risk of personal exposure of any individual if he feels the data collected about him are damaging or that the analysis of such data will result in conclusions that are overcritical of his performance.

The giving of individual feedback can be illustrated from several cases. In the Apex Company I met with each of the vice-presidents whose groups had been interviewed and gave them a list of comments which had been made about their respective managerial styles. I knew each man well and felt that he would be able to accept the kinds of comments which were made. In each case we scheduled at least a one-hour session, so we could talk in detail about any items which were unclear and/or threatening.

These discussions usually become counseling sessions to help the individual overcome some of the negative effects which were implied in the feedback data. Since I knew that I would be having sessions such as these, I urged each interviewee to talk at length about the style of his boss and what he did or did not like about it. In cases where the boss was an effective manager, I found a tendency for subordinates to make only a few vague generalisations which I knew would be useless as helpful feedback. By probing for specific incidents or descriptions, it was possible to identify just what the boss did which subordinates liked or did not like.

Making suggestions

The consultant must make it quite clear that he does not propose any particular solution as the best one. However frustrating it might be to the client, the process consultant must work to create a situation where the client's ability to *generate his own solutions* is enhanced. The consultant wants to increase problem-solving ability, not to solve any particular problem.

In my experience there has been only one class of exceptions to the above " rule. " If the client wants to set up some meetings specifically for the purpose of working on organizational or interpersonal problems, or wants to design a data-gathering method, then the consultant indeed does have some relevant expertise which he should bring to bear. From his own experience he knows better than the client the pros and cons of interviews or questionnaires; he knows better what questions to ask, how to organize the data, and how to organize feedback meetings; he knows better the right sequence of events leading up to a good discussion of interpersonal process in a committee. In such matters, therefore, I am quite direct and positive in suggesting procedures, who should be involved in them, who should be told what, and how the whole project should be handled.

For example, I recall that in the Apex Company the president decided at one of their all-day meetings to try to give feedback to all the members. He asked me to suggest a procedure for doing this. In this instance I was not at all reluctant to suggest, with as much force and logic as I could command, a particular procedure which I thought would work well. Similarly, when it was proposed to interview all the members of a department, I suggested exactly how this procedure should be set up; I explained that all the members had to be briefed by the department manager, that a group feedback meeting would have to be held, and so on. I have not been at all hesitant in refusing to design a questionnaire study if I thought it was inappropriate, or to schedule a meeting on interpersonal process if I thought the group was not ready.

In conclusion, the process consultant should not withhold his expertise on matters of the learning process itself; but he should be very careful not to confuse being an expert on *how to help an organization to learn* with being an expert on the *actual management problems* which the organization is trying to solve. The same logic applied to the evaluation of individuals; I will under no circumstances evaluate an individual's ability to manage or solve work-related problems; but I will evaluate an individual's readiness to participate in an interview survey of his group or a feedback meeting. If I feel that his presence might undermine some other goals which the organization is trying to accomplish, I will seek to find a solution which will bypass this individual. These are often difficult judgments to make, but the process consultant cannot evade them if he defines the *overall health of the organization* as his basic target. However, he must always attempt to be fair both to the individual and the organization. If no course of action can be found without hurting either, then the whole project should probably be postponed.

3. Evaluation of results

Considerable value change and skill growth occurred over the course of the first year. During this time I spent a great deal of time in two major activities: (1) sitting in on various meetings of the top-management group; and (2) conducting interview and feedback surveys of various key groups, as managers decided they wanted such interviews done. In addition there were periods of individual counseling, usually resulting from data revealed in the interviews.

I have already given examples of the kinds of specific activities which occurred in the group meetings, interviews, and feedback sessions. It was clear that with increasing experience, the group was learning to tune in on its own internal processes (skill), was beginning to pay more attention to these and to give over more meeting time to analysis of interpersonal feelings and events (value change), and was able to manage its own agenda and do its diagnosis without my presence (skill). The group first discovered this from having to conduct some of its all-day meetings in my absence. Where such meetings used to be devoted entirely to work content, the group found that even in my absence they could discuss interpersonal process with profit. The members themselves described this change as one of " climate. " The group felt more open and effective; members felt they could trust each other more; information was flowing more freely; less time was being wasted on oblique communications or political infighting.

During the second year, my involvement was considerably reduced, though I worked on some specific projects. The company had set up a committee to develop a management-development program. I was asked to sit in with this committee and help in the development of a program. After a number of meetings, it became clear to me that the kind of program the group needed was one in which the content was not too heavily predetermined. The problems of different managers were sufficiently different to require that a formula be found for discussing the whole range of problems. One of the reflections of the value change which had taken place in the managers was their recognition that they should be prime participants in any program which they might invent. If a program was not exciting or beneficial enough to warrant the committee's time, it could hardly be imposed on the rest of the organization.

We developed a model which involved a series of small-group meetings at each of which the group would set its own agenda. After every third meeting or so, a larger management group would be convened for a lecture and discussion period on some highly relevant topic. Once the first group (the committee plus others at the vice-president level) had completed six to eight meetings, each member of the original group would become the chairman for a group at the next lower level of the organization. These ten or so next-level groups would then meet six to eight sessions around agenda items developed by themselves. In the meantime the lecture series would continue. After each series of meetings at a given organizational level, the model would be reassessed and either changed or continued at the next lower level with the previous members again becoming group chairmen.

My role in this whole enterprise was, first, to help the group to invent the idea; second, to meet with the original group as a facilitator of the group's efforts to become productive; third, to serve as a resource on topics to be covered and lecturers to be used in the lecture series; and fourth, to appear as an occasional lecturer in the lecture series or as a source of input at a small-group meeting. As this procedure took form, my involvement was gradually reduced, though I still meet with the original committee to review the overall concept.

In recent months I have met occasionally with individual members of the original group and with the group as a whole. My function during these meetings is to be a sounding-board, to contribute points of view which might not be represented among the members, and to help the group assess its own level of functioning. I have been able to provide the group with some perspective on its own growth as a group because I could more easily see changes in values and skills. It has also been possible for the group to enlist my help with specific interpersonal problems. A measure of the growth of the group has been its ability to decide when and how to use my help, and to make those decisions validly from my point of view in terms of where I felt I could constructively help.

4. Disengagement: reducing involvement with the client system

The process of disengagement has, in most of my experiences, been characterized by the following features where:

(i) reduced involvement is a mutually agreed upon decision rather than a unilateral decision by consultant or client;

(ii) involvement does not generally drop to zero but may continue at a very low level;

(iii) the door is always open from my point of view for further work with the client if the client desires it.

In most of my consulting relationships there has come a time when either I felt that nothing more could be accomplished and/or some members of the client system felt the need to continue on their own. To facilitate a reduction of involvement, I usually check at intervals of several months to see whether the client feels that the pattern should remain as is or should be altered. In some cases where I have felt that a sufficient amount had been accomplished, I have found that the client did not feel the same way and wanted the relationship to continue on a day-a-week basis. In other cases, I have been confronted by the client, as with the Apex Company, with the statement that my continued attendance in the operational group meetings was no longer desirable from his point of view. As the president put it, I was beginning to sound too much like a regular member to be of much use. I concurred in the decision and reduced my involvement to periodic all-day meetings of the group, though the initiative for inviting me remained entirely with the group. Had I not concurred, we would have negotiated until a mutually satisfactory arrangement had been agreed upon. I have sometimes been in the situation of arguing that I remain fully involved even when the client wanted to reduce involvement, and in many cases I was able to obtain the client's concurrence.

The negotiation which surrounds a reduction of involvement is in fact a good opportunity for the consultant to diagnose the state of the client system. The kinds of arguments which are brought up in support of continuing (or terminating) provide a solid basis for determining how much value and skill change has occurred. The reader may feel that since the client is paying for services, he certainly has the right to make unilateral decisions about whether or not to continue these services. My point would be that if the consultation process has even partially achieved its goals, there should arise sufficient trust between consultant and client to enable both to make the decision on rational grounds. Here gain, it is important that the consultant not be economically dependent upon any one client, or his own diagnostic ability may become biased by his need to continue to earn fees.

5. Memo on control systems

In this study with the Apex Company the following memo was prepared, distributed and later discussed in a meeting:

Some ideas why internal auditing is seen as nonhelpful or as a source of tension:

(1) Auditors often feel primary loyalty to auditing group rather than company as a whole; they tend, at times, to feel themselves outside of the organization. Managers, on the other hand, feel primary loyalty to organization.

(2) Auditors are typically rewarded for finding things wrong, less so for helping people get their work done. Managers, on the other hand, are rewarded for getting the job done, whether things were wrong or not.

(3) Auditors tend to be (a) *perfectionists*, and (b) focused on *particular* problems in depth. Managers, on the other hand, tend to be (a) " *satis-ficers* " rather than maximizers (they tend to look for workable rather than perfect or ideal solutions), and (b) *generalists*, focusing on getting many imperfect things to work together toward getting a job done, rather than perfecting any one part of the job.

(4) The auditor's job tempts him to *evaluate* the line operation and to propose solutions. The manager, on the other hand, wants *descriptive* (nonevaluative) feedback and to design his own solutions.

Some possible dysfunctional consequences of tension between line organiza-tion and auditing function:

(1) Members of the line organization tend to pay attention to doing well, primarily in those areas which the auditor measures, whether those are important to the organizational mission or not.

(2) Members of the line organization put effort into hiding problems and imperfections.

(3) Management tends to use information about their subordinates in an unintentionally punishing way by immediate inquiries which gives sub-ordinates the feeling of having the boss on their back even while they are already correcting the problem.

(4) Members of the line organization are tempted to falsify and distort information to avoid punishment for being " found out, " and to avoid having their boss " swoop down " on them.

(5) *Detailed* information gathered by the auditing function tends to be passed too far up the line both in the auditing function and the line organization, making information available to people who are too far removed from the problem to know how to evaluate the information.

351

Some tentative principles for the handling of auditing :

(1) *Line involvement:* The more the line organization is involved actively in decisions concerning (a) which areas of performance are to be audited, and (b) how the information is to be gathered and to whom it is to be given, the more helpful and effective the auditing function will be.

(2) *Horizontal rather than vertical reporting:* The more the auditing information is made available, *first* to the man with the problem (horizontal reporting), then to his immediate boss only if the problem is not corrected, and then only to higher levels in either the line or the auditing group if the problem is still not corrected, the more likely it is that auditing will be effective (because line organizations will be less motivated to hide or falsify information and less likely to feel punished).

(3) *Reward for helping rather than policing:* The more the managers in the auditing group reward their subordinates for being *helpful* (based on whether they are being perceived as helpful by the line) rather than being efficient in finding problem areas, the more effective will be the auditing function.* (* Auditing people tend to be undertrained in how to use audit information in a helpful way; an appropriate reward system should be bolstered by training in how to give help.)

(4) *Useful feedback:* The more the auditing information is *relevant* to important operational problems, *timely* in being fed back as soon after problem discovery as possible, and *descriptive* rather than evaluative, the more useful it will be to the line organization.

PERSON-TO-PERSON COMMUNICATION IN CONSULTING

This appendix is intended to provide an overview of some of the essentials required in consulting practice, emphasising that the person-to-person form of communication should be viewed not simply as an art and a skill, but as a downright necessity.

1. Importance and purpose of person-to-person communication

Person-to-person communication is vitally important for two reasons: primarily, because it is the means of linking the consultant and the client and, secondly, because of its role in bridging the concepts and practices of change between the management and the staff within the client organisation.

Reviews of management consulting practices suggest that on assignments approximately 30% of the time is spent on problem analysis and related matters on an individual basis, whereas 70% is spent in communicating with others. Thus, for the consultant and his client, communication represents a large slice of the available time and effort.

Listening is considered to be the single most important component, accounting for 45% of the total communication time. Next in importance comes speaking (30%), reading (16%), and writing (9%).[1] A quick glance at these figures reveals that three-quarters of management's time involves person-to-person communication viz. listening and speaking. Considering that the consultant has to provide functional expertise coupled with its application, it is inevitable that considerable emphasis should be placed on training in this form of communication. In most training programmes 20% of the total time is devoted to this task.

---

[1] H. and Z. Roodman: *Management by communication* (Toronto, Methuen Publications, 1973), p. 146.

Finally, it stands to reason that ease of communication facilitates comprehension and acceptance of new ideas which is, after all, the main purpose of the consulting assignment.

Communication is the vehicle for transmitting knowledge and introducing attitude change. Person-to-person communication is its most effective form essential for all counselling work. It is the basis for the preparation of written reports, which usually do no more than confirm agreements previously reached.

Communication is also the source of power for two accelerators creating the greatest impact on the management scene today, viz. changes in technology, and changes in management concepts and methods. Person-to-person communication is the final link in the chain required to bring them into effect.

Additionally, such communication is a vital part of the synergy phenomenon, which explains why the collaborative efforts of members of a team are often more effective than the individual efforts of those same people. Whereas motivation may be the key to productivity improvement due to synergy, communciation is undeniably the basis of that motivation.

Mastery of person-to-person communication adds to the stature of the consultant and sets him on the path to becoming a senior or supervising-level practitioner.

2. General issues and problems

Person-to-person communication can be viewed as a scalar dimension moving from formal meetings and conferences at one end of the scale to informal social gatherings at the opposite end of the scale. In all instances effective communication depends upon certain universals which include:

  (i) knowledge of the mechanics of speaking, listening, interpreting gestures, etc.[1];

 (ii) practice in these mechanics which should take place under appropriate guidance;

(iii) development of empathy defined as the ability to understand, feel and predict how others will react.

The consultant should be aware that person-to-person communication possesses distinct advantages and disadvantages compared with other forms of communication. Major advantages include *immediacy* and *association*. Immediacy offers opportunities to raise questions and provide answers on relevant issues as needs arise. Association permits a clearer understanding of spoken

---

[1] See recommended reading at the end of this appendix.

words by associating them with accompanying gestures, intonation, emphasis, etc., and so provides appropriate interpretation. Such interpretation is necessary because the 500 most frequently used words of the English language possess more than 14,000 different meanings [1] (an average of more than 28 per word), which leaves a good deal of room for possible error.

One major drawback to this form of communication is that permanent records are not usually maintained, and residual interpretations may not be faithful reproductions of original messages due to problems created by distortion, omission, addition, etc. To reduce errors of this nature the following considerations should be kept in mind:

- brevity (keep the message to a minimum),
- relevance (don't confuse the audience),
- draw conclusions (don't rely on inferences being properly made),
- consider audience level (communicate to express, not impress),
- use own natural style to best advantage (you cannot pretend to be what you are not, but you should, at least, perform to the best of your ability).

Critical elements in the communication process are represented in Figure 13.

References to the model shown in Figure 13 can be found in most literature on this subject. Critical areas, from a consultant's point of view, occur throughout the system and are noted in the Figure. They are discussed in the next section.

3. Specific points relevant to consulting

In consulting, person-to-person communication deals with either the reception or the presentation of information, During the life-cycle of an assignment composed of a " beginning ", a " middle " and an " end ", the emphasis for the consultant usually switches from reception to presentation of information. In the initial stages the consultant is mostly fully absorbed obtaining relevant information, and presentations at this time are usually confined to explaining his presence in the organisation.

---

[1] H. and Z. Roodman, op. cit., p. 7.

Figure 13.   Critical elements in reception and transmission of person-to-person communication

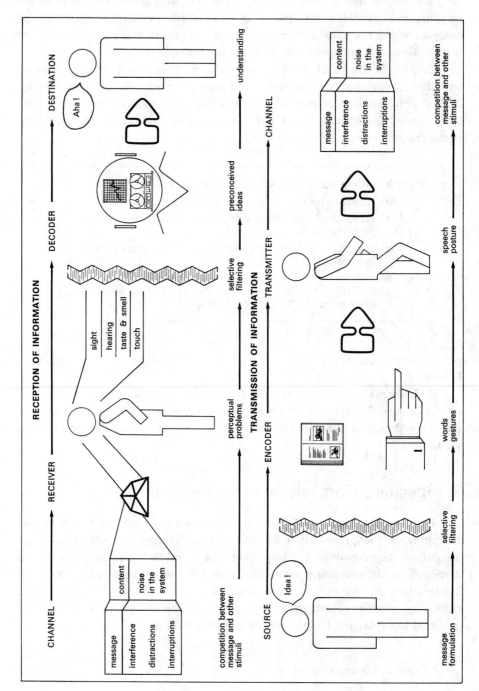

Reception techniques at the "beginning" stage

Reception techniques involve listening and observing, which have to do with receptivity and assimilation. They might be thought of as "passive" exercises; but this would be entirely wrong, since full concentration is called for, and expected, during this crucial stage. Most people can absorb four times more information than can be delivered verbally; thus there is the ever-present danger of distraction.

Measures to facilitate information gathering include:

● soliciting permission to write down important facts (especially figures);

● using the pregnant pause, i.e. when the speaker stops talking, don't hurry to speak yourself, but look as if expecting further information—when it comes it may be most revealing;

● encourage elaboration of points by asking "anything else?" or "yes, go on please";

● ask for examples to illustrate generalities that are offered;

● try not to be involved in speculation, or answering questions in the fact-finding stage; advise that you will certainly give your opinion at a later stage but that you would first prefer to hear all other impressions;

● if necessary answer a question with a question, e.g. to a question put to you, reply with "why do you ask that?" or "behind all good questions usually lies an answer—I would like to know your answer to your own question".

Because so much time is involved in listening and observing and the consultant may be impatient to proceed as rapidly as possible, it is quite possible that bad habits will develop. Some elementary precautions that might be taken to prevent this are indicated in Table 26.

Table 26. Precautions to facilitate the listening process

Bad habits	Possible remedies
Becoming distracted	Try to analyse individual statements and evaluate them (award theoretical marks, e.g. 7 out of 10)
Taking too many notes	Select key points and write digest-style telegram notes
Making snap decisions	Record pertinent data
	Draw your conclusions after the meeting or interview
Lack of concentration	Try to anticipate the next idea, sentence or phrase
Selective listening	Look for new or hidden meanings
Interrupting the speaker	Wait until there is a natural break in the delivery

Case-building during the " middle " stage

In the " *middle* " stage of the communication process a large percentage of time becomes allocated to building a case for the proposed changes and preparing the necessary supporting documents and material. There can be insufficient time allowed for preparation, but only rarely can too much time be allocated; material which is not used can always be discarded.

Preparation involves the development of a structure for the presentation of conclusions and proposals whether it be for formal or informal presentation. There is no guarantee that your presentation will be heard in its entirety, so prepare summaries for delivery at its commencement, during its course, and on its conclusion so that early-leavers and late-comers (who may be important persons) can be provided with some idea of the total scope of your case.

An outline of your presentation may be in note form, on cards, etc., but should be available. If time and conditions permit, it is advisable to use audio-visual aids. Rehearsal will improve performance, and opportunities should be taken, whenever possible, to practise before a critical audience.

Delivering the presentation : the " end " stage

The " *end* " stage of the process usually revolves around presentations by the consultant. Critical elements to be kept in mind at this stage are:

- introduce the presentation with a summary outline of what is to follow;

- at the conclusion of discrete sections of your delivery, reference to the outline might usefully be repeated, e.g. " let's see where we are, up to this stage ";

- if you are delivering a tightly knit presentation advise that questions will be handled only after the presentation has been completed or at set times during your delivery; in many cases you will probably have answered likely queries during the course of your presentation, and continuity of delivery and timing will not suffer;

- unless specifically warranted, do not commence with an apology: there is always a chance that it might not be accepted; confidence and a positive approach are priority personal qualities required to induce change;

- most people have an " image " of what they expect to see in a consultant in much the same way as they view doctors, lawyers, engineers and other professionals; by and large, neat but " neutral " clothing styles and a highly organised presentation are expected; anything else may detract from the presentation;

- when handling questions, answer them one at a time; if objections are raised, deal with them as recommended earlier in the text of this book;[1]

- always make due acknowledgements to persons who have assisted you in your work—it may be necessary to make this a " thank you " to the whole organisation;

- if delivering from a written, fully prepared text try to read each sentence to yourself, pause, look at your audience and say it aloud; pause, glance at the next sentence again silently and then repeat it aloud to your audience while looking at them; with practice, a flowing style can be developed which will convert a script-reading session into an imposing delivery;

- if the consultant is convinced that his proposal will supply the changes necessary to assist the organisation, he must have the strength and the will to fight for his case; this does not mean that he should seek to humiliate any opposition, if there is room for compromise; however, if compromise would be to the detriment of the organisation, he should resist it by every possible means.

Consultants bring a wealth of education and experience in communication with them to the profession. A young consultant should have his particular style observed and analysed by experienced colleagues and subsequently try to capitalise on his acknowledged strengths and take appropriate steps to remedy weaknesses.

4. Literature on communication

Blatner H.A.: *Acting-in: practical applications of psychodramatic methods* (New York, Springer Publishing Co., 1973); 152 pp.

Carvell F. J.: *Human relations in business* (New York, Macmillan, 1975); 408 pp.

Dyar D. A., Giles W. J.: *Improving skills in working with people: interaction analysis* (London, Her Majesty's Stationery Office, 1974); 38 pp.

Honey P.: *Face to face: a practical guide to interactive skills* (London, Institute of Personnel Management, 1976); 150 pp.

Murphy H. A., Peck C. E.: *Effective business communications* (New York, McGraw-Hill, 1976); 703 pp.

Rockey E. H.: *Communicating in organizations* (Cambridge, Mass., Winthrop, 1977); 156 pp.

---

[1] See Chapter 4, p. 42.

Roodman H. and Z.: *Management by communication* (Toronto, Methuen Publications, 1973); 340 pp.

Rosenthal R., Jacobson L.: *Pygmalion in the classroom* (New York, Holt, Rinehart and Winston, 1968); 240 pp.

Schneider A. E., Donaghy W. C., Newman P. J.: *Organizational communication* (New York, McGraw-Hill, 1975); 367 pp.

Sidney E., Brown M, Argyle M.: *Skills with people: a guide for managers* (London, Hutchinson, 1973); 232 pp.

Sigband N. B.:*Communication for management and business* (Glenview, Ill., Scott, Foresman & Co., 1976); 657 pp.

Simpkin R., Jones R.: *Business and the language barrier* (London, Business Books, 1976); 291 pp.

CONSULTANT REPORT WRITING

The reports written by consultants for their clients are mentioned in various chapters of the book according to the occasions and purposes that call for them. The purpose of this appendix is to review the essential factors in the writing and production of all reports used in consulting.[1] The consultant's general strategy should be to make report writing as easy for himself as possible. Ease of writing leads to ease of reading.

1. Reports in perspective

In consulting work written communication complements oral communication, but in some special cases the written report may become the main communication channel.

In addition to conveying information, reports to clients have other important functions. They contribute by their quality and presentation to the impact the consultant makes during the assignment. They also affect the consultant's general reputation. When the personal contacts between consultant and client are limited (for example, if the client obtains written survey reports from several consultants and will select one on the basis of those reports), persuasion may be a vital feature of a report.

As a matter of principle, consulting reports do not repeat information obtained from the client or well known to him, with the exception of information which directly justifies proposals. The essence of information is *news*. Thus, the information content of reports should be on:

— facts discovered for the first time by the consultant;

— newly discovered significance of known facts;

---

[1] There are good books on report writing in general; some references will be found at the end of this appendix.

— newly found connections between known effects and hitherto unknown causes;

— solutions to the problems, and their justification.

For his own check, the consultant should ask himself about the *necessity* and *purpose* of any report he intends to produce:

— why is the report necessary?

— what will it achieve?

— is there a better way of achieving the purpose?

— is now the time for it?

It is not a bad thing to try drafting an introduction, starting with " The purpose of this report is . . . ". If there is any difficulty in finishing the sentence there is some doubt about the need for the report. The length of time since the last report does not matter, as long as the assignment has progressed satisfactorily in the meantime and the client knows it.

2. Structuring the report

The contents need to be arranged in the best *sequence* for the nature and purpose of the report and for the desired reaction to it. This may be difficult. Although the author hopes the reader will start at the beginning and read through to the end, there is no guarantee that he will. This is one of the hazards of written communication. Persuasion requires careful build-up through a reasoned sequence—which the reader may not choose to follow.

A solution to this may be in a well-presented *summary* at the beginning of the report. Many busy executives will read the summary and this will provide them with over-all guidance to the structure of the report even if they do not read all chapters.

A *table of contents* is essential (except in very short reports); it is regrettable that many reports do not have one.

The whole report should be carefully planned. It will contain certain main ideas and topics, some of which will have subdivisions. It may help to write headings and briefly sketch the subject matter on separate sheets or cards. The sheets may then be sorted into the best order for deciding the outline and for the drafting.

Marshalling the body of a report into a logical structure is aided by having a formal system of numbers and/or letters for main headings, sub-headings and so on. The wording after each number may be typed in a different style.

A decimal system may be used, such as:

    1.   *MAIN HEADING*

    1.1.   SUB-HEADING

    1.1.1 Sub-sub-heading

or numbers and letters, as:

  I. MAIN HEADING

    1. *Sub-heading*

       A. Sub-sub-heading

          (i) listed item

         (ii) listed item

The advantage of such a scheme is that it makes the writer think about his priorities and determine which topics are genuine subdivisions of others. It promotes the orderly organisation of the structure and points the way to economy of layout and avoidance of repetition.

For example, a report covering three subject areas: Buying, Stores and Production deals with three statements about them: Findings, Conclusions and Recommendations. Which of the three layouts below may be the best?

1. *Findings*	1. *Buying*	1. *Buying*
1.1 Buying	1.1 Findings	1.1 Findings
1.2 Stores	1.2 Conclusions	1.2 Conclusions
1.3 Production	1.3 Recommendations	
2. *Conclusions*	2. *Stores*	2. *Stores*
2.1 Buying	2.1 Findings	2.1 Findings
2.2 Stores	2.2 Conclusions	2.2 Conclusions
2.3 Production	2.3 Recommendations	
3. *Recommendations*	3. *Production*	3. *Production*
3.1 Buying	3.1 Findings	3.1 Findings
3.2 Stores	3.2 Conclusions	3.2 Conclusions
3.3 Production	3.3 Recommendations	
		4. *Recommendations*
		4.1 Buying
		4.2 Stores
		4.3 Production

For any particular report one of these may prove easiest, but if " Findings " tell the client nothing new, there is no point in belabouring them.

" Conclusions " usually lead straight into " Recommendations ". It could even be that the whole report needs to be written as for section 4 in the third column above: the recommendations themselves being written so as to make the findings and conclusions quite clear.

Everything depends on priorities, weights, balance and purpose; a scheme of marshalling helps to sort them out.

Appendices are useful for taking out of the body of a report detailed tables, charts, diagrams, etc., that would break up the continuity of reading and would be difficult to fit in. The body of the report is essentially for reading and quick examination of summary data. Appendices can takes items which, though contributory, require a more lengthy examination. It does not help to make a case if the reader is suddenly confronted with several pages of closely tabulated figures. A small table or diagram, however, is not disturbing.

If a report included, for example, the complete specification of an office system, this would almost certainly be in an appendix. Such an appendix may later become part of a general manual of procedures for the client, while the report may remain under confidential cover.

Acknowledgements have to be made especially in final reports on consulting. This may require some tact. If names are mentioned there must be no obvious omissions: every genuine helper likes to see his name on the list. At the same time, to include someone who has been more hindrance than help—and knows it—may cause mixed feelings all round. If the list would be too long, it is better to leave it out and settle for general thanks and the remark that " it would be an impossible task to mention everyone who . . . ".

3. Writing the report

At the present time executives are flooded with reports and hate long and badly written ones.

It is useful, therefore, to observe certain principles, which have been summarised in the following checklist [1] (Table 27).

When the author has the time, the first complete draft should be put aside for a day or two, after which anything wrong is more easily seen and revised. When it looks right, someone else should read it. An operating consultant's draft will certainly be read by his supervisor, who usually has a knack of finding things a junior consultant never suspected. There are, however, some dangers at this point: any report can always be improved, and the temptation to work on it until it is " perfect " may be hard to resist. As with most things, there is a point of diminishing return.

---

[1] Some of the principles are adapted from R. Gunning: *The technique of clear writing* (New York, McGraw-Hill, 1952).

Table 27. Principles of clear writing

1.	Keep report as short as possible
2.	Consider your reader, his outlook and experience
3.	Write to express, not to impress
4.	Write naturally; style that flows smoothly and does not draw attention to itself is the most effective
5.	Keep sentences short; vary their length but let the average be under 20 words
6.	Avoid complex sentences and carefully blend short and long words
7.	Use familiar words, avoiding rare or far-fetched ones
8.	Avoid jargon unless it is sure to be familiar to the reader and you know what it means
9.	Avoid unnecessary words that give an impression of padding
10.	Use terms the reader can picture: call a crane a crane, not " a lifting facility "
11.	Put action into your verbs; use the force of the active voice; use the passive to vary the style
12.	Keep every item of a report relevant to the purpose
13.	Ensure the contents include all the points necessary to the purpose
14.	Keep a proper balance—giving space and emphasis to each item according to its importance
15.	Keep a serious " tone " as befits a serious purpose; do not tempt the reader to read between the lines: if you do, you are at the mercy of his imagination
16.	Be careful in the use of numbers: figures tend to draw attention to themselves; decide when absolute values have more significance than percentages, and vice versa; when quoting figures from other sources, be exact; when estimating, consider the order of accuracy and round off

4. Printing the report

The report must look professional in every respect. Its cover and binding should give a good first impression. Inside, the typescript should allow a generous binding margin, be impeccably typed on a well-adjusted machine and free from extraneous marks or alterations. Any graphs, charts and diagrams must be well drawn and in every respect up to the standard of the typescript.

The consulting unit may have its own standard format that not only distinguishes its reports but caters for filing and control in its report library. Within the covers, the body of the report may also have a standard layout for division and subdivision of the contents.

The final draft prepared for reproduction should leave the typist in no doubt as to precisely what is required. The author should take the trouble to lay out the text as he wants to see it typed. He is also completely responsible for ensuring that no mistakes remain.

5. Literature on report writing

BACIE: *Report writing* (2nd ed.) (London, British Association for Commercial and Industrial Education, 1973); 24 pp.

Brown L.: *Effective business report writing* (Englewood Cliffs, N. J.. Prentice Hall, 1973).

Casson J.: *Using words* (London, Duckworth, 1968).

Ewing D. W.: *Writing for results* (New York, Wiley, 1974); 466 pp.

Gowers E.: *The complete plain words* (Harmondsworth, Middx., Penguin Books, 1968); 270 pp.

Gunning R.: *The technique of clear writing* (New York, McGraw-Hill, 1968).

Schneider, A. E., Donaghy W. C., Newman P. J.: *Organizational communication* (New York, McGraw-Hill, 1975); 367 pp.

Sigband N. B.: *Communication for management and business* (Glenview, Ill., Scott, Foresman & Co., 1976); 657 pp.

Strunk W.: *The elements of style* (New York, Macmillan, 1959); 70 pp.

Weaver P. C., Weaver R. G.: *Persuasive writing: a manager's guide to effective letters and reports* (New York, The Free Press, 1977); 239 pp.

TRAINING FILMS

Note: The list includes selected 16 mm sound films which are good discussion generators.

" *The Newest Profession* " (1970, 25 minutes)—A film about consultancy showing four assignments in the United Kingdom.
The Institute of Chartered Accountants in England and Wales—in colour.

" *A Class of Your Own* " (1966, 25 minutes)—A film about instruction and how to ensure best value.
Ministry of Defence, UK—in colour.

" *The Floor is Yours* " (1972, 26 minutes)—The stages in preparing a successful presentation.
Guild Sound and Vision, UK—in colour.

" *Overcoming Objections* " (1956, 30 minutes)—One of the Borden and Bussey films giving six rules for overcoming objections.
Dartnell Corporation, USA—in black and white.

" *Right First Time* " (1963, 20 minutes)—A case study in quality control.
British Productivity Council, UK—in black and white.

" *The Man in the Middle* " (1961, 27 minutes)—Looks at the work of a foreman, the pressures on him, and the effect of supervisory training.
British Productivity Council, UK—in black and white.

" *Successful Staff Appraisal* " (1972, 29 minutes)—A film on the performance review and appraisal.
Guild Sound and Vision, UK—in colour.

" *Face to Face* " (1973, 26 minutes)—A film about personal conflict at work in a small chemical factory.
Guild Sound and Vision, UK—in colour.

" *Creativity* " (21 minutes)—Explains ways of overcoming barriers to creative thinking.
American Management Association, USA—in black and white.

" *Looking at Paperwork* " (1968, 17 minutes)—Explains the nature and importance of organisation and methods.
British Productivity Council, UK—in black and white.

" *The Engineering of Agreement* " (1958, 21 minutes)—Suggests ways of gaining acceptance of proposals.
Roundtable Films, USA—in black and white.

" *Method Study—Basic Principles* " (1968, 20 minutes)—Explains the systematic approach to method study.
British Productivity Council, UK—in colour.

" *Hardy Heating Co. Ltd.* " (1970, 5 hours)—A series of ten films on the meaning and purpose of accounting records and statements.
British Broadcasting Corporation, UK—in black and white.

" *Problem Solving—Some Basic Principles* " (1971, 18 minutes), and
" *Problem Solving—A Case Study* " (1971, 22 minutes)—Two films showing how to solve business problems.
Rank Aldis, UK—in colour.

" *The Beaver Report* " (1976, 20 minutes)—Three case studies in management consulting.
Companion Guides Limited, UK—in colour.

" *Management Survey—The Technique* " (1975, 12 minutes) and "*Management Survey—In Action* " (1975, 14 minutes)—Techniques used in a management survey as demonstrated in a hospital.
World Wide Pictures, UK—in colour.

" *The Goya Effect* " (1975, 23 minutes)—Portrays two contrasting styles of management in a manufacturing department.
Rank Aldis, UK—in colour.

" *Focus on Results* " (1973, 20 minutes), " *Focus on Decisions* " (1973, 25 minutes) and " *Focus on Organisation* " (1974, 30 minutes)—Films

looking at three aspects of the manager's job: planning and controlling, decision-making, organisation.
Guild Sound and Vision, UK—in colour.

" *The Challenge to Change* " (1977, 23 minutes)—Overcoming resistance to change; women in management.
Roundtable Films, USA—in colour.

" *Meeting, Bloody Meetings* " (1976, 29 minutes)—Shows the disciplines and techniques that should be used to shorten meetings and make them more productive.
Video Arts, UK—in colour.